A.D.R.Student Simplified Text Series

C++
Simplified

Adam Shaw

A.D.R. (London) Limited
2-4 Wellington Road
Bridlington
YO15 2BN
England

Second Edition
Best Buy

Student Simplified Text Series

C++ Simplified

Acknowledgement

I would like to thank Robin Taylor for his encouragement and support during the writing of this book. and David Dunn for his very helpful comments and advice on its drafting.

Copyright

© A.D.R. **(London)** Limited 1998

British Library Cataloguing in Publication Data

A catalogue record for this book is available from the British Library

ISBN 1 901197 99 9

. First published 1997   . Second enlarged edition published 1998

Trademarks and Registered Trademarks

Direct Order

In case of difficulty. you can obtain this book from the publishers.

A.D.R. (London) Limited
2-4 Wellington Road
Bridlington
East Yorkshire YO16 7SS
England

Tel: 01262 672905
 Fax: 01262 605538 & 400851

Printed in Great Britain

For
my wife Armenoui
for her patience, and above all love

<u>Preface</u>

The C++ Programming Language

C++ was derived directly from the C programming language in the 1980s. The letter C is not an abbreviation of any name; it is simply the name of a programming language. Because C++ is associated with C, the symbols ++ were added to C in order to distinguish one from the other. This book concentrates on C++, and does not refer to C requirements. Indeed, there are some similarities and some differences between these two languages; but I have made no attempt to compare or contrast them.

In the 1990's C++ has been widely used in the world of work to develop programs for business information systems, scientific systems and the like. It can be said that it is the language for the decades in the next millennium. It is for this reason that it is increasingly taught on many courses in both further and higher education.

C++ is available in a variety of implementations, including Windows 95. Each implementation has its own mechanism for creating, editing, compiling, debugging, and linking source files. To learn C++ through this book, you need:

. Microsoft Windows 95 or Windows NT

. C++ compiler (Borland Turbo C++ 4.5 or version 5.00 or another product)

. A one-gigabyte hard disk

. CD-ROM drive

. Between 16 -32 megabytes of RAM

. A Pentium PC running at a fast speed (no less than 90 MHz)

. A high-density floppy disk drive

. A good quality monitor (at least SVGA type)

My many years experience has convinced me that programming is best learnt by practice. Thus the focus of this book is practical rather than theoretical; and therefore it introduces C++ through work-related examples. These examples were tested by using the essential hardware and software requirements listed above. The book demonstrates the application of C++, and helps you to apply learnt techniques and skills to write workable programs.

It is designed for readers who wish to learn the fundamentals of C++. It is therefore based upon the assumptions that you are a newcomer to C++; and you have access to a computer system. You will find it as a straightforward practical workshop companion, helping you to master the basic techniques and equip yourself with essential skills needed to develop programming expertise. It will lay a solid foundation for your continued expertise in C++ programming.

The book is filled with examples which are coded and explained. For each example the code and program output are depicted in a diagram or in a number of diagrams. The output is an important part of an example, as it will enable you to fully comprehend the code. You are advised to try these out on your computer as you progress through the book. Programming is best learnt by a hands-on approach, therefore you are advised to work though the examples, and try your best to write and test programs for programming exercises. Try not to read the solutions which are given in chapter 12 until you have attempted the exercises.

This second edition of C++ Simplified is the revised and enlarged version based on the first edition. It includes:

. Chapter 13 - Glossary of Terms for ease of reference, and

. Chapter 14 - Exploring Java. It will give you the opportunity to learn similarities and differences between C++ and Java programming languages.

The book will enable you to achieve your objective to write workable practical programs. I hope you derive as much pleasure and satisfaction from it as I enjoyed in its writing.

Adam Shaw
Bridlington
England

CONTENTS

Preface

Chapter 9 Mixed Data Structure.......................157

Chapter 10 File Processing 166

Chapter 11 Object Oriented Programming (OOP)...............185

Index does not include references to chapters 13-14

Chapter 1

Introduction to C++ Programming

Before you can start writing a program it is desirable
that you learn the following fundamental requirements, so that you
can start with confidence, and make good progress.

Towards a computer

A computer is a machine. It has to be instructed by human beings in the same way as one person instructs the other person in a language that is understood by both the instructor and the person to whom instructions are given. For instance, if you ask a police officer to direct you to the Houses of Parliament in London, you have to ask the officer in English. It is due to the fact that English is the language spoken in London. The officer will direct you using the English language. Let's assume the officer gave you precise directions and that you were able to understand and follow the route until you reached your destination. In this case, we can say that the police officer programmed you using the English language, by giving you a set of instructions (directions), and you were able to complete the task (reached your desired destination) successfully.

Programming Languages

In the above example, we have assumed that the police officer and the enquirer communicated with each other using the English language. Of course, being human both are able to think, remember and recall. In fact, a computer can perform tasks not only so simple, but much more complicated, providing someone has already thought out **instructions,** and the **sequence** of these instructions for the computer. From this illustration, we can see that a set of **instructions arranged in sequence** for a computer, is known as a **program**. The program tells the computer what to do and how to carry out a task step-by-step. The set of instructions, that makes up the program has to be given in a particular **programming language**, that a computer can understand. Indeed, a computer can solve most of our day-to-day problems, if we can relay these to it in a particular programming language, such as C++.

Languages spoken by people tend to be ambiguous and metaphorical. Our phrases can mean different things to different people. We may use words to confuse other people. Therefore, programming languages have been developed to remove such difficulties. They have precise syntax rules (governing arrangements of words), and are concise in their meanings. These computer languages can be broadly classified as **Low Level and High Level Languages**.

Low Level Languages use binary codes. These codes are complex and cannot be easily transferred from one computer to another. It is not easy to learn a Low Level Language. One very important advantage of these languages is their speed. A program written in a Low Level Language hardly requires any translation into machine codes. Therefore a Low Level program operates faster than a High Level Language program.

High Level Languages such as C, **C++**, COBOL, and PASCAL use English-like words. This makes computer programming easier to learn. They are not machine-based, and therefore can be used on most computers. The program written in any language is known as the **source program**, that contains **source code**.

Before a High Level Language source program can be run, it has to be translated into the **object program**, that contains machine codes. It is the object program that the computer can understand, as it is in machine code. A single instruction written in a High Level Language (source code) may become several lines of machine code. **How is this done?**

Comparison between an interpreter and a compiler

This is achieved by means of **Interpreters** and **Compilers**. These are program translating systems.

Interpreter

- Translates and carries out the instruction immediately line by line as it meets each line.
- Source code and the interpreter are together in memory.
- Memory space for data is reduced due to the presence of the interpreter.
- Speed of translation and run, is slower than that of the compiler.

Compiler

- It translates the whole source program into a self-contained program.
- The self-contained program can be run independently, immediately or later.
- During the run neither the source program nor the compiler has to be in memory.
- Efficient use of memory space for data.
- Speed of translation and run is faster than that of the interpreter.

Every computer needs an **operating system** to organise its operations. Usually, the operating system is stored in RAM (Random Access Memory). Microsoft Windows 95 is an operating system. An operating system itself is a large program. It manages the memory, interprets the user's keyboard operation, operates the screen, allows the user to create, delete, move, print, read and write on disks, run other programs and so on.

The integrated development environment

The compiler converts C++ programs into machine code. There are a number of compilers available on the market. The most popular is **Borland C++** compiler package for Windows, which the author has used for all programming illustrations. It contains all the necessary tools and utilities one needs for programming in C++. The initial screen for its compiler's IDE is shown in figure 1. The IDE helps you to develop Windows applications. It is easy to use, once you have some practice of using it. The Borland package is menu-driven. It is easy to understand for those who are familiar with Windows.

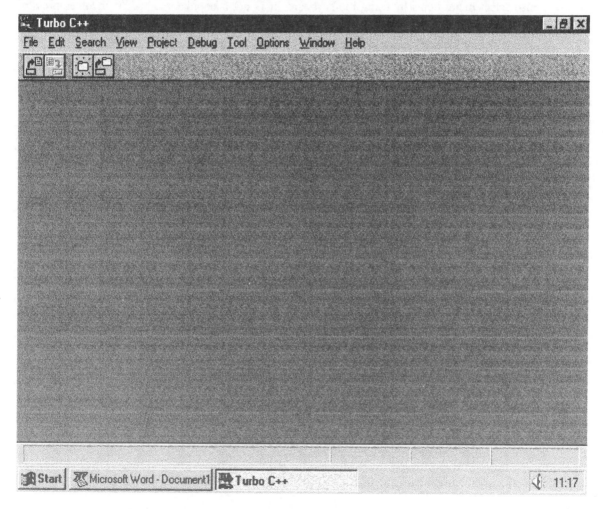

Figure 1 The Integrated Development Environment (IDE)

It is of paramount importance that you gain some working knowledge of menus. It does not matter which version you use, your program will run on any C++ compiler. You can activate or select a menu by clicking it using the mouse. You place the mouse pointer over the desired option and then click the left mouse button. When you do so, the menu's commands will appear on the screen. If a command is not relevant to a present situation, its name is displayed in grey letters, and you cannot select it. This way IDE warns you that this particular option is currently unavailable. It implies that IDE is lacking some prerequisite for that particular option to be available. For example, the **File menu's option Save** will be grey if the Edit window is empty. The Save command knows that there is nothing to save.

You can also select menu items by using the keyboard. It is not a popular method. It involves pressing simultaneously **Alt key** and **the letter in the item** you wish to select. For example, you can select File menu by pressing simultaneously **Alt** and **F** keys. From this menu, you can select any of the **8** items (commands) described below.

In Figure 1, the grey space is the **edit window**, the line above the grey area is the **speed bar**, and above this bar lies the **menu bar**. The bar menu consists of File, Edit, Search, View, Project, Debug, Tool, Options, Window, and Help items, which are shown in Figure 1. Each menu items consists of some commands. These commands perform specific functions. Edit window contains the editor, which allows you to create and edit your program code. Let us first consider **File Menu items,** so that you can understands the working of commands. File Menu items or commands are shown in Figure 2 below. At the top of the list is **Menu item New** - it allows you to open a new file.

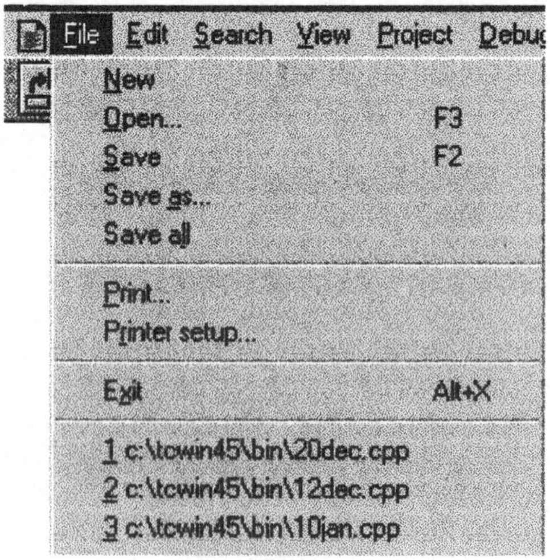

Figure 2

The IDE automatically gives a name and a number to the new edit dialogue box, which contains your new file. The name that is given by IDE is '**noname**'. It is followed by a number, which is followed by .**cpp**.

The first edit dialogue box or window (for short edit window) will be '**noname00.cpp**'. Our Figure 3 shows the edit window with an empty file namely, **noname00.cpp**. Each time a new file is opened, Borland C++ titles the file, noname; and the number 00 is incremented. Of course, you can use a name or a name and a number without any space between the name and the number to open a new file. You will soon learn how to do so.

File menu items

Let us first consider **File Menu items,** so that you can understand the working of commands. File Menu items or commands are shown in Figure 2 above. At the top of the list is **Menu item New** - it allows you to open a new file.

The IDE automatically gives a name and a number to the new edit dialogue box, which contains your new file. The name that is given by IDE is 'noname'. It is followed by a number, which is followed by .cpp. The first edit dialogue box or window (for short edit window) will be '**noname00.cpp**'.

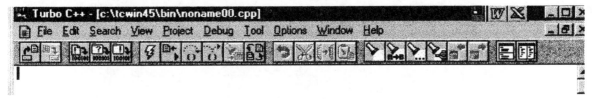

Figure 3

Figure 3 shows the path to file **noname00.cpp**.

c:\tcwin45\bin\noname00.cpp

where

drive	= c:
directory	= \tcwin45\
sub directory	= \bin\
file name	= noname00
extension	= .cpp

Open - it opens a file, which is already stored under a given name. Our Figure 4 contains 12 files, the path to these files and the name of drive on which these files are stored. You can select any of these files for opening and using it as desired.

Save - When the active window contains a previously unsaved file, and you select the **Save** command, it will automatically invoke the **Save as** dialogue box as shown in Figure 5.

Save all - command is more powerful than Save. If several files are opened, it can save the contents of all files. In addition, if one of the files is a new file, and has never been saved before, this command will invoke the Save as dialogue box , and you can give the file a valid name. It certainly allows you to name and save all files (windows) if they were not saved previously. See Figure 5.

Print - it allows you to obtain a hard copy of the file. Just click the print command item in the File Menu and the IDE will open Print Option dialogue box, which is shown in Figure 6. It is easy to select the desired option (s) by placing the mouse pointer on the option(s).

Print setup - it allows you to select a printer, together with size of the paper, colour and other print requirements. Figure 7 shows all the options available the author's printer.

Options... box within the print setup dialogue box which contains some more related print characteristics. You must explore your system to find out its capabilities for printing a hard copy.

Exit - by clicking this command you can quit the Borland C++ IDE. If you have not saved a file (s), the IDE will display the following warning message box, shown in Figure 8.

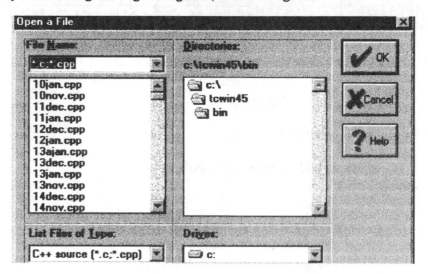

Figure 4

You are given three choices. If you select **yes**, it will save **noname10.cpp** file. If you click **NO**, the IDE will take you back to the current window and you have another chance to save it either as **noname10.cpp** or under another valid name. **How nice!**

How to flash cursor at a particular place in the edit window?

It is easily achieved. Take the mouse pointer to the location where the cursor should be placed. Once the pointer is placed at the desired location, click only once the left button on your mouse and then release it.

How to select a portion of text or the whole text?

Take the mouse pointer to the place in the active window from where you wish to select the text. Keep holding the left mouse button, drag the mouse to the right along the same line and then down the next line until the desired text displayed in the shaded or reverse background. Once you have marked the desired text than release the left button.

Borland's Turbo C++ and the latest version 5 meet the needs of programmers working in the Windows 3.11, Windows NT and Windows 95 environments.

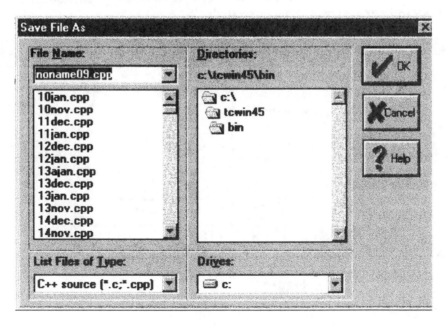

Figure 5

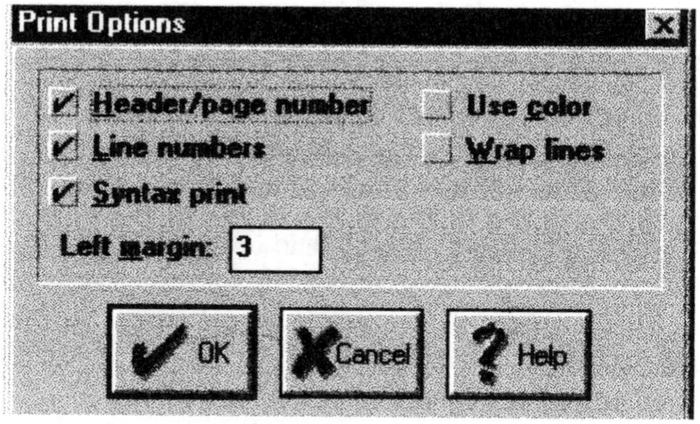

Print Options

☑ Header/page number   ☐ Use color
☑ Line numbers   ☐ Wrap lines
☑ Syntax print
Left margin: 3

✓ OK   ✗ Cancel   ? Help

Figure 6

This chapter started by drawing an analogy between computer language and the English language, a communication between the police officer and the enquirer, and the need to give precise, step-by-step directions. The sequence of instructions (directions in our analogy) is at the heart of solving any problem which involves systematic thinking. This is exactly what the programming is all about, giving a set of instructions, that is organised in sequence. If the sequence of instructions is systematic, free of syntactic errors, the computer will **execute** the program successfully.

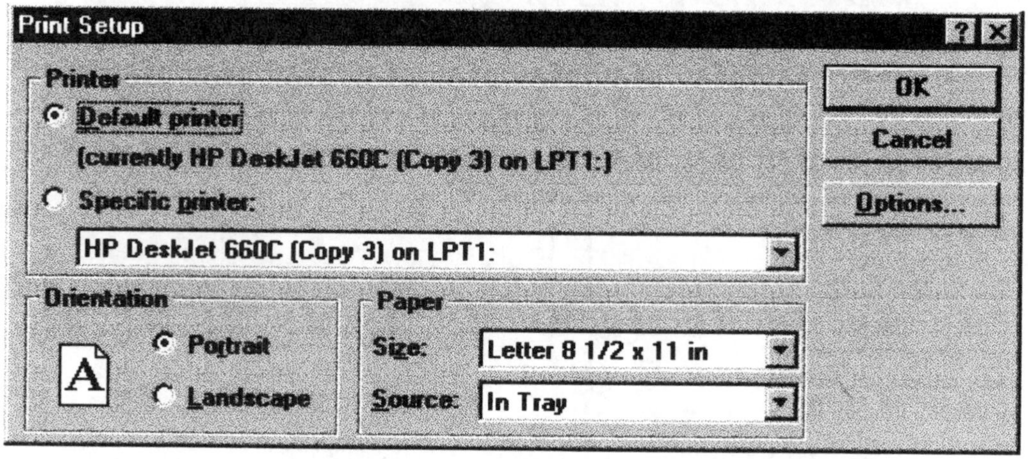

Print Setup

Printer
● Default printer
(currently HP DeskJet 660C (Copy 3) on LPT1:)
○ Specific printer:
HP DeskJet 660C (Copy 3) on LPT1:

OK
Cancel
Options...

Orientation
A
● Portrait
○ Landscape

Paper
Size: Letter 8 1/2 x 11 in
Source: In Tray

Figure 7

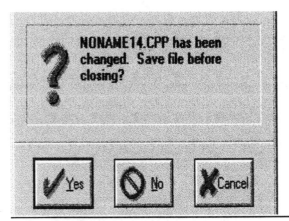

Figure 8

.Entering the Source Code

It is your **Source code**. This source code is entered into the computer's memory via IDE. How? By choosing the **File | New** found in the main menu, as shown in Figure 1. . The IDE opens the edit window with an empty file, for keying in the source code in this empty file (active window).

.Saving the Source Code File

In order to save the source file , which you just entered into the active window, choose the **File | Save** command. This command has a **hot key** , **F2**. You can use this hot key instead of choosing File | Save option. Whichever of these methods you use, the IDE opens **the Save File** dialogue box as shown in Figure 5. Now you can enter a suitable name for this file, say **oct15**, and then click on the save button. The compiler adds **.cpp** to the source code file. Thus your file's full name is **oct15.cpp**.

. Compiling the Saved Code File

C++ compiler produces an independent program which is capable of being executed by itself. The **compilation** process involves analysing the language structure of the source program. It checks the accuracy of C++ syntax rules. Once the source code is valid, it produces an intermediate file which is known as **object file**. It has **.obj** extension. The Borland IDE has three options for compiling .cpp file. **Option Compile** is most suitable for our purpose. **Figure 9** shows the outcome of this option.

You can scroll through the message box, navigate to the program lines listed in the message box, highlight one program line after another in the source code and correct each highlighted line accordingly.

The other method is to choose from the main menu **Project | Build all** command. The build all compiling process detects syntax errors and displays these in the output window. Figure 10 shows the outcome of this option. It illustrates that our source file has been compiled successfully. The compiler has found no syntax errors but one warning is issued.

Now click Ok button to open output window message box as shown in Figure 11. It highlights one **linker warning**.

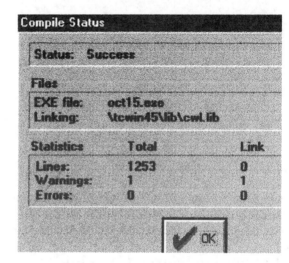

Figure 9 　　　　　　　　　　　　　　　　　**Figure 10**

A linker or **linker editor** is the software tool. It allows already compiled object code files or modules to be combined with the compiled program and any library functions that the original program called for, and then converted directly into an **executable file**. This has the **.ex** extension, as shown on third line in Figure 11.

The command **Project | Build all** is for compiling a project which usually has a number of files. We used it to compile a single file. This warning indicates that the default-definition settings are being used. It is expected as we have not created a module-definition file, with extension **.DEF**. This is the reason for issuing this warning; but the program has been compiled successfully. See compile status: success. A program compiled with warnings can be executed. It is not always a good idea to ignore warnings.

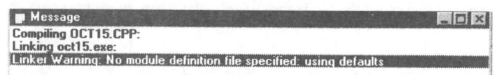

Figure 11

The third option is **Project | Make all** which will be demonstrated when we discuss projects.

Executing or Running a Program

In order to execute the program, choose the **Debug | Run** option. Now the IDE will display the output of this program. You can see in Diagram 1 the source code and the desired output in a small box within this diagram. <u>You can execute or run a single file program by choosing **Debug | Run** from the main menu.</u>

Debugging a Program

Our program may contain errors or bugs. We have to detect, locate and correct all bugs.
These errors are classified as follows:

Syntax errors are due to violation of the rules of C++ language for whatever reasons. For instance, you might have misused a key word, or punctuation mark, or used upper case letters instead of lower case letters. **Remember that C++ is a case-sensitive language**. The IDE lists these errors. These errors are not always easy to correct. For example Figure 12 reveals our syntax due to } missed out at the end of our source code. Here the program is incorrectly terminated. These are detected during the compilation and are thus also known as Compilation Errors.

Message

Compiling OCT15.CPP:
Error OCT15.CPP 6: Compound statement missing } in function main()

Figure 12

Run-time errors or Execution errors are due to a breach of logical or mathematical rules. These errors are detected during program execution as shown in Figure 13. Here the run-time error is due to dividing a number by 0. Because of this error, the processor has stopped running this program.

Logical Errors - such errors are due to poor program design. They are mistakes in the program design. During the compiling process, the IDE does not list any logical errors. A program containing a logical error or errors may appear to be running correctly but its output is undesirable. Logical errors can be recognised because the program outputs the wrong result or it just does not produce or display anything at all.

Linking errors - A linking error occurs when a compiled program is linked to a library function. It may be that the required function or subroutine is not available or incorrect parameters are given. Our Figure 11 above shows a linking warning. This could have been a linking error detected during the operation of **Project | Build** all option.

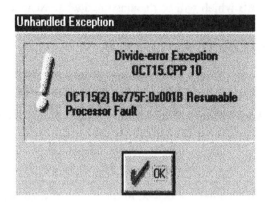

Figure 13

Program Testing

It can be argued that the development of an information system is the development of the computer programs. These programs are the backbone of the workable information system. It is vitally important that programs are rigorously tested. The testing plan should include already worked out, required and acceptable results; so that these can be compared with the actual results generated by your program. The compiling, executing, and debugging cycle to modify the programs, and repeating the testing cycle are essential phases of a program development.

You should always know your expected outputs before you test your program.

An Overall View

This section is not intended to give you an overall view of programming. A program is a set of instructions, which tells the computer what to do. Irrespective of the language in which the program is written, the computer obeys the sequence of instructions one at a time. The set of instructions is in fact an **algorithm** that leads to the solution of a problem. The problem's algorithm is tackled by a program. Therefore, the first step is to establish **the nature** of the problem. A clear understanding of the nature of the problem is essential to **planning a solution**.

In the real world of work, usually the problem is complex and involves many inter-related things and some uncertainties. It is therefore often highly desirable to sketch out the algorithm in the form of a diagram such as a **structure chart**. A diagram enables the programmer to think about the overall structure of the program. It helps to decide how many program modules will be required and what tasks are to be assigned to different modules of the program.

It is no use to staring to code a program without knowing precisely what is involved in the given situation. Program writing is almost the same activity as telling someone how to solve a problem or perform an activity. Often the poor program design is due to the lack of precise knowledge of what must be done to solve the problem.

A programmer must fully understand the **program specification**. A program specification must contain all the essential **input-process-output** requirements. This complex and lengthy task can be broken down into procedures or modules and each procedure can be coded, tested and documented by different programmers. These procedures or modules can be linked together to form the **main program**.

The **source code** is entered into the computer, saved and compiled. The compiler manages the source code. It converts it into an intermediate file which is known as an **object file**. It also merges it with any required (called functions) library functions prior to generating an executable program. The executable program is known as an **executable file** which has the **.EXE** extension.

Your **executable file** (program) may have **bugs** (errors) and these must be found and corrected (debugging). You must test (run) your program by using different test values in order to demonstrate that your program works correctly and outputs the correct results in the required format(s). You may find that your program does not perform the required task due to a variety of errors.

A **poor program design** leads to some serious problems and it is very time consuming to put it right. It is best to give all the consideration to the program development before coding it. A program should solve the problem efficiently, reliably, and it must be **user friendly** so that it can be used with great ease and confidence by users without any computing background.

An efficient design of a program is based upon its reliable **documentation**. A reliable documentation is necessary for current program maintenance and its future development. It must be clear and concise so that it can be followed by other programmers without any further aid to understand it. It should help other programmers to implement its contents.

Procedural Programming VS OOP

What has been said so far about the program specification concerns procedural programming, where the problem is analysed in terms of **input-process-output** and the code is written. The code is usually subdivided into procedures to make sure that the program is manageable.

Object Oriented Programming (OOP) differs from this procedural approach. In OOP objects have to be used. First you have to identify all the objects which are needed and then decide which functions and data are necessary. The collection of all related data and functions in the form of an object is an interface to the object. This collection is known as **encapsulation**. The great advantage of the object is that you can use it in another program. That is what is known as software re-use. It is recommended that you read a specific book on OOP as there are several formal OOP program design methodologies. This books starts with procedural programming and progresses to the introduction of OOP.

Chapter 2

C++ Program Structure

Soon C++ will not be a mystery to you. Be patient!

Your First C++ Program

The program is designed to display a message on your screen. It introduces the essential requirements for a C++ program, how to run (**execute**) it, and achieve the result successfully. This program consists of 6 lines of source code but lays the foundation for much longer programs.

A program consists of instructions, which are written here in C++. It is suggested that you compile and run each example in order to understand the language and gain some experience of programming skills. It will help you if you would store them on your disk for future programming development.

The first step towards a program development is to know precisely the nature of the problem that you want to solve. Therefore your source code or just code should be written to generate a solution to the problem. The code shown in Diagram 1 is written to display, "**Soon C++ will not be a mystery to you. Be patient!**". We now analyse each instruction of this code.

Pre-processor statement

#include <iostream.h> is called **Pre-processor directives**. A pre-processor directive is an important part of C++ program, as it instructs the compiler to retrieve the code stored in a <u>pre-defined</u> file into the **source code** (your program).

For this program the pre-defined file is **iostream.h**.
This file is known as the **Header File**. On the first line **# include** directive plus the name of the required header file in $<\ >$ (**angle brackets**) make up the essential **pre-processor directive** .

<u>#include <iostream.h></u>
↓   ↓
Directive + Header file = **pre-processor directive**

For this program, we need **iostream.h** header file. It is a **Standard C++ Library file.** In **iostream.h** file pre-defined information about **I/O - input-output** is kept. These files can be used in any program written in C++. They are external to a program, but they are part of C++ language. On line 5, we have an output statement, and therefore, we have to have **iostream.h** file as **#include directive**.

// **comments** are shown on the second line. Some meaningful comments can be included in a program. The idea is to assist someone to follow your program. A program can have more than one line of comments. There are no rules concerning comments, except that a comment must not insult someone's intelligence. In this book, // symbol is used before a comment. It is recommended to include a meaningful comment at the beginning of your program. The comment (s) should highlight the purpose of your program.

Main Function

void main (void) is a declaration of the function called **Main**.

All C++ programs have at least one function. Each function is given a name. **Void** is a **keyword**. A keyword is already defined and is reserved in C++. It has a special purpose. Here, first void means the function **main( )** does not return a value. The second void within the **parentheses** shows that the function takes no arguments. Void indicates the absence of any values. All programs in C++ must have a starting point, beginning with the external function called **main ( )**. Its meaning will become more clearer as you progress further. Functions are the basic blocks of C++ Program design. See more below.

Function Declarations

A function name must begin with a letter followed by as many letters and digits as you like, but C++ considers only first **31** characters. In fact, a function name should follow the same rules as are described below for variable names. A function declaration may look like:

(a)
$$\underset{\downarrow}{\textbf{int}} \; \underset{\downarrow}{\underline{\textbf{do}}} \; (\; \underset{\downarrow}{\underline{\textbf{int}}} \;)$$

Type of value function   **do** name   Data type of the parameter
returns is an   of the   function **do** takes
integer value   function

. Function **do** returns an integer value, and it takes integer type data.

. int is an abbreviation for integer.

(b)   int account (<u>int x, char y</u>)
                                 ↓

Two different data types of parameters
that function **account** takes

In this declaration, there are two parameters namely **int x** and **char y**, and their data types are integer and character respectively. This function has multiple parameters. It is therefore, important that you specify the type for each parameter. Here x and y are identifiers for the parameters.

. **char** is an abbreviation for character.

(c)   **int wages (int a, int b, int c, int d)**

                             ↓

       All three parameters of the same data type - **integer**, but
       must be specified separately.

(d)   **void main (void)**

The function main returns no value of any data type, and it does not need any parameters. This function may be declared as **main ( )**.

. Void function type is self-contained. We will discuss functions in detail.

Body of the program

In fact the body of this program consists of only one statement. This statement is shown within a pair of braces { } known as **curly brackets**.

The statement uses the keyword **cout**. It is pronounced as see out. This is an abbreviation for 'console output'. It refers to the **standard output stream**, which is the screen. << is known as output operator or the insertion operator or put to operator. All these names mean the same thing when they are used with cout. cout is used to display the message on the screen. **cout <<** sends an item or items of data to a stream. In the above program, statement online 5 sends one item of data to the screen. This data item is enclosed within " " marks. You can send several data items to output stream by writing these on the same line. You will soon learn through our program in Diagram 3 how to write such statements.

The braces { } enclose the body of the main (void) function. These are essential. There are other occasions when { } are used in a program. You will learn about other uses through other programs.

What you have learnt through our simple program is not trivial. Why ? Because you will require this knowledge over and over again irrespective of the length of a C++ program.

The print screen , a small window, within diagram 2 on page 17, shows the output of this simple program designed to print an encouraging message for you, " Soon C++ will not be a mystery to you. Be patient!". The program works well, as the message is printed by the computer.

Your first program and the desired output

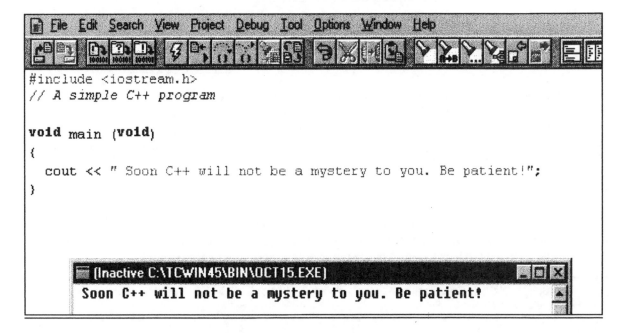

```
#include <iostream.h>
// A simple C++ program

void main (void)
{
   cout << " Soon C++ will not be a mystery to you. Be patient!";
}
```

(Inactive C:\TCWIN45\BIN\OCT15.EXE)
Soon C++ will not be a mystery to you. Be patient!

Diagram 1

The shortest C+ + program

Note that the shortest C++ program is

```
main ( )
{
}
```

. What can it do ?

It can do nothing, except to show you the skeleton of a C++ program.

Let us analyse diagrams 2, which depicts another simple small program. The program is designed to display a two-line message on the screen, followed by a new line.

.Explanation

This time we have declared main ( ), on line 3, and on line 7 shown **return (0)** statement.

The purpose of return statement is to terminate the execution of the program, and return control to the operating system. Usually a program without this statement runs successfully. It must be noted that when return statement is not included, and you try to compile the program by choosing **Project | Compile** command, the compiler issues a warning message, "Function should return a value in function main[ ]". This warning message is shown in Diagram 2A. If you compile it by choosing **Debug | Run** command, this programs runs successfully, without giving you any warning message. Most compilers do not require return (0) statement.

On line 5, see the symbolic constant **endl**. This is a pre-defined **iostream** manipulator. You place it at the end of cout line, followed by a semicolon. It is equivalent to the symbol **\n**, which is ASC II code for feed or a new line. **\n** is required here to meet our requirements as part of our desired solution.

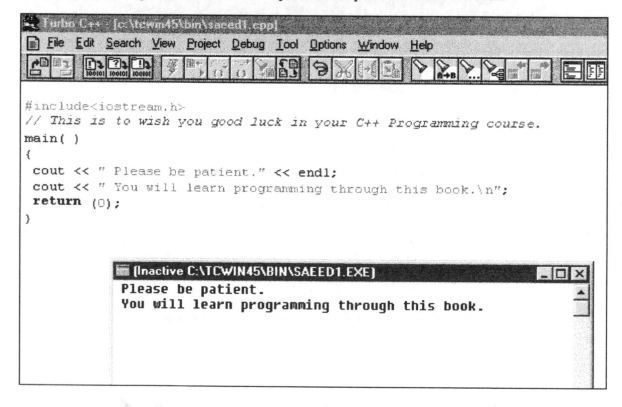

Diagram 2

The message is loud and clear, as shown in the small box within the Diagram 2. Our program was compiled successfully, displaying our message, followed by a new line.

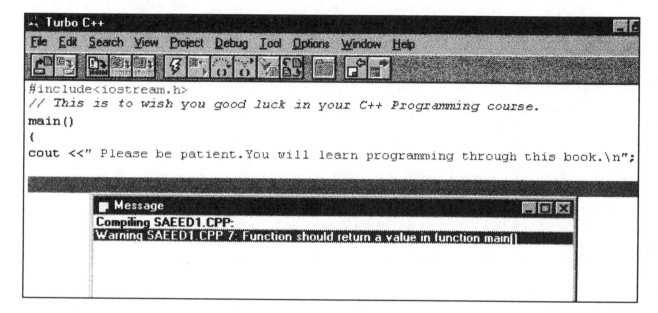

Diagram 2A

Practical Hints

1. No punctuation marks at the end of Pre-processor directives (they begin with #).
2. A semicolon is required at the end of each statement.
3. Semicolon is used as a statement terminator.
4. C++ is case sensitive. It distinguishes between upper and lower case letters.
5. Do not interchange lower and upper case letters.
6 Do not miss } and { punctuation marks or enter an additional symbol.
7. Enter <iostream.h> without any space; otherwise you will get unnecessary messages.

A Variable and its value

You can think of computer memory as a row of houses on a street, each house having its own unique number. The occupants of a particular house can be approached by means of its unique number allocated to it.

Similarly, a computer memory consists of many thousands of cells. We can give unique names to each of these memory locations. In any of these memory locations (cells), we can place a **value** and recall it by referring to it by its unique name or symbol. This name or a symbol is called **variable**. In our next program, on line 6, 'Account' is a unique name given to a memory location. The data/information stored in the cell is the value of this variable, 'Account '. The computer system must know the type of this value. In this case, its type is **int** (**integer**). We will discuss the impact of line 6 in more detail below. At this stage, we must discuss variables and their declaration.

Variables and their Declarations

C++ requires declarations of all variables and their types at the start of a program. A declaration statement such as '**int** Account' is a simple declaration that gives information about the variable 'Account' and its type. A declaration may be a compound statement. For example: <u>int age, name, retirement, pension.</u>

It declares four variables and their type - all integers. An **int** is an abbreviation for integer. In C++ variables come under the broad category known as **identifiers**. An identifier is a name chosen by the programmer to represent a variable, a function, a data type or any other element defined within a program. We will discuss other types of identifiers as we meet them in our programs. Now, we can list the most used variables below:

Variable	Type	Example of Declaration
Numeric whole number	**int**	**int** n;
Numeric real or float number	**float**	**float** x;
*textual data	**char** (character)	**char** surname;

Table 1. Types of Variables

A **Character (char)** is any symbol on the keyboard. Most computers use the ASCII (American Standard Code for Information Interchange) code. **A, M, N, b,",/,** and **|** are examples of characters. Each character is converted to its equivalent in ASCII code, which is in binary code. A binary code is a combination of two digits 0 and 1. This is called <u>two's complement</u> form or <u>int type</u>.

The letters of the alphabet are stored using numeric values, which are in the integer range of zero to 127. Altogether there are 128 characters. For instance, the binary code for capital letter S is 0101 0011. This character set is extended to 256 on most PCs. Now you can appreciate that **char** type is also one of the integer types.

Think !

Integer Types & Range of Values

. An **integer (int)** is a whole number: 0,1,2,3,4,5,6,7,8,9, -4, -3,-5 and so on. It is any whole number without a fractional part. The reserved word **int** is modified as unsigned, short and long. These modifiers are used to store variables within the range of values available on your PC. Our Diagram 7 depicts a program which prints out integers, characters and modifiers, together with their range of values. All these values are shown as output in Diagram 7A. You can find out sizes of these in bytes, that your computer uses, if you run the program shown in Diagram 8.

An **unsigned int** is <u>not</u> a negative integer. Examples are 3, 5, 0. On the contrary, a signed int is either negative or positive. For example -89 is a signed integer.

. A **float or Floating-point** is a *real* number. Example 12.76 is a float. In C++ , you can declare real numbers as <u>float, double and long double</u>. The size of float, double, and long double in bytes on my computer are shown in Diagram 8.

Size and Precision of Information

In the business world you have to be well aware of the level of accuracy of numeric information held in computer memory. Much of the business data is of numeric type. The size of numeric data is not always predictable. A number may be very small or very big, positive, negative, a whole number or a fraction. The way numbers are stored involves a compromise between the range of values needed and the accuracy with which these values can be represented. My PC uses 16 bits to an integer, this gives a range of values between:

- 32,768 to 32,767, as shown in Diagram 7A.

It is likely that your PC has a similar range of integer values. For the world of business this range is not big enough to comply with the accuracy requirements. C++ has a large integer range between - **2147483648 to + 2147483647**. See Diagram 7A for other ranges. It is big enough for any real-life problem solving. Similarly for handling floating-point calculations, the precision range for double is 15 digits, and for the long double 19 digits of precision. A large number requires a bigger memory space. For instance, every floating-point variable of type long double needs 10 bytes of memory, whilst a float needs only 4 bytes of memory. See Diagram 8 for other memory sizes.

How to name a variable
The following rules are important to remember as a guideline for giving names to variables.

. A variable name can have one or more letters, digits or the underscores (_) character.
A variable beginning with an underscore character may lead to some errors, and therefore it is advisable not to begin a variable name with it.

. **In** theory a variable name can be as long as the programmer wants, but only the first **31** characters are significant to the C++ compiler.

. **C++** is case-sensitive language. This means it makes a distinction between upper-case and lower-case letters. Thus the compiler will not accept a variable if it is referred by a case other than in which it is declared.

. **Start** a variable name with a letter.

. **Make** sure your variables names make sense to other programmers.

. **Do not** use keywords as variable names. **A Keyword or reserved word is a pre-defined word in C++**. For instance **FOR** is a keyword in C++, and therefore, you cannot use it as a variable.

Some Examples of legal and illegal identifiers

legal Names	Illegal Names	
Account	101 Account	→ does not start with a letter
gross	Pay Roll	→ space is not allowed
Gross	# x	→ begins with a # symbol
b	0	→ zero is not a letter but a number
sumDiff	pay-rate	→ '- ' is not underscore
O (upper-case 'O')	overtimeRate£	→ ends with illegal character £
o (lower-case 'o')	stop!	→ ends with illegal symbol
pay_rate [(_) is underscore]	friend	→ reserved or keyword forbidden

It is wise to use names that are descriptive. For instance Account rather than c.

asm	auot	break	case	catch	char	class	const	continue	default	delete	do	double	else
enum	extern	float	for	friend	goto	if	inline	int	long	new	operator	overload	private
protected	public	register	return	rtti	short	signed	sizeof	static	struct	switch	template	this	
throw	try	typedef	union	unsigned	virtual	void	volatile	wchart	while				

Table 2. Some Reserved Words or Key Words in alphabetical Order

There are some more Borland Turbo C++ keywords, that are not part of the ANSI (American National Standards Institute) conventions. These are unique to C++ for Windows.

Using Variables

Diagram 3 depicts another program that is designed and tested in order to introduce you to further

C++ language structure. You can learn the basic principles of user-computer interaction, **input-output**, and how to declare and use variables. Before we can discuss this program, it is desirable that you understand the following text.

Code shown in Diagram 3 illustrates in the simplest way how to communicate with the computer via the screen. The statement on line 5 must now make sense as it declares the variable, ' Account' and its type as **int**. This declaration falls within our above explanation. On line 7, our new statement is **cin >>Account**. cin stands for console-input. Here **cin** is the input stream, and >> is the extraction or get from operator. The >> is also known by two other names: input operator and extraction operator. **cin >>** enables the user to input (key in) the required value for the variable named.

How does it work?

Let us now examine each statement in this program.

Line 1 shows #include directive. Here **iostream.h** is needed for input-output processes. If this file was not included the compiler would not have understood **cout** and **cin** statements.
Line 2 is a comment line. It begins with // (double slashes).
Line 3 shows the function header that is essential. It tells the compiler that the function is self-contained. It is the same as void main (void).
Line 4 has {. It is required in order to begin with the main body of the program.
Line 5 contains variable declaration. This is essential for memory location.
Line 6 holds the insertion / put to statement. It displays on the screen statement written within the " ". In computer jargon:

The statement cout<< "Key in Account Number: " ;

instructs the computer to send the message within the quotation marks to the standard **output stream** which is the screen. Thus on the screen **" Key in Account Number: "** appeared without the quotation marks.

How could the user respond to this question or statement?

. After obeying the instruction on line 6, the control passed on to **line 7: cin >> Account;** cin is input stream as described above. When the control reached to line 7, the system paused, and waited for an answer - the input. The user keyed in the required data -101. This could have been any number. This is **how** the user was able to respond to the statement generated by line 6.

<u>Line 7</u> It reads the value from the keyboard and stores it in the variable account. As soon as the user finished keying in the account number 101, and pressed return/ Enter key the control passed on to the next statement on **line 8** to be executed.

. In our previous program, the **<u>insertion operator</u>** << performed the action of sending the value of the expression within the quotation marks listed on its right side to the output stream (screen) shown on its left. In this program, it is the same action, but here the expression is complex and it deserves an explanation. **Line 8 reads**:

cout << " Account Number" << " = " << Account << " which you have typed in.";

The message is in four parts. According to our above explanation, line 8 is executed from left to right. This means first of all " Account Number" is sent to output stream (screen), followed by " = " , then data value '101', and finally , " which you have typed in ". Note that variable name or identifier has been replaced by its data value, which was already in the memory location. It was keyed in by the user.

<u>Line 9</u> is return (0) . This indicates the termination of the execution of the program.
You have already met this statement. **No value to return**.

<u>Line 10</u> is essential in order to enclose the main body of the program. Without } the compiler will not allow you to run this program successfully.

```
# include <iostream.h>
// To illustrate input and output on screen

main()
{
int Account;
cout << "  Key in Account Number: ";
cin >> Account;
cout <<" Account Number" << " = " << Account << " which you have keyed in.";
return(0);
 }
```

```
 [Inactive C:\TCWIN45\BIN\SAEED3A.EXE]          _ □ ✕
    Key in Account Number: 101
 Account Number = 101 which you have keyed in.
```

<u>Diagram 3</u>

- It is worth remembering that the general form of cout is:

cout << expression << expression << ....<< expression;

Our line 8 has four expressions. • **Can you identify these expressions ?**

The small box within our Diagram 3 contains the required output.

.Using Integer and Character Variables

Diagram 4

The design and coding in diagram 4 illustrate the application of integer and character data types. The program displays on the screen question-answer dialogue, for the user to key in the required answers. The output of the interactive session includes a suitable complimentary message.

.Explanation

We have already discussed the meaning and use of **pre-processor statement**, and function **main**. Now is the time to discuss **data types and their declarations**. In this program we have declared two types of data or variables. These are **Surname**, and **age**. Surname is declared as <u>character variable</u>, size 40 characters. It tells the compiler to reserve space for up-to 40 characters in memory which is identified as Surname. The **identifier** is Surname. Here, we place 40 within [ ]. This will be explained under arrays. The statement is:

```
char Surname [40];
```

char is a reserved word. Write it using lower case letters. The declaration always ends with ; punctuation mark. Our other variable declaration is:

```
int age;
```

int is another reserved word. It should be typed in lower case letters. It informs the compiler to allocate memory space for an identifier declared as age. Note that this time our declaration does not mention any size, like the above declaration, and no [ ]. It is due to the fact that most microcomputers have integer range between -32,768 to 32,767. We will discuss integer type later on.

```
cout <<"Type now your surname, and then Please press return key: ";
```

This statement sends the message within the "   " to the screen.

```
cin >> Surname;
```

Because of this statement the program pauses for any **Surname** to be keyed in, and then the **Enter key** to be pressed by the user. The surname, **Johnson** is entered and the Enter key is pressed by the user. This is then stored in the memory location, which we have called **Surname**. If the **Surname** exceeds 40 characters, it will be rejected.

```
cout <<" " << endl;
```

This statement produces an empty line (a space) between two lines. See the output.

```
cout <<"Your surname is Mr. " <<Surname <<"." << " How nice!" << endl;
```

It sends **Your surname is Mr. Johnson. How nice!** to the screen. Johnson was already in the memory space known **Surname.** The computer has copied Johnson for Surname in the statement.

```
cout <<"Type now your age, and then please press return key: ";
cin  >> age;
cout <<" " << endl;
cout << "Mr. "<< Surname << " you are " << age << " years young." << endl;
```

These statements work in the same way as our last three statements, except that this time two pieces of data, which are Johnson and 23 are copied from the memory locations labelled Surname and age. These are then sent to the screen for display as required.

```
cout <<" " << endl;
cout <<" " << endl;
cout <<"          .... ................" << endl;
cout <<"          Keep smiling!" << endl;
cout <<"          ...................." << endl;
```

Here our first two statements are meant to separate the result of question-answer session from the complimentary message. Statements 3 and 5 draw two lines, so that our complimentary message can be displayed between these two lines, almost in the centre of our screen.

Source code and the output of this program are shown in diagram 4 below. It is suggested that you experiment with this program. **Remember**

Practice makes perfect!

Diagram 4. Source code and the required output

```cpp
# include <iostream.h>
// screen input/output practice.
main( )
{
  char Surname [40];
  int age;
  cout <<"Type now your surname, and then Please press return key: ";
  cin  >> Surname;
  cout <<" " << endl;
  cout <<"Your surname is Mr. " <<Surname <<"." << " How nice!" << endl;
  cout <<" " << endl;
  cout <<"Type now your age, and then please press return key: ";
  cin   >> age;
  cout <<" " << endl;
  cout << "Mr. "<< Surname << " you are " << age << " years young." << endl;
  cout <<" " << endl;
  cout <<" " << endl;
  cout <<"                    .... ................" << endl;
  cout <<"                    Keep smiling!" << endl;
  cout <<"                    ..................." << endl;
  return (0);
}
```

================================ Program output================================

```
[Inactive C:\TCWIN45\BIN\SAEED4.EXE]
Type now your surname, and then Please press return key: Johnson

Your surname is Mr. Johnson. How nice!

Type now your age, and then please press return key: 23

Mr. Johnson you are 23 years young.


                  - - - - - - - - - - - -
                  Keep smiling!
                  - - - - - - - - - - - -
```

Initialisation & Assignment

Diagram 5

It contains another program and its output. It is designed to initialise three variables, and display their assigned values on separate lines, one after the other. This program also illustrates how to assign an initial value to a variable.

Explanation

The first four lines of this source code do not need any explanation, as we have already discussed these through Diagrams 1 to 4.

int a = 10;	int b = 15 ;	int c = 30;

These are three assignment statements. The variables a, b and c are assigned initial values 10,15 and 30 respectively within their declarations. All three variables are of integer type. It is suggested to initialise variables when they are declared. Note the use of assignment operator =. It must be placed between the variable and the value assigned.

These statements allocate three separate memory locations, and called them **a**, **b** and **c**. In these locations initial values of 10,15 and 30 are stored. After initialisation, the next statement for execution is:

cout << a << endl;.

This statement sends the value of variable **a** to the screen for display, and generates a **next line**. (because of endl;). The same process is repeated for the next two lines. The output is shown in the grey area in Diagram 5A.

```
# include <iostream.h>
// To illustrate how to assign values to variables
 main( )
 {
      int a  =  10;
      int b  =  15 ;
      int  c =  30 ;
      cout << a << endl;
      cout << b << endl;
      cout << c << endl;
      return(0);
}
```

Diagram 5

```
========================= Program Output =========================
                              10
                              15
                              30
```

Diagram 5A

Diagram 6

It contains another small program which is designed to allow the user to read two values of two different variables from the keyboard (input), add them up together, and display their sum on the screen. It demonstrates further application of variable values, and how these are assigned to a variable for computation and displayed the output on the screen.

When the statement **cin >> b >> o;** executes, the system pauses for input data for two variables namely **b** and **0**. The user enters the value of b, and presses the return key, enters a value for o, and then presses the return key. These values are then assigned to **b** and **o** in the statement **gross = b + o;**

The statement **gross = b + o;** is evaluated from the right of the assignment operator as 126 + 67, and the resulting value 193 is assigned to gross. The value 193 is stored in the memory location, which we have labelled **gross**.

cout << "gross = " << gross; - it copied 193 from the memory, substituted it for gross in this statement, and sent it with the message within the quotation marks to the screen. See the dark grey area of diagram 6 for the output.

```
#include <iostream.h>
 //  To use keyed in values in an assignment statement
 main ( )
{
  int b, o , gross;
  cin  >> b >> o;
  gross =  b + o;
  cout  << "gross = " << gross;
  return ( 0 );
}
```

```
                             126
                              67
                          gross = 193
```

Diagram 6

Practical Hints

1. A variable is a symbol used to name a space in the computer's memory.
2. Give meaningful names to variables, so that you can recognise these after sometime.
3. Data or information held in the memory is the value of the variable.
4. An assignment statement has two parts. These are separated by an assignment operator. For instance:

$$K = \underline{a + (\ b * 77\ )}\ ; \text{ should be red as } \mathbf{k}\ \mathbf{becomes} \text{ instead of equals to}$$

     ↓   ↓

   Variable   **expression**

5. The expression is evaluated first, arriving at a single number.
6. The single number is then stored, that is **assigned** to a variable on the right side of the assignment operator for further execution.
7. = read as becomes.

Arithmetic Operators

We have already met one arithmetic operator + in our last program. The following is a full <u>list of arithmetic operators in C++.</u>

Operator	Meaning
+	addition or sum
-	subtraction
*	multiplication
/	division
%	reminder of integer division or modulus

Table 3. Arithmetic Operators

The order of calculation is as follows:

- Starts calculation from innermost brackets **( )**
- then performs multiplication *****
- next performs division **/**
- next performs modulus or division calculation **%**
- next addition is carried out **+** and lastly subtraction **-**

What happens when all the operators have the same priority?

In such a case, the order of calculation is from left to right.

Algebraic Convention

Addition, subtraction, multiplication perform their basic algebraic calculations on all data both integer and floating point. Division using modulus operator cannot be performed on floating point type data. For instance 200 % 25.75 is not allowed. **Why?**

Because 25.75 is not an integer, but a floating point.

What do you when an integer is divided by another integer?

When you divide an integer by another integer, say 4/2 , you get 2, which is an integer. There is no remainder value. If you divide 7/2 , you get integer 3 as the answer, and 1 as the remainder. **What happens to this remainder?** The remainder is discarded.

How will you divide an integer by another integer to get the remainder?

You should perform calculations using modulus operator %. By this method the remainder is kept and the result of the division is discarded.

Diagram 7

It contains a program which is designed to display on the screen **types of integers and their ranges** on my PC, running Borland Turbo C++ for Windows compiler. Try this on your own computer in order to find out its ranges for each integer type. Most PCs have similar ranges.

Explanation

<limits.h> is another header file, which contains parameters about limitations, ranges of integers, and compile time. This library file is required here besides **<iostream.h> include file**. Note header files are also known as **include files**. The compiler recognises INT_MIN, INT _MAX , and other 12 definitions, which are used to find out the range values. These definitions and ranges are in header file **< limits.h >**.

\t is horizontal tab. It is used in this program to design the layout of its output. It is an ACII code, just like **\n**, which gives new line or line feed. Consider now

```
cout << "\t Minimum int          = " << INT_MIN    << endl;
```

In this statement, **"\t Minimum int   = "** displays exaactly as within the quotation marks. \t moves the cursor to one tab position along the horizontal line for displaying the size of **Minimum int**. **endl;** - this produces a new line. Other statements follow the same pattern in order to display other required sizes.

In this program we do not have a **return (0);** statement. It is not required here, as we have:-

void main (void) function.

 If you run this program without the return statement, the compiler will not display any warning message. The rest of the program consists of **output stream <<** . The desired output of this program is shown in Diagram 7A.

```
#include <iostream.h>
#include <limits.h>
// Types of integers and their ranges my PC running Borland Turbo C++ compiler V 4.5
void main ( void )
{
cout << " " << endl;
cout << "\t..................................................\n" << endl;
cout << "\tInteger Types and Ranges on My PC   \n" << endl;
cout << "\t..................................................\n" << endl;
cout << "\t Minimum int                = " << INT_MIN    << endl;
cout << "\t Maximum int                = " << INT_MAX   << endl;
cout << "\t Minimum short int          = " << SHRT_MIN  << endl;
cout << "\t Maximum short int          = " << SHRT_MAX << endl;
cout << "\t Minimum long int           = " << LONG_MIN  << endl;
cout << "\t Maximum long int           = " << LONG_MAX << endl;
cout << "\t Maximum unsigned short     = " << USHRT_MAx << endl;
cout << "\t Maximum unsigned int       = " << UINT_MAX  << endl;
cout << "\t Maximum unsigned long int  = " << ULONG_MAX << endl;
cout << "\t Minimum char               = " << CHAR_MIN <<  endl;
cout << "\t Maximum char               = " << CHAR_MAX << endl;
cout << "\t Minimum signed char        = " << SCHAR_MIN << endl;
cout << "\t Maximum signed char        = " << SCHAR_MAX << endl;
cout << "\t Maximum unsigned char      = " << UCHAR_MAX << endl;
cout << "\t..................................................\n" << endl;
}
```

Diagram 7

```
.........................................................

Integer Types and Ranges on My PC

.........................................................

Minimum int                    = -32768
Maximum int                    = 32767
Minimum short int              = -32768
Maximum short int              = 32767
Minimum long int               = -2147483648
Maximum long int               = 2147483647
Maximum unsigned short         = 65535
Maximum unsigned int           = 65535
Maximum unsigned long int      = 4294967295
Minimum char                   = -128
Maximum char                   = 127
Minimum signed char            = -128
Maximum signed char            = 127
Maximum unsigned char          = 255

.........................................................
```

Diagram 7A

Diagram 8

This program is designed to display the size of integer types. **See diagram 8 on page 35**.

Explanation

This program follows the same pattern of source code as the previous program. It does not need
< limits.h> file. Here we are applying **sizeof operator** to find the sizes of integer types in bytes. The sizeof operator gives the size in bytes. In general, it is **sizeof < type>**.

```
cout << " Int  "       << "\t\t\t\t\t" << sizeof (int)  << endl;
```

In this statement, **" Int "** displays exactly as within the quotation marks. The symbol **"\t\t\t\t\t"** moves the cursor to five positions along the horizontal line for displaying the size of int. **endl;** This produces a new line. Other statements are simple output streams. You should run this program on your computer in order to gain further practical experience.

C++ Relational Operators

The next chapter will introduce you to the programming techniques of testing the relationship between values, under some given conditions. When a particular condition is evaluated as **true** then a specific line of action is followed. When the condition is evaluated as **false** an alternative action is taken. C++ has the following relational operators, which enable you to include test conditions in your program.

Relational Operators	Test Condition
==	equal to
!=	not Equal to
<	less than
<=	less than or equal to
>	greater than
>=	greater than or equal to

Table 4. Relational Operators

Practical Hints

1. Use **float-point** for numerical values involving a decimal point.
2. **Type short** defines the set of integer values between −32,768 and 32,767.
3. **Type void** defines the empty set of values, thus you cannot use it to declare a variable.
4. **Void function** returns no value.

Programming Exercises

1. Write a program that assigns three numerical values to three different variables, and performs the Following tasks:

   a) add all values together and print on the screen their sum;
   b) add two of the three variables together, divide their sum by the third variable and then display the answer on the screen; and
   C) find the average value of these variables and display it on the screen.

For questions 2 and 3, see page 36.

```
#include <iostream.h>
// To illustrate the application of sizeof operator.
//  To find out the size of  integer types in Bytes.
 main ( )
 {
cout << " \t The Size of  Integer  Types in Bytes " << endl;
cout << " \t ........................................... " << endl;
cout << " Integer Types "   <<  "\t\t\t Size in Bytes" << endl;
cout << " ....................."   <<  "\t\t\t....................\n" << endl;
cout << " char "        << "\t\t\t\t" << sizeof (char) << endl;
cout << " signed char"  << "\t\t\t\t" << sizeof (signed char) << endl;
cout << " unsigned char" << "\t\t\t\t" << sizeof (unsigned char) << endl;
cout << " Int  "        << "\t\t\t\t\t" << sizeof (int)  << endl;
cout << " short int"    << "\t\t\t\t" << sizeof (short int) << endl;
cout << " long int"     << "\t\t\t\t" << sizeof (long)<< endl;
cout << " float"        << "\t\t\t\t\t" << sizeof (float) << endl;
cout << " double"       << "\t\t\t\t\t" << sizeof (double)<< endl;
cout << " long double"  << "\t\t\t\t" << sizeof (long double) << endl;
cout << " unsigned int" << "\t\t\t\t" << sizeof ( unsigned int) << endl;
cout << " unsigned short int" << "\t\t\t" << sizeof (unsigned short int) << endl;
cout << " unsigned long int" << "\t\t\t" << sizeof (unsigned long int) << endl;
cout << " ...........................................\n" << endl;
}
```

The Size of Integer Types in Bytes
....

Integer Types	Size in Bytes
char	1
signed char	1
unsigned char	1
Int	2
short int	2
long int	4
float	4
double	8
long double	10
unsigned int	2
unsigned short int	2
unsigned long int	4

....

Diagram 8

2. cout >> " Why",
   cout << I am fine;
   cin << " Well done";
   cin >>n <<endl;

The above is a segment of a code. Is this correct? If not, why?

3. Convert the following into C++ assignments:

    a)   Balance is equal to old balance plus current sales
    b)   Discount = (Sales*5)
    c)   Y = L (1+X)

Programming Questions for Chapter 11

1. create a class called **customer** that uses a **structure** called **cust_name** to collect the following related data items:

first name, middle name, last name, status (Mr, Mrs----), sales account number and credit limit allowed. The user should be able to input values for these data items from the keyboard. Your Program should also display the Personal Finance Credit Control Information on the screen.

Hints Use **Void cust_input ( )** function for data input and **void cust_output ( )** function for displaying the required information. Create **sales_infor** object to associate it with these functions.

2. **a)** Develop a program that makes use of **nesting structure** within the **class** called **personnel** to collect the following data items to be stored in **Staff File** for the personnel dept.

name, national insurance number, sex, status, born (the year employee was born), school qualifications, further or technical qualifications, university or professional qualifications, present, recent past and past relevant work experience, present post, date appointed, salary and any other information.

   b) Your program should allow the user to enter values for the above items from the keyboard.
   c) Use the relevant values to calculate the age of the employee at his/her next birthday.
   d) Display the information under **Staff File : Information Held** as a long list consists of the following headings and the correct information against each heading:

       Name, national Insurance Number, Date of Birth, Age at Next Birthday, Marital Status, Sex, School, Qualifications, Technical/FE Qualifications, University/Professional Qualifications, Present Post, Relevant Recent Experience, Relevant Past Experience, Post Title, Date Employment Commenced, Current Salary, and Any Other Relevant Information.

Chapter 3

Conditions Testing (1)

Computers' strength lies in their ability to repeat groups of instructions at electronic speeds within a program , and to choose which instructions to execute first.

Control Structures

Some programming techniques have been developed to exploit computers' ability and power, which enable programmers to control the flow of execution. Therefore, programmers can include different means by which a group of instructions can be repeated, and executed accordingly. You can design a program which has a mechanism for controlling how many times an instruction or group of instructions is to be obeyed by the computer. You can direct your program to execute another part of the program. You can tell the computer to do something a fixed number of times and so on. You have to build a control structure in your program by means of loops and conditional statements as shown in our Table 5.

Table 5 . Control Structures Statements

Type of Conditional Statement	Action of the Condition
if	Allows conditional execution of a statement(s).
if ......else	Allows selection from two alternatives.
if......then	Allows selection when a condition is met.
for loop	Allows fixed number of times repetition.
while loop	Allows unknown number of times repetition until a condition is met.
do-- while loop	Executes the statement(s) first, and evaluates test condition at the end of the first iteration.
nested loop	Allows inside loop to be executed unknown number of times for each execution of the outer loop.
case , switch...	Allows multiple selection. Some group of statements may be executed at a time when a particular requirement is satisfied, whilst the other group is not executed.
goto	Allows repeats - a kind of jump, use label with it.
break	Allows early exit from the loop - jump statement.
continue	Returns control to the start of a loop's block.

This chapter contains a number of well structured programs. These will enable you to learn how to design programs with a control structures.

.If statement application

Diagram 9

This program enables the user to enter an account number. It tests the account number against the condition laid down. When the account number is **1000** or **greater than 1000**, it displays a message, "Wrong number. Try again!".

Source Code and the output from this program

```
#include <iostream.h>
//  To illustrate how simple if statement works.
void main ( void )
{
int account;
cout << " Enter account number: ";
cin >> account;
if ( account >= 1000 )
cout << " Wrong number. Try again! " << endl;
}
```

```
[Inactive C:\TCWIN45\BIN\FEB11.EXE]                    _ □
Enter account number: 1200
Wrong number. Try again!
```

Diagram 9

Explanation

The variable declaration is int account. It is the account which is given different numbers. The user is allowed to input any account number, because of **cin >> account;** statement. Once a number is entered the next statement is executed. Let's examine this vital statement.

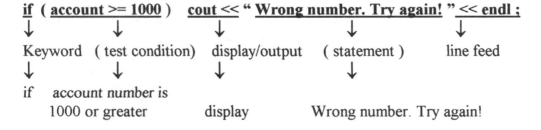

if (	account >= 1000)	cout <<	" Wrong number. Try again! "	<< endl ;
↓	↓	↓	↓	↓
Keyword	(test condition)	display/output	(statement)	line feed
↓	↓	↓	↓	
if	account number is 1000 or greater	display	Wrong number. Try again!	

To execute an **if statement,** the test condition must evaluate to TRUE or FALSE.
In this statement the test <u>condition is an integer expression</u>. When an integer expression is evaluated as a test condition, it must evaluate to TRUE or FALSE. In C++, a nonzero value, which is !0 is interpreted as a logical <u>TRUE</u>, and a zero value as a logical FALSE. In our example, the statement,

if (account >= 1000) cout << " Wrong number. Try again! " << endl ;

was evaluated to a nonzero value, !0 when the user entered 1200. For this reason, the message, " Wrong number. Try again!" was displayed on the screen. There is enough evidence to prove this in Diagram 9 above. You can see this in the print screen, a small box within this diagram. <u>The syntax for a simple **if** statement is</u> :

if (test condition) statement;
and TRUE evaluation to be executed.
. What happens when a test condition is FALSE?

The above program is not designed to evaluate TRUE and FALSE. It evaluates only nonzero value, logical True. To take any of the two separate actions, on the basis of TRUE or FALSE, you have to use BI-conditional **if....else statement**. The syntax for if....else is as follows:
if (test condition) statement 1;
else statement 2;
In this case, **statement 1** is executed, when the test condition is evaluated to a logical TRUE, **and statement 2** is executed, only when the test condition is evaluated to a zero value, **a logical FALSE.**

Diagram 10 - The previous program cannot evaluate the statement when the account number is less than 1000. It takes only one action. The program in diagram 19 can test two alternative statements:
a) display a message when the account number is equal or greater than 1000; and
b) display a different message when the account number is less than 1000.

Explanation

Let's analyse the following segment of this program.

```
if ( account >= 1000 ){
cout << " Wrong number. Try again! " << endl;
}
else
cout << " The number you have entered is:  " << account << endl;
}
```

When the user entered 1200 as an account number in response to **cin >> account;**

the test condition was executed, and a comparison was made. Since **1200** is greater than **1000**, it was evaluated to a logical **True** value. As a result of this, the statement **1** was executed, which has displayed the message, " wrong number. Try again!". See small box within diagram 10.

The user run the program once again. This time, **950** was entered. The same test condition was applied. Since it is less than **1000**, it was interpreted as a logical **False**, and the alternative action followed, " The account number you have entered is 950", was displayed on the screen. This output is shown in Diagram 10 A.

```cpp
#include <iostream.h>
//  To illustrate how simple if statement works.
void main ( void )
{
int account;
cout << " Enter account number: ";
cin >> account;
if ( account >= 1000 ){
cout << " Wrong number. Try again! " << endl;
}
else
cout << " The number you have entered is: " << account << endl;   }
```

(Inactive C:\TCWIN45\BIN\FEB11.EXE)
```
Enter account number: 1200
Wrong number. Try again!
```

Diagram 10

(Inactive C:\TCWIN45\BIN\FEB11.EXE)
```
Enter account number: 950
The number you have entered is: 950
```

Diagram 10 A

A **limitation** of this program is its inability to let the user key in more than one account number, without running the program once again. <u>How do we solve this problem ?</u> The solution is simple, use **goto** statement. In C++ a **goto statement** is a kind of jump statement. Therefore, it allows the control of the program to jump over other statements. Its destination from one place in the program to another place is determined by a **label** within the statement. Let's analyse the body of the program in Diagram 11.

```
#include <iostream.h>
// To illustrate how goto statement operates with if...else statement
void main ( void )
{
int account;
again:
cout << " Enter account number: ";
cin >> account;
if ( account >= 1000 ) {
cout << " Wrong number. Try again! " << endl;
goto again;
}
else
cout << " The number you have entered is: " << account << endl;
goto again;
}
```

Program output

```
Enter account number: 1000
Wrong number. Try again!
Enter account number: 567
The number you have entered is: 567
Enter account number: 1289
Wrong number. Try again!
Enter account number: 799
The number you have entered is: 799
Enter account number: 999
The number you have entered is: 999
Enter account number: _
```

Diagram 11

Diagram 11 - it contains an improved source code for allowing the user to input account numbers. The program checks the input against 1000. If the input account number is equal to 1000 or greater than 1000, the computer displays a message, " Wrong number. try again!". The user can continue entering account numbers. Whenever the account number is less than 1000, the computer displays a message that includes the number entered by the user, and allows user to enter account number again.

Explanation

The body of this program starts with a declaration of two variables namely, **int account, and int again;**. You have already met int account. int again has to be declared first , before it can be used as a label with a goto statement.

A label identifies a destination for a **goto** statement. It is terminated by a colon (**:**), and placed at a location, where the **goto** statement returns the control action.

The keyword goto has to be used with the declared label. The syntax for a goto statement is **goto label;** In this source code, it is **goto again;**. In this program, we have placed **again:** On the second line. On line 3, **cin >> account;** lets the user input data item. As soon as the user entered the account number 1000, the control passed on to the next line, which is a conditional statement:

> if (account >= 1000) {cout << " Wrong number. Try again! " << endl;

Since the entered number is **1000**, the statement is evaluated as a logical true, the message within the quotation marks displayed on the screen. Now the next line had to be executed. This is a **goto again;** statement. Because of this, program control jumped out of the sequence of instructions, and returned to **label again:**. Once again, the user was able to input another number, **567**. Since 567 is smaller than 1000, the control was passed on to the following segment of the program.

```
else
cout << " The number you have entered is: " << account << endl; goto again;
```

The computer displayed the message within the " " , and inserted 567 in the blank space, because of **<< account**. Program output is shown in the lower part of Diagram 11.

Practical Hints on goto statement

- **A goto** statement is useful when a repetition is desirable. In this chapter we have used **goto** statements in order to demonstrate the repeated application of a segment of a program, or to illustrate that a program can be run several times successfully.

- It is important to remember that **goto** statements can lead to codes that are difficult to read, understand, and debug.

- C++ has some excellent facilities for structured programming, some of which you will learn through this book.

Compund Conditions

Until now, we have used simple conditions. Relational operators can be used to create compound conditions, combined with logical operators. **The logical operators that can be combined are defined in our table 5.**

Logical Operator	How to read It	Definition
&&	And	**a & & b** must evaluate to 1, that is return nonzero value - logical Truth
||	Or	**a | | b** must evaluate to 1, when a and b evaluate to 1 - logical truth. Also **a | | b** must evaluate to 1, when either a or b evaluate to 1 - logical truth
!	Not	**! a** must evaluate to 1 when either a evaluates to 0

Table 5. Logical Operators & their definitions

We can draw the same conclusions from the following Truth Tables. These tables may help you to implement these rules, when testing compound conditions. These tables are from **Boolean Algebra**. In Boolean Algebra, truth values are manipulated in accordance with these rules. The value of **1** for **true**, and the value of **0** for **false**.

And Truth Table			OR Truth Table			Not Truth Table	
a	b	a && b	a	b	a || b	a	!a
1	1	1	1	1	1	1	0
1	0	0	1	0	1	0	1
0	1	0	0	1	1		
0	0	0	0	0	0		

In these tables, 1 stands for logical truth or true, and 0 for logical false or false. The next program in Diagram 12 illustrates the use of a compound statement.

Diagrams 12 & 12A

The aim of this program is to enable the user to enter customer account numbers. These numbers are to be tested against the test condition. It states that a customer account number must be greater than 1000, but less than 10000. If the entered customer number satisfies this condition, the computer should display a message, " This is our regular customer. When the current order exceeds £1000, refer to the credit controller.". If not an alternative message, "This is not our regular customer. For credit over £100, refer to our sales manager." to be displayed.

Explanation

This program follows the same pattern as our previous program, except that here the following test condition:

(account > 1000 && account <= 10000)

is a compound statement. In this test condition, it is required to implement correctly the rational operators, > and <= , combined with the logical operator **&&**, in order to achieve the desired program output. To convert the requirements into a compound test condition can be a bit tricky.

Customer account number **1234** was input by the user. The program found out that **1234** is not less than **1000** and not even **1000**, but greater than **1000**. The test condition also requires that the number must not be greater than **10000**. Indeed, 1234 is less than 10000. The test condition was satisfied, and the correct required message was displayed, as shown in Diagram 12A. Next the **goto** statement returned the control to the beginning of the program, the label, **again**. The user entered **700**, which did not meet the test condition.

Thus the control passed on to **else**, and the second required message was displayed. The program works well!

```
# include <iostream.h>
// Credit control information - application of if ...else conditional statement
void main ( void )
{
 int account, again;
again:
 cout << " Customer Account Number: ";
 cin >> account;
 if ( account > 1000 && account <= 10000 ){
        cout << "This is our regular customer. When the current order " << endl;
        cout << "exceeds £1000, refer to the credit controller." << endl;
        goto again;
    }

    else
        cout << "This is not our regular custmer." << endl;
        cout << "For credit over £100,";
        cout << " refer to our sales manager." << endl;
        goto again;
}
```

Diagram 12

Customer Account Number: **1234**
This is our regular customer. When the current order
exceeds £1000, refer to the credit controller.

Customer Account Number: **750**
This is not our regular customer.
For credit over £100, refer to our sales manager.

Customer Account Number:

Diagram 12A

* Boldface is used to highlight the input data in this diagram, and other diagrams to follow.

Non-numeric Variables

Programming is not only about handling numerical data. Programs manipulate alphabetic data as well as special characters such as *, & and so on. For instance a mailing list contains alphabetic characters. Databases hold large volumes of non-numeric data. C++ has some efficient techniques for non-numeric data manipulation. You have already met character variables. It is to repeat that eventually all data is stored and manipulated in numeric forms, that are combinations of 0 and 1. The following program illustrates how an alphabetic single character held in the store, can be detected by the computer.

Diagrams 13 & 13A

This program is designed to test if variable x holds a letter. The user has to enter a character. If this character is a letter than the test is successful, and a message, **" The letter you have just entered is =   "** to be displayed ; otherwise the alternative message, **" The number you have just entered is =   "** is printed on the screen. The blank space in both messages is filled in by the character entered each time the test condition is executed.

Explanation

We have declared **char x**, and **int s**. Variable character x holds the value of the variable that is entered by the user. The user entered T. Its value was then put in the store, labelled x. The second part of the compound test condition shown below was evaluated to logical true, because 'T' is a capital letter. It matched the required test condition.

$$((\ \underline{x >= \ 'a'\ )\ \&\&\ (\ x <= \ 'z'\ )}\ \ ||\ \ \underline{(\ x >= \ 'A'\ )\ \&\&\ (\ x <= \ 'Z'\ )}\ )$$

• First part of the test condition	• Second part of the test condition
• tests whether variable **x** holds any lower case single letter of the alphabet or not	• tests whether variable **x** holds any upper case single letter of the alphabet or not

Next the following statement was executed. This displayed the required message.

" The letter you have just entered is =   "   << x << endl;

               In this blank   Its content fills the blank space
           space **T** was printed

The goto s; statement returned control to the beginning of the program. Once again, the user entered a character. This was 9. Both parts of the compound test condition were evaluated.

Number 9 is not any of the letters of the alphabet, and thus the statement was evaluated to a nonzero value. This is a logical **false**. The control passed on to **else**, and then the following statement was executed. The second message was printed, inserting 9 in the blank space.

cout << " The letter you have just entered is =   " << x << endl;

Once again, the **goto** statement returned the control where the **label s:** is, and the execution of the program started. The output of this program is shown in the screen print below.

```
# include <iostream.h>
// single-character variable manipulation. Tests if x holds a single letter
void  main (void )
{
char x;
s:
cout << " Enter a character: ";
cin >> x;
if ( ( x >= 'a' ) && ( x <= 'z' ) || ( x >= 'A' ) && ( x <= 'Z' ) ) {
cout << " The letter you have just entered is = " << x << endl; goto s; }
else
cout << " The letter you have just entered is = " << x << endl; got s;
}
```

Diagram 13

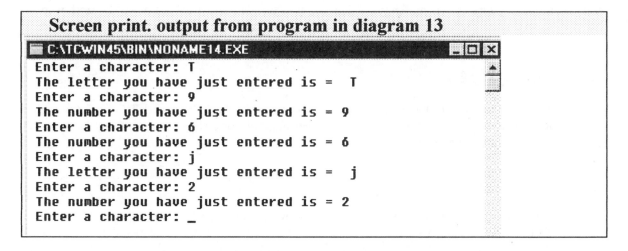

Screen print. output from program in diagram 13

```
C:\TCWIN45\BIN\NONAME14.EXE                              _ □ ×
Enter a character: T
The letter you have just entered is =  T
Enter a character: 9
The number you have just entered is = 9
Enter a character: 6
The number you have just entered is = 6
Enter a character: j
The letter you have just entered is =  j
Enter a character: 2
The number you have just entered is = 2
Enter a character: _
```

Diagram 13A

Iteration - it means the process of repetition of a statement or a number of statements in a program. It involves a loop, which is repeated or iterated until a specified condition is met. C++ has the following three iteration statements:

（ 1 ）　　　　　　　　（ 2 ）　　　　　　　　　（ 3 ）

while loop;　　　　**do--- while loop;**　　　**for statement;**

All three statements are illustrated in this book.

The while Loop It is executed continuously **while** some condition is true. It only ends when a particular condition or some conditions become(s) **false**. It is very useful where the number of repetitions is unknown. The while loop tests for exiting out of the loop, before the execution of any instructions inside the loop. It is therefore, worth using for testing conditions where no action is required. It can be used with more than one exit condition.

The While statement syntax:　**while (test condition) statement;**
　　　　　　　　　　　　　　　↓　　　　↓　　　　↓
　　　　　　　　　　　keyword　　condition　statement to be executed when true

The while statement syntax when multiple actions are involved:

```
while ( test condition)
  {
    action 1;
            action 2;
  }
```

Note the use of **{ } braces** when multiple actions are possible. The test is carried out at the start, when a loop begins. All actions will be carried out only when the test condition is satisfied, that is **true**. There is no loop, when the condition is **false**.

Diagrams 14 & 14A

The program in this diagram illustrates the application of a **while** loop. It is written to read any whole number that is entered from the keyboard, and then calculate its **cube** value. The program lets the user compute cubes as many times as necessary.

Explanation

The statement **cout << " Enter a whole number: " ;** allows the user to key in any number. The user entered number 6. In accordance with the test condition: **while (n! = 0)**, this number was then compared with 0. Since the test condition is **true**, that is number 6 is not equal to zero, the five statements within the loop were executed. The last statement: **cout << " Enter another number, if you wish: " ;** inside the loop allowed the user to enter 15. Number 15 was compared with **0**. It is not equal to 0; thus the test condition was again **true**. Lastly, the user entered 0. On comparison with **n!= 0**, the test condition proved **false**, and the execution of the program finally terminated. Each time control reached the last statement inside the loop, the condition was tested once again. You can see the output in diagram 14A.

```
#include <iostream.h>
// Work out the cube for a whole number. How to apply while statement
main(   )
{
 int n, x;
 cout << " This program is for computing cubes" << endl;
 cout << " ......................................................" << endl;
 cout <<" " << endl;
 cout << " Enter a whole number: " ;
 while (n! =  0){
     cin  >> n;
     x  = ( n*n*n );
     cout << " cube of the number keyed in is: " << x << endl;
     cout << "............................................." << endl;
     cout << " Enter another number, if you wish: " ;
     }
     return ( 0 );
}
```

Diagram 14

The output from the program in diagram 14

```
This program is for computing cubes
.................................................

 Enter a whole number: 6
 cube of the number keyed in is: 216
.............................................
Enter another number,if you wish: 15
 cube of the number keyed in is: 3375
.............................................
Enter another number,if you wish: 0
```

Diagram 14A

Diagram 15 - Using the **while loop** control structure, write and run a program that will increase the initial value 1 of the variable called <u>counter</u> by 2, each time the loop is executed, until the value of the counter is 20. Calculate the values of variables x and y, whose initial values are: x = (counter + 1) and y = (counter -1). Display the values of x and y under two columns.

Explanation

The program shown in diagram 15 perfroms the required calculations in order to generate two columns of figures, **counter** was used to control the loop.

while (counter <= 20) test condition was set up. To repeat the loop, the variable counter was incremented by 2, each time the statements:

```
x = ( counter + 1 );   y = ( x -1 );    cout << x << "\t\t\t" << y << endl;
```

inside the loops were executed. Eventually, the loop reached 20, and the test condition was then false. That terminated the loop. The computed values are shown in the lower part of the diagram.

```
#include <iostream.h>
// How to apply while statement
 void main( void  )
{

 int x, y, counter;
 cout << " x Values" << "\ty Values" << endl;
 cout << "........" << "\t ........." << endl;
 counter = 1;
         while ( counter <= 20){
                 x = ( counter + 1 );
                 y =  ( x -1 );
                 cout << x << "\t\t\t" << y << endl;
                 counter = counter + 2;
                 }
}
```

===================== Program Output =========================

```
(Inactive C:\TCWIN45\BIN\NONAME14.EXE)

 x Values          y Values

 .........          .........
 2                    1
 4                    3
 6                    5
 8                    7
 10                   9
 12                   11
 14                   13
 16                   15
 18                   17
 20                   19
```

Diagram 15

Practical Hints - while loop

- As long as the **(test condition)** is **true**, the statement or statements within { } braces
  will be executed.

- Use a while loop when you do not know how many repetitions are needed to process the data.

Do -- while loop

This loop is the only loop which executes the statement(s) first, and then tests the condition at the end of the first <u>iteration</u>. The syntax for do -- while is :

do

{

    statement;

}

while (<u>condition</u>);

test condition ↵

<u>Its general structure for multiple statements is:</u>

do

{

    statement 1;

    statement 2;

    statement 3;

}

while (<u>condition</u>);

test condition ↵

<u>Diagram 16</u> - The program is designed to read 10 different values of an integer, and display these values under column, 'number'. Use these values to generate two more columns of figures. Column 'b values' to be computed by adding 2 to each value in column 'number'; and the other column 'c values', to be the 'square' of each value in column b. Display all three columns.

Explanation

The variable **int n** was initialised to zero outside the loop. When the program reached the keyword **do,** the loop began. A block of four statements within the { } was executed, as first iteration. At the end of first iteration, the **while condition** was tested. It was found **true.** The loop entered the block of statements again, and repeated the execution of the block, until the **while condition** became **false.** The loop terminated, and the next statement

```
cout << "..................................." << endl;
```

was executed which drew a dotted line under three columns. The output is shown in diagram 16.

```
# include <iostream.h>
// illustration of do---while loop
void main ( void )
{
int b, c;
int n = 0;
          cout << "Number" << "\t\tb values" << "\tc values" << endl;
          cout << "......" << "\t\t........." << "\t........." << endl;
do {
                n = n+1;
                b = ( n +2 );
                c = ( b * b);
                cout << n << "\t\t" << b << "\t\t" << c << endl;
        }
          while ( n<=9);
          cout << "......................................" << endl;
}
```

Output

```
[Inactive C:\TCWIN45\BIN\NONAME14.EXE]
Number                 b values            c values
- - - - - -            - - - - - - - - -   - - - - - - - -
1                      3                   9
2                      4                   16
3                      5                   25
4                      6                   36
5                      7                   49
6                      8                   64
7                      9                   81
8                      10                  100
9                      11                  121
10                     12                  144
- - - - - - - - - - - - - - - - - - - - - - - - - - - - -
```

Diagram 16

while (n<= 9); above has ended at 10 not at 9, because the initial value was incremented by 1 each time.

Diagram 17

A program is designed to allow the user to enter any letter of the English alphabet. The entered letter is to be displayed. The execution of the program will be terminated, as soon as 0 that is zero is entered, by displaying, " **The end!** ".

Explanation

The source code of this program follows the same pattern as the previous program. In order to terminate the do--- while loop, it was necessary to use **logical not operator** != in the while statement:

while (alpha != '0');

When the user entered the letter v, the loop was executed immediately, performing first iteration without testing the while statement. Next the user keyed in the letter B. The test condition was evaluated and it was executed as logical true. On all subsequent entries of the data, the test condition was evaluated true, until **0** (zero) was entered. The test condition became logical false and the control was returned to the

cout << " The end!" << endl;

statement, from where the program continued. <u>The output is shown in Diagram 17A</u>

```
# include <iostream.h>
// do -- while loop operation

void main ( void )
{
char alpha;
cout << " Enter any letter of English alphabet: ";
cin >> alpha;
do
    {
    cout << " You have entered: " << alpha << endl;
    cout << " Enter any letter of English alphabet: ";
    cin >> alpha;
    }
    while ( alpha != '0' );
                    cout << " The end!" << endl;
                    cout << "........." << endl;
}
```

Diagram 17

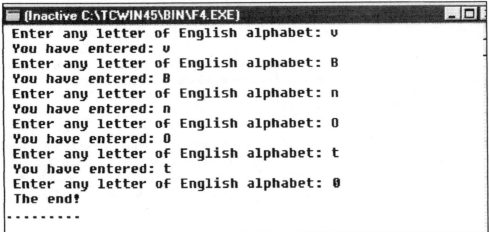

```
(Inactive C:\TCWIN45\BIN\F4.EXE)
Enter any letter of English alphabet: v
You have entered: v
Enter any letter of English alphabet: B
You have entered: B
Enter any letter of English alphabet: n
You have entered: n
Enter any letter of English alphabet: O
You have entered: O
Enter any letter of English alphabet: t
You have entered: t
Enter any letter of English alphabet: 0
The end!
. . . . . . . . .
```

Diagram 17

Practical Hints - do---while loop

• The do---while loop executes at least once.

• It is in fact a **post-test loop**, because the condition is only tested after the first iteration inside the loop (cycle).

For loop

A **for** loop can be complex.: In generl the syntax for the **for statement** is as follows:

for (initialisation value ; condition for the repetition of the loop ; counter to update the loop)
{
  statement or a block of statements;
}

Example

<u>for</u> (<u>int a = 0</u>; <u>a <= 10</u>; <u>a ++</u>)
   ↓   ↓   ↓   ↓

keyword   variable **a**   test   initial value of **a** to be updated by 1 each time loop
          assigned initial condition   is repeated to 10
          value **0**   for repetition
                      of loop up-to 10 times

{
  statement or statements;
}

Diagrams 18 & 18A

The program is designed to generate, and display 10 Customer Account Numbers, starting at 1000. These numbers to be listed under an appropriate list heading. It illustrates the application of **for loop**.

Explanation

This program has two header files. The second file **<conio.h> defines clrscr ( )** function. This function clears the output screen. The program declares account as an integer variable to hold variable values.

A **for loop** repeats the instruction for a fixed number of times, until a condition is satisfied. Here the loop was repeated 10 times. Let's analyse our for loop statement below.

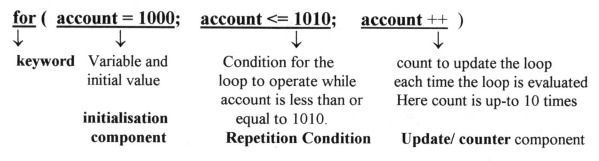

for (　account = 1000;　account <= 1010;　account ++)

keyword	Variable and initial value	Condition for the loop to operate while account is less than or equal to 1010.	count to update the loop each time the loop is evaluated Here count is up-to 10 times
	initialisation component	**Repetition Condition**	**Update/ counter component**

The output of this program is the required list shown in the print screen format in **Diagram 18**.

```
# include <iostream.h>
# include <conio.h>                    // header file for clearing display screen
// to illustrate how for loop statement operates
 void main ( void )
 {
 clrscr ( );              // to clear the screen
 int account ;
        cout << "\t\t Customer Account Numbers " << endl;
        cout << "\t\t ----------------------- " << endl;
               for ( account = 1000;  account <= 1010;  accunt++ )
                      cout << "\t\t\t " << account << endl;
}
```

Diagram 18

```
[Inactive C:\TCWIN45\BIN\CUSTOMER.EXE]                _ |□|
                Customer Account Numbers
          ----------------------------
                        1000
                        1001
                        1002
                        1003
                        1004
                        1005
                        1006
                        1007
                        1008
                        1009
                        1010
```

Diagram 18A

Diagrams 19 & 19A

The purpose of this program (**diagram 19**) is to read a variable 10 times. For each value of the variable compute its square and add square value to the number itself. Print on the same line the number, sum and square for each value that is being red.

Explanation

Statement **int a;** declared integer variable, which was used to control the **for** loop. **a =1;** initialised the variable **a** to hold 1. Let's analyse:

1.   **for (a = 1; a <= 10; a ++)**

   Keyword   initial value   test condition   each time the number is red, it
               set to 1   1 to 10 numbers   is incremented up-to 10 only as
                                to be red in the   per test condition
                                variable a

The loop repeated 10 times, and each time computed the required values in accordance with the following statement, which is an initial component of the **for loop** in this program.

2.   cout <<" Number: " << a << " Square; " <<a*a<<" Sum: "<<(a+ (a*a))<< endl;

When the counter **a** reached 10, the loop was terminated. That ended the program - no other instructions were there to execute outside the loop. Output is shown in **diagram 19A**.

```
#include <iostream.h>
// To illustrate the for statement - a simple loop.
void main (void)
{
  int a;
  cout << "\t\t\t  A Simple Calculation Program" << endl;
  cout << " \t\t\t ............................." << endl;
  cout << " " << endl;
  for ( a = 1; a <= 10; a ++ )
  cout <<" Number: " << a << " Square; " <<a*a<<" Sum: "<<( a+ (a*a))<< endl;
}
```

Diagram 19

```
========================= Program Output =========================
                     A Simple Calculation Program
                     .................................

Number: 1 Square; 1 Sum: 2
Number: 2 Square; 4 Sum: 6
Number: 3 Square; 9 Sum: 12
Number: 4 Square; 16 Sum: 20
Number: 5 Square; 25 Sum: 30
Number: 6 Square; 36 Sum: 42
Number: 7 Square; 49 Sum: 56
Number: 8 Square; 64 Sum: 72
Number: 9 Square; 81 Sum: 90
Number: 10 Square; 100 Sum: 110
```

Diagram 19 A

Pseudo Random Numbers
with for loop

It can be said that computers produce the same output for the same input. This makes them deterministic. Because of this programs cannot generate true random numbers, that are required for simulating many real life situations, such as marketing decision making which involves uncertainties. For this reason, a pseudo random number generator is used.

This random generator produces numbers by using its own pre-defined function, that uses its own defined variable. This variable is known as **seed**. By default, this seed, will always be the same; no matter how many times you run a program. C++ has a library function called **strand ( )**, that allows you to initialise your own seed. The computer program can thus generate pseudo random numbers.

Diagram 20

The diagram 20 contains another illustration of **for loop** for generating Pseudo-random numbers by using **srand library function**. The program is designed to generate 10 Pseudo- random numbers for a given **seed** , and display these in the desired format.

Explanation

```
# include <stdlib.h>
```

This program needs two header files. The above header file will enable the program to compute pseudo random numbers. **int s** is declared for the following reasons:

. when **cin >> s;** is executed, the value has to be stored in a memory cell called **s**.

. the content of **s** is then placed within **srand ( )** function in order to initialise the seed:

srand (10);

. This value is thus used as a starting point for the loop.

. To generate a set of 10 random numbers, using a **for** loop, a test condition is needed in

for (s = 0 ; s < 10 ; s++).

   int s is used here for the initial value. for test condition, as well as up-dating the counter, until it reaches 10.

The output from this program reveals that the user entered number **5** in response to a request from the computer. The computer generated a sentence acknowledging the number entered. This followed by a list of **10** random numbers generated. Since the program has included a **goto** jump statement, the control returned to **again;** statement, and the process started all over again. See the last line of the output in dagram 20A, waiting for another input data.

Practical Hints - for loop

. Use it when you already know how many times the loop needs to be executed.

```
# include <iostream.h>
# include <stdlib.h>
// To generate random numbers by applying srand ( ) function.
void main ( void )
{
  int s, again;          // s stands here for seed to be entered by you
  again:
  cout << "\t\t The Random Number Program" << endl;
  cout << "\t\t -----------------------\n" << endl;
  cout << " Please enter any whole number of your choice: ";
  cin >> s;
  srand ( s );                     // to initialise the seed
  cout << " You have just entered: " << s << endl;
  cout << " The following Random Numbers are generated" << endl;
  cout << " .........................................\n" << endl;
  srand ( s );
        for ( s = 0 ; s < 10 ; s++ )
            cout << "\t" << rand ( )<< endl;
            cout << " .........................................\n" << endl;
              goto again;
}
```

```
Please enter any whole number of your choice: 5
You have just entered: 5
The following Random Numbers are generated
- - - - - - - - - - - - - - - - - - - - - - - - - - - - - - - - - - - - - -
        1731
        32036
        21622
        27059
        21151
        21729
        26739
        27230
        23546
        31068
- - - - - - - - - - - - - - - - - - - - - - - - - - - - - - - - - - - - - -

              The Random Number Program
              ---------------------------

Please enter any whole number of your choice: _
```

Diagram 20

Programming Exercises on page 79

Chapter 4

Conditions Testing (2)

. Nested Conditional Loops

You can include a particular loop within the compound statement of another loop. A nested loop occurs when a conditional statement of a particular loop is used within the conditional statement of another loop. There is no limit to how many loops you can nest in a program. If you use too many loops, it can be very complex to sort them out. One should keep nesting simple and logical. The mechanics of nesting loop is that the **inside loop** is executed *n* times for each execution of the outer loop.

In previous examples, you have already seen the impact of a **goto** statement, which restarted the loop within the **label** and **goto** statement. The inner loop was executed *n* times, each **goto** statement was executed. The following programs illustrate nested conditional control structures.

Diagrams 21-23

The program in diagram 22 is designed to do the following tasks:

1) Create an interaction session between the user and the computer. Ask the user if he or she wants to compute a set of numbers, their squares and cubes and display them.
2) If user is not interested then a message, " goodbye!" is printed; otherwise, user is asked to enter a positive number, and how many different numbers, and their squares, and cubes are required, starting from the first number entered.
3) Built-in loops let the user re-start all over again, and compute as many sets of values as desired.
4) Only lower case letters are permitted for the interactive session.

Explanation

The program in diagram 22, has used nested conditional statements. These are depicted in diagram 21. The program displays a simple heading, informing the user of the purpose of this program. The following segment of the program invites the user:

cout << " Would you like to compute a set of numbers?" ;
cout << " Enter y for yes otherwise n: ";
cin >> canswer;

The question-answer session is self-explanatory. In order to comprehend the flow of the program, and the working of the nested conditional statements, within **if, if---else**, and **for** loops, and **goto** jump statements, now study diagram 21. The program worked very well. Its output is shown in diagram 23.

Skeleton of nested statements in the program shown in Diagram 21

Conditional statements	What they do in this program
label:	goto statement to return
if (test condition)	if the user wishes to use the program
{	
multiple	
statements	for printing a message -use lower case key
goto statement;	for the re-start if the lower case key is not used
}	
else	if the lower case key is used
if (test condition)	if user is not interested in any computation.....
{	
multiple	
statements	for printing Goodbye message
goto statement;	for the re-start
}	
else	if the user is interested in computation.....
multiple statements	for entering a number for computation ....
if (test condition)	tests if the number meets the requirement
{	
statement;	advising the user to response correctly
goto statement;	for the re-start
}	
for (initial value; test condition; increment or count;) statement;	
goto statement;	for the re-start

* for statement for printing the computed values as many times as required

Diagram 21

```
# include <iostream.h>
// To illustrate if--else, for and goto statements. All operating together.
void main (void)
{
 int a,c;
 char canswer;
 again:
 cout << " * This program generates numbers, squares and cubes.*" << endl;
 cout << " * .................................................................*" << endl;
 cout <<   " " << endl;
 cout << " Would you like to compute a set of numbers?" ;
 cout << " Enter y for yes otherwise n: ";
 cin  >> canswer;
 cout << " " << endl;
if ( canswer != 'y' &&  canswer != 'n'){
                cout << " Please enter again using a lowercase key." << endl;
                cout << " _____ " << endl;
                cout << " " << endl; goto again;
        }
 else
 if ( canswer != 'y' )
        {  cout << "          Goodbye!" << endl;
                cout << "      _____ " << endl;
                cout << " " << endl;
                goto again;
        }
 else
        cout << " Please enter a positive whole number: ";
        cin >> a;
        cout << " Please enter how many numbers,their squares and cubes"<< endl;
        cout << " to be computed, starting from the number entered above: ";
        cin >> c;
 if (c < a)
     {
       cout <<" It must be greater than the number entered above. Try again." << endl;
      goto again;
      }
       a = a ;
       for ( a = a ; a <= c; a ++ )
       cout <<" number: " << a <<" Square: " <<a*a <<" cube: " <<a*a*a << endl;
       goto again;
}
```

Diagram 22

* This program generates numbers, squares and cubes.*
* .... *

Would you like to compute a set of numbers? Enter y for yes otherwise n: **N**

Please enter again using a lowercase key.

---

* This program generates numbers, squares and cubes.*
* .... *

Would you like to compute a set of numbers? Enter y for yes otherwise n: **Y**

Please enter again using a lowercase key.

---

* This program generates numbers, squares and cubes.*
* .... *

Would you like to compute a set of numbers? Enter y for yes otherwise n: **y**

Please enter a positive whole number: **10**
Please enter how many numbers, their squares and cubes
to be computed, starting from the number entered above: **7**
c must be greater than a. Try again.
* This program generates numbers, squares and cubes.*
* .... *

Would you like to compute a set of numbers? Enter y for yes otherwise n: **y**

Please enter a positive whole number: **10**
Please enter how many numbers, their squares and cubes
to be computed, starting from the number entered above: **15**
number: 10 Square: 100 cube: 1000
number: 11 Square: 121 cube: 1331
number: 12 Square: 144 cube: 1728
number: 13 Square: 169 cube: 2197
number: 14 Square: 196 cube: 2744
number: 15 Square: 225 cube: 3375

Diagram 23 Output from the program in diagram 22

Program output

The user's first response **N** was not accepted. The program directed the user to re-enter. The user's next response **Y** was also rejected, and re-directed the user.

The user entered **y,** which was accepted, and therefore, the user was allowed to enter **10.** Next the user entered **7** which was not accepted.

Again the user was re-directed, and entered the **nested** loop again. This time, the user entered **y, 10** and **15**, which were acceptable in accordance with the conditions laid down. The program worked out numbers 10 to 15, their squares and cubes, and displayed them as per the following statement:

```
cout <<" number: " << a <<" Square: " <<a*a <<"  cube: " <<a*a*a << endl;
```

Diagrams 24-26

The program shown in diagram 25 illustrates the **nesting of conditional statements**. These are **if---else** loops. It demonstrates that every **for** statement is not necessarily followed by **else** in a nesting loop. It provides invaluable credit control information in accordance with the following rules:

a) Any orders less than £50, no credit is given.

b) if a new customer, the amount of the order is more than £49, but less than £500, charge
   15% interest over 2 years; otherwise charge 10% over 2 years.

c) if a new customer, the value of the order is £500 or more than refer to the manager;
   otherwise 15% interest over 2 years is allowed.

The program is user-friendly. It allows the user repetitions of the process involved.

Explanation

The program starts with a simple heading, asking the user to enter the amount of credit required and then to find out the customer's status. It asks the user to enter **e** for an established customer, and **n** for a new customer. It follows the rules embodied in the conditional statements, which are the rules listed above. The question-answer session is self-explanatory. In order to comprehend the flow of the program, and the working of the nested conditional statements, within **if, if---else** loops, and **goto** jump statements, now you must read diagram 24, and run this program on your own computer. The program worked very well on my system. Its output is shown in diagram 25.

Skeleton of nested statements in the program shown in Diagram 25

Conditional statements	What they do in this program
label:	for jump to start all over again
if (test condition)	test for credit worthiness
{	
statement;	Action - no credit
goto statement;	re-start again
}	
if (test condition)	test for establishing order value
if (test condition)	test for establishing order value
if (test condition)	test for establishing customer type
statement;	information on interest/ action
else	when last three test conditions **false**
statement;	information on interest/ action
if (test condition)	test for establishing order value
if (test condition)	test for establishing customer type
statement;	action for the manager
else	when last two test conditions **false**
statement;	information on interest/action
goto;	start all over again

Diagram 24

```
# include <iostream.h>
// This program demonstrates the use of nested if-else statements.

void main (void)
{
    int amount ;
    again:
    char canswer;
    cout << "\tCredit Control Information" << endl;
    cout << "\t........................................" << endl;
    cout <<  " Please enter the amount of credit required: ";
    cin >> amount;
    cout << " Please enter customer status, e for established customer."<< endl;
    cout << " Enter n for a new customer: " ;
    cin >>  canswer;
        if ( amount <= 49 ){
           cout << "\t\t\t No credit available\n" << endl; goto again; }
         if ( amount > 49 )
            if ( amount <= 499 )
              if ( canswer != 'e' )
                 cout << "\t\t\t 15 % interest over 2 years\n" << endl;
                   else
                     cout << "\t\t\t 10 % interest over 2 years\n" << endl;
                     if( amount >= 500)
                       if ( canswer != 'e')
                         cout << "\t\t\t Refer to the manager\n" << endl;
                       else
                         cout << "\t\t\t 15% interest over 2 year\n" << endl; goto again;
}
```

Diagram 25

Credit Control Information
....
Please enter the amount of credit required: **500**
Please enter customer status, e for established customer.
Enter n for a new customer: **n**
                Refer to the manager

Credit Control Information
....
Please enter the amount of credit required: **49**
Please enter customer status, e for established customer.
Enter n for a new customer: **e**
                No credit available

Credit Control Information
....
Please enter the amount of credit required: **49**
Please enter customer status, e for established customer.
Enter n for a new customer: **n**
                No credit available

Credit Control Information
....
Please enter the amount of credit required: **750**
Please enter customer status, e for established customer.
Enter n for a new customer: **n**
                Refer to the manager

Credit Control Information
....
Please enter the amount of credit required: **10000**
Please enter customer status, e for established customer.
Enter n for a new customer: e
                15% interest over 2 year

Credit Control Information
....
Please enter the amount of credit required:

<u>Diagram 26</u>

switch-case and break statements

The general structure of a **switch-case** and **break** statements:

.... a switching variable. It may
↓   be a number or character/s

keyword →   **switch (variable)**
                {
Keyword →   **case 1:**
                        statement;
                        statement;
                        .
                        .
                        break;
                case 2 :
                        statement;
                        statements;
                        .
                        .
                        break;
                        .
                        .
                        .
Keyword →   **default :** statements;   ← optional statement or statements
                        to which the program branches out
            }

When to use switch-case statement?

You can use switch-case statement with break, when **if---else nesting** loop may be difficult to follow and implement. A switch-case statement can enable you to easily code a program, which involves multiple choices.

How does it operate?

The switch statement starts with evaluating the switching variable. It searches for its value amongst the cases listed. If a match is made with the variable in case 1, then statement(s) in case 1 will be executed. If not, it will look for a match until the variable value amongst the remaining cases is found. When a match is made, then a statement (s), in that particular case will be executed. If no match is found, then the default statement will be executed until the break statement. If there is no default statement, then the program finds its exit through the }.

Reason for a break statement with switch-case:

When a match is made in a particular case, and statement(s) is/are executed, it is the **break** statement that causes the remaining switch-cases to be skipped. Without the break statement, all other statements from the next case would be executed. If the next case does not include a break statement, then all statements from this case that follow it would also be executed and so on. It is therefore important to include a break a statement at the end of each case to avoid disorder.

Diagrams 27-28

The program in diagram 27 is written and tested to demonstrate the application of switch-case and break statements. The code is aimed at allowing the user to input four pieces of numeric data a, b, c, and d, and then select any of the four cases to perform the following calculations:

a) add up **a** and **b** together, and display their sum;
b) subtract **c** from **b**, and display the result;
c) add **c** and **d** values together, divide their sum by 2, and display the answer;
d) add up all four pieces of data together, divide the sum by four, and show the result on the screen.

Explanation

The variable declaration included four **int** variables for computation, and fifth **int start** for using it as switching variable. The switch statement started with the keyword **switch**. This was followed by a switching variable in brackets. It is shown here: **switch (start)**. A simple routine of **cout** and **cin** statements invited the user to input four variables. The user entered 34, 20, 55, and 70. The next **cout** and **cin** statements required a value for the switching variable to be input. In response to this requirement, the user keyed in 1, which replaced start in switch (start) to become **start (1)**. This value set the switch to 1. The switch statement started by comparing 1 (switching variable) with the variable in **case 1**.

The program matched this with case 1 and executed the **cout** statement in case 1. This statement added up the values of a and b, and displayed then as **(a + b) = 54**. After this the control was passed on to the break statement that caused the program to terminate. The program was run four times, using different set of values. The case values were not input in the order of 1 to 4. It is not necessary. If a variable is not found, the default value is executed, as demonstrated below. see diagram 28A.

.What will happen if a switching variable value is not within the case variable range?

This is well illustrated by the following code segment, which was added to the program in diagram 27. It was placed under the case 4, before the end of switch statement. Code:

```
default: cout << "\t\t\t It is out of range " << endl;
```

The program asked to input the switching value. The user keyed in **6**. It was compared with the case values, and was found outside the range. Thus the default statement was executed, which displayed the message, "**It is out of range**". **See diagram 28A.**

Program: switch-case and break statements illustration

```
# include <iostream.h>
// Switch- break statements
 void main ( void )
 {
int a,b,c,d, start;
cout << "A simple program to demonstrate how switch & break operate" << endl;
cout << " _____ " << endl;
cout << " Enter four numbers: " << endl;
cin >> a >> b >> c >> d;
cout << "Enter start: ";
 cin >> start;
 switch (start ){
         case 1: cout << "\t\t\t ( a + b )  =  " <<( a + b ) << endl; break;
         case 2: cout << "\t\t\t ( b - c )  =  " <<( b - c ) << endl; break;
         case 3: cout << "\t\t\t ( c + d )/2  =  " <<( c + d )/2 << endl; break;
         case 4: cout << "\t\t\t(a+b+c+d)/4  =  " <<( a + b +c + d )/4 << endl;  break;
     }                                           // end of switch statement
}
```

Diagram 27

Output with the following code added to the program in diagram 28

default: cout << "\t\t\t It is out of range " << endl;

```
A simple program to demonstrate how switch & break operate
_____
 Enter four numbers:
78
89
67
90
Enter start: 6
          It is out of range
```

Diagram 28 A

A simple program to demonstrate how switch & break operate
_____
 Enter four numbers:
34
20
55
70
Enter start: 1
        (a + b) = 54

A simple program to demonstrate how switch & break operate
_____
 Enter four numbers:
56
90
100
78
Enter start: 4
       (a+b+c+d)/4 = 81

A simple program to demonstrate how switch & break operate
_____
 Enter four numbers:
56
89
0
67
Enter start: 3
       (c + d)/2 = 33

A simple program to demonstrate how switch & break operate
_____
 Enter four numbers:
67
89
90
100
Enter start: 2
       (b - c) = -1

<u>Diagram 28</u>

Continue statement

The **continue** statement stops the execution of all statements below it in the loop and returns to the beginning of the loop to start the next iteration. The iteration of the loop continues as long as the test condition is satisfied.

In what way do continue and break statements differ ?

The **continue** statement returns to the start of the loop but the **break** statement terminates the loop. The **continue** statement causes iteration. The **break** statement terminates the loop, and stops iteration process altogether. The following two small programs in diagrams 30 & 31 illustrate how these two statements operate.

Diagram 30

The program in diagram 30 is aimed at allowing the user to enter all together **5** account numbers. These account numbers must not be less than **9999**. If a user enters any account number greater than 9999, the computer should display, "you have entered   ". In this message, computer should insert the account number, which is greater than 9999.

Explanation

long int accNum is declared for variable account. In order to keep a count of account numbers to be entered, a **for loop** is required. The initial value of accNum = **1**. The test condition is set to AccNum <= 5, and the counter to update the initial value up-to 5 is accNum++.

To check the account number is less than 9999, **if** statement is included within the **for** loop. The output from this program shows that the user entered 7776, 9090, 9999, and 10000 account numbers. Because 10000 is greater than 9999, the statement which is below the **continue** statement was executed. The message, "**You have entered: 10000**" was displayed, and then **continue** returned to the start of the **for loop** to begin iteration.

The user was able to enter another account number, "777". Since this was the 5th and last account number to be allowed, the test condition failed, and loop terminated. You can confirm this action for yourself by examining the program output in this diagram.

Combining continue and break statements

Diagram 31

It contains the same program as in diagram 30, but the **break** statement is included. The user entered

654, 1239, 9999 without any message displayed by the computer. When **12345** was entered, the computer responded by displaying: **You have entered: 12345**, and the loop was terminated. Now you can be sure of the effects of both **continue** and **break** statements on the loop. Break statement does not return to the beginning of the loop, instead it terminates the loop.

```
# include <iostream.h>
// How to use continue statement
void main ( void )
{
    long  int accNum;
     for ( int counter = 1; counter <= 5; counter ++ ){
    cout << " Please enter account number: ";
     cin  >> accNum;
         if ( accNum <= 9999)continue;
             cout << " You have entered: " << accNum << endl;
         }                  // to end loop
}
-------------------------------Program output-----------------------------------------------
Please enter account number: 7776
Please enter account number: 9090
Please enter account number: 9999
Please enter account number: 10000
You have entered: 10000
Please enter account number: 777
```

Diagram 30

Enumerated types

Its general syntax is as follows:

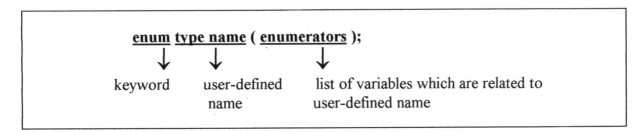

```
# include <iostream.h>
//  Effects of break and continue statements when combined
void main ( void )

{
      long  int accNum;
       for ( int counter = 1; counter <= 20; counter ++ ){
       cout << " Please enter account number: ";
       cin  >> accNum;
                if ( accNum <= 9999) continue;
                  cout << " You have entered: " << accNum << endl;
                  break;
          }    // to end loop
}
-------------------------- Program OutPut----------------------------------------
Please enter account number: 654
Please enter account number: 1239
Please enter account number: 9999
Please enter account number: 12345
You have entered: 12345
```

Diagram 31

Enumerated types are also known **as user-defined types**, because they are defined by the user.

Example

enum month { january =1 , february, march, april, may, june, july, august,
                    september, october, november, december };

In the above example **enum** is the keyword, that is always required. **month** is the name given by the user. The list month consists of 12 members, which are 12 months in any year. This way you can define your own data types. **For instance**:

enum season (spring, summer, autumn, winter);

↓

enumerators

In the above example, there are four different seasons (variables) in any year. These are then enumerators. The user can define the values of enumerators as **integer type**. In our example **enum** month, the first enumerator is defined as **january = 1**, where 1 is in fact an **integer value**. Because the first enumerator is defined as 1, the other enumerators in this list are automatically assigned the values of 2,3,4.................12. Once an enumerator is assigned a value, then the following enumerators are defined as next consecutive values. You can override the values 0,1,2,3,.....n of the enumerators, if there is a need to do so.

The prime reason for using the enumeration is that the code is easier to read and understand. Now you should examine the code in diagram 32.

Diagrams 32 & 32A

This program is designed to demonstrate the use of **enumeration** and **if** statements. The program allows the user to input any number between 1-12, as there are 12 months in a year. The computer will display a message in accordance with the number entered.

In this diagram you can see the outcomes of user-computer dialogue. When the computer displayed:

"**Enter any number from 1 to 12 for months in a year :**" The user entered 2. In response to it:

"**It is winter time in England.**" was displayed.

Program Output

Enter any number from 1 to 12 for months in a year :2
....
 It is winter time in England.

Enter any number from 1 to 12 for months in a year :6
....
 It is summer time. Enjoy your long days!

Enter any number from 1 to 12 for months in a year :4
....
 It is spring time in the UK. Be happy!

Diagram 32A

```cpp
# include <iostream.h>
// Enumeratoion type is an integer type
void main ( )
{
enum month { january =1 , february, march, april, may, june, july, august,
                september, october, november, december };
int m;
cout << "\t Enter any number from 1 to 12 for months in a year :";
cin >> m;
cout << "\t ................................................." << endl;
if ( m ==1 || m == 2 || m == 12 ) {
cout << " It is winter time in England" << endl;
                        }
        if ( m == 3 || m == 4 || m ==5 ) {
cout << " It is spring time in the UK. Be happy!" << endl;
    }
                if ( m == 6 || m == 7 || m == 8 ) {
cout << " It is summer time. Enjoy your long days!" << endl;
    }
                        if ( m == 9 || m == 10 || m ==11 ) {
cout << " It is autumn now. Get ready for winter" << endl;
    }
 }
```

Diagram 32

Diagram 33

This program illustrates that you can achieve similar results **without user-defined** type data. It is another interactive program, that allows the user to enter a response to:

"Please enter 1 to 7 for days of the week: ".

The user can choose any one of the seven 'correct' responses. Diagram 34 lists all responses input by the user, and the corresponding messages displayed by the computer.

The program can detect an **error**, if any number other than 1 to 7 has entered. When the user entered **8**, the computer responded by displaying: **"Wrong number. Try again!"**.

```cpp
# include <iostream.h>
// The application of if statement without using enum statement to achieve the same result
void main ( void )
{
  char monday, tuesday, wednesday, thursday, friday, saturday,sunday;
  int d ;

  cout << "\t Please enter 1 to 7 for days of the week: " ;
  cin >> d;
  cout << "\t .............................................................\n" << endl;

  if ( d < 1 || d > 7 ){ cout << " Wrong number. Try again!\n"<< endl;  }

      if (d == 1 ){
  cout << "On Monday we have weekly Mass lecture at 14.00\n" << endl;  }

          if ( d == 2 ){
  cout << "Tuesday is IT workshop with Dr. Nobody\n" << endl; }

            if ( d == 3 ){
  cout << "Wednesday is private study day\n" << endl; }
                if ( d == 4 ){
  cout << "Lectures all day along on Thursday\n" <<endl; }

            if ( d == 5 ){
  cout << "Friday is programming day. I enjoy learning C++\n"<< endl; }

              if ( d == 6 ){
  cout << "Saturday morning I go to our university library\n"<< endl; }

            if ( d == 7 ){
  cout << "On Sunday I take it easy, but study in the morning\n"<< endl; }
}
```

Diagram 33

Output from program in Diagram 33

Please enter 1 to 7 for days of the week: **8**
....

Wrong number. Try again!

Please enter 1 to 7 for days of the week: **2**
....

Tuesday is IT workshop with Dr. Nobody

Please enter 1 to 7 for days of the week: **1**
....

On Monday we have weekly Mass lecture at 14.00

Please enter 1 to 7 for days of the week: **7**
....

On Sunday I take it easy, but study in the morning

Please enter 1 to 7 for days of the week: **5**
....

Friday is programming day. I enjoy learning C++

Please enter 1 to 7 for days of the week: **4**
....

Lectures all day along on Thursday

Please enter 1 to 7 for days of the week: **3**
....

Wednesday is private study day

Please enter 1 to 7 for days of the week: **6**
....

Saturday morning I go to our university library

Diagram 34

Programming Exercises Chapters 3-4

1. Design and test a program that is user-friendly. It must allow the male user to enter the year in which he was born. Use the year entered to work out the year the person will reach his statutory retirement age, which is 65. Display the following message,

"You will be happily retired in ---- years time. Be happy!".

Your program must forecast the number of years.
If the user has already reached his statutory retirement age , print the following message:

Sir you are a senior citizen. Keep enjoying yourself !

The interactive user-friendly session must begin with a simple message, informing the user, what the program can tell or work out.

(In your own interest write and run the designed program first. See the suggested program and its desired output on page 220).

2. Write and run a program that will generate retirement information for ladies, under the following requirements:

(a) if she is under 60 years of age:

. numbers of years before she will reach her statutory retirement age.
. year when statutory retirement year to commence.
. the year she was born.
. the above information should include her first name, and a cheerful remark.

(b) if she already has reached her statutory retirement age:

. you are already a senior citizen.
. the year you reached your pensionable age.
. the year she was born.
. the above information to be printed with a cheerful remark.

Screen layout should begin with the a brief heading, describing the aim of this program. For both cases, all the required information to be worked out by applying input data.

Hint: variables for this program: **int age, retirement, pension; currentYear, birth, retire;**

Further hint: char name [30] ; This will be explained under arrays.

3. Write and run a program that tests if a variable holds a single digit or not. The program should enable the user to apply this test more than once.

4. Write and run a program that will demonstrate the use of a **while loop control structure**. This program must generate three columns, containing values of

$$n, \ b = (n+1), \ and \ c = (b* \ b)$$

respectively. The initial value of **n = 0**. No more than six values to be displayed in each column.

5. Write and test a program that will generate **10 random** numbers. You should use your own **seed 2**. Show these numbers in the form of a list with an appropriate heading.

6. Your PC has the **maximum random number**. Write and run a program to find out this number on your own computer, and display it. (solution on page 78).

7. Develop a program that will distinguish between a normal year and a leap year. A leap year is one year in every four years, with an extra day (29 February). Your program must be interactive, so that the user has the opportunity to find out past or future leap years. Display both input and output on the screen.

Leap Year Programming Problem

To compute a leap year requires first the year be divided by 4. However, if the year is also divided by 100 then it is not a leap year, unless it is also divisible by 400. **Why is it so?** The fact is that the earth does not go around the sun four times in exactly **1461 (3*365+366)** days. Because of this, every so often a correction is needed. Year 2000 is a leap year. The following is the required test condition for computing the leap year.

```
if ( y % 4 == 0 && y % 100 != 0 || y % 400 == 0)   // Leap Year condition
```

8. Write and run a program that will perform the following tasks:
   input data:

   a) ask the user to supply surname, first initial, and second initial, each on a separate line;
   b) let the user enter subject code numeric number; and
   c) let the user enter final grade, using upper case letter only.

These grades are: **P** for pass, **F** for fail, **R** for referral, **M** for merit, and **D** for highest pass grade.

output information

a) use these grades as **char** case values in **switch-case** statement.

b) display first initial, second initial, and surname on the same line.

This should be followed by an appropriate message. The required appropriate messages are:

. Your pass grade is P. Successful!   for grade P
. You are unsuccessful.   for grade F
         Please make an appointment to see your course tutor.
. Your grade is referral. You will receive a letter soon.   for grade R
. Your pass grade is merit. Good!   for grade M
. Your grade is the highest pass grade.   for grade D
         Well done!

If a grade is entered in **lower** case letter, display an error message, **" Error: grade is out of range"**.

Hint: switching variable: **grade.** use **break** statement with **switch-case** statement.

switch (grade) ↵

9 Develop and test a program that will perform the following tasks.

a) Allow the user to enter any number between 1 and 7 as there are seven days in a week. Monday is day one.
b) the user should be able to enter any number of his or her choice.
c) In response to the number to be entered, an appropriate message, from the following messages to be displayed on the screen:
    when 1 is entered: On Monday we have weekly Mass lecture at 14.00
    when 2 is entered: Tuesday is IT workshop all afternoon with Dr. Nobody
    when 3 is entered: Wednesday is private study day
    when 4 is entered: Lectures and seminars all day along on Thursday
    when 5 is entered: Friday is programming day. I enjoy learning C++
    when 6 is entered: Saturday morning I go to our university library
    when 7 is entered: On Sunday I take it easy, but do study in the morning
d) when 8 or any other number, other than 1 to 7 is entered, display this message:

Wrong number. Try again!

The answer to this question is on page 77-78. You should write a similar program about your daily routine.

Chapter 5

Functions

Most programs that deal with real life situations are large and consist of a number of small programs or modules. These modules are known as functions. Functions are at the heart of C++ programming. You have already met main ( ) function, which is the vital part of all C++ programs. Functions simplify programs, which is an important aspect of structure programming. C++ has a library of pre-defined functions, accessible through header files. You have already leant the use of clrscr ( ), rand ( ) and other library functions.

Let's first consider the **main ( )** function:

```
        main ( )    ← execution of the program begins from this point
    {               ← body of function main ( ). It begins here.
      statement;        )
      statement;        )
            .           )   Body of function main ( )
            .           )
      return statement;  )
            ↓
        returns value in accordance with
        return type. For instance int type will return int type value, and
        void will not return any value.
    }  ← body of function main ( ) ends here
```

● Why should you use simply **main ( )** instead of **int main ( )?** **int type** is the **default** return type for any function. Usually it is sufficient to write **main ( )** instead of **int main ( )**

If you do so, Borland compiler will issue a warning.

● **main ( )** has nothing within ( ). **Why is it so?** It simply means that function **main ( )** has no arguments or parameters. **main ( )** is known as **void** function. It does not return any value to be used in the rest of the program.

.Function calling another function

Since most programs have a number of functions, **main ( )** function is conventionally the first function and other functions appear underneath. However, it is not a hard and fast rule. Let's examine first **diagram 35** on page 85.

It contains a program that displays information about company, its address and telephone number, each on a separate line. <u>Each line of this program has an arrow head pointing to it, with some explanation</u>. The program illustrates the use of functions. and each function's role within this program.

Explanation

The program execution starts from the function **main**. This function **calls** or **invokes** the function **Company**. The computer begins execution of function **Company**. The function **Company** requires data to carry out its task. Thus the computer executes the statement:

cout << " A.D.R. (London) Limited" << endl;

which is within this function definition. It displays the required company name. There are no more instructions/statements to execute in this function and therefore, the control passes to the function **Address** and statement :

cout << " A.D.R. (London) Limited" << endl;

in this function definition is executed. It displays the required address. As with the previous function call, there is only one statement to execute. At the end of this function, the control passes to the next function **Tel**. Like the previous function, it has only one statement:

cout << " 01262 60011" << endl;

which is executed. This statement displays the required telephone number.

Prototype

From the above it is evident that the function **main ( )** has made use of three functions. It is for this reason that we have declared important information about these functions within the body of the function **main**. It is just enough information about functions namely, Company, Address, and Tel. This information has enabled the compiler to be aware of the <u>types and arguments these functions have used</u>. This declaration is called **function prototype**. It is also known as **function declaration**. It tells the compiler of the type of data to be returned and type of data and number of arguments that function will use. Because of this prototype the compiler can check that the data and argument (s) that are passed to the function are of the same types. Usually the function prototype is simple. Its general format is shown on page 84.

<u>**type to be returned**</u>   <u>**Name (argument types)**</u> **;**

↓	↓	↓	↓
it can be	any legal	it can be	it is essential
void, int, float...	name	void, int float...	

Prototypes are usually placed below **main ( )** <u>It should be remembered that a function's declaration does not end with a semicolon, like the declaration of its prototype.</u> You can see this in diagram 35. You should run the program as you have done before, and analyse its working to understand how control passes from one function to another function. The next example in diagram 36, will further illustrate how to declare the prototype, how functions work, and how control passes from one function to another function to complete the execution of a program.

Diagram 36

This program is designed to illustrate how to declare prototypes. The program has two functions, besides the **main ( )**. Function **displayMessage1** and **displayMessage2** will generate and display on the screen two different messages. **<u>How does it work?</u>**

Explanation

This time we have declared **int main (void)**.

Because of **int type** return, we have to include **return (0)**; otherwise, the compiler will issue an error message. Like the previous program, prototypes of both functions are declared within the boundaries of function **main**. In this program function **main** makes use of two functions. Each function has a body that is composed of a number of statements, which is enclosed within { }, a pair of braces.

The program execution starts at the beginning of function **main**, which calls the function **displayMessage1**. Its execution begins and statements within its boundaries are executed sequentially. This function generates and displays the required message:

"Hallo my friend! Welcome to the wonderful world of functions!"

As soon as the execution of function **displayMessage1** ends, the control or the execution returns to the function **displayMessage2** and a number of statements within this function are sequentially executed. This function generates and displays as required:

> **I must tell you our next motto**
> **Live each day as it comes!**

....

At the end of the execution of the last statement within this function, control passes to the function that calls it. As there are no more functions to execute, the program execution is terminated. The output from this program and the program are shown in diagrams 36 and 36A on pages 86-87.

```
# include <iostream.h>  ← HEADER FILE for the input & output routines
void main ( void)          ← Program execution starts here with this function
{
void Company ( void );   ←    function Company header /declaration

Company ( );      ← function Company needs data to carry out its task/ declaration
                        Without it, function Company will not perform its task, and
                        computer will not  display any error message.
void Address ( void );  ← function Address header/ declaration

Address ( );      ← function  Address requires data to carry out its task/declaration
                     Without it, function Address will not perform its task, and
                     computer will not  display any error message.


void Tel ( v oid );   ← function Tel/declaration

 Tel ( );                    ← function Tel needs data to carry out its task/declaration
                               Without it, function Tel  will not perform its task, and
                               computer will not  display any error message.
}
void Company ( void )        ← function Company/ definition
{
cout << " A.D.R. (London) Limited" << endl;      ←   task for function Company
}

void Address ( void )            ← function Address/definition
{
 cout << " Bridlington England" << endl;     ← task for function Address
}

void Tel ( void )                ← function Tel/ definition
{
 cout << " 01262 60011" << endl;             ← task for function Tel
 }
================= Output from the Program =================
A.D.R. (London) Limited
Bridlington  England
01262 60011
```

Diagram 35

```
# include <iostream.h>
//  Prototypes and how to use them
int main ( void )
{
                                            // Function displayMessage1 prototype
      void displayMessage1 ( void );
      displayMessage1 ( );
                                            // Function displayMessage2  prototype
      void displayMessage2 ( void );
      displayMessage2 ( );
   return ( 0 ) ;
}
 void displayMessage1 ( void )                  // function displayMessage1
{
      cout << " " << endl;
      cout << " " << endl;
      cout << "          ........................ " endl;
      cout << "            Hallo my friend!"  << endl;
      cout << "          ........................." << endl;
      cout << " " << endl;
      cout << "  Welcome to the wonderful world of functions!" << endl;
      cout << "  ........................................................" << endl;
      cout << " " << endl;
}
void displayMessage2  ( void )                  // function displayMessage 2
{
  cout << " " << endl;
  cout << "    I must tell you our next motto  " << endl;
  cout << " " << endl;
  cout << "    Live each day as it comes! "  << endl;
  cout << "      ........................... " << endl;
  cout << " " << endl;
}
```

Diagram 36

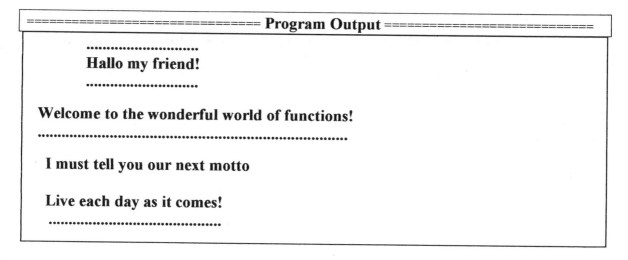

```
============================== Program Output ==============================

          ........................
          Hallo my friend!
          ........................

    Welcome to the wonderful world of functions!
    ................................................................

    I must tell you our next motto

    Live each day as it comes!
          ...........................................
```

Diagram 36 A

Return statement and the likely pitfalls due to its incorrect use

What happens when return statement is either missing or incorrectly coded for int type to be returned?

Borland compiler issues a warning or error message, if you have not coded **return** statement correctly. The following messages were issued when **return** statement was incorrectly coded:

1) Without **0** in ( ) , the compiler issued the following error message, and the program was <u>not</u> compiled successfully:

> **Compiling XX.CPP:**
> **Error XX.CPP 10: Expression syntax in function main( )**

2) When tried to compile the program with **return** statement coded just **return;**
the compiler issued the following error message:

> **Compiling XX.CPP:**
> **Error XX.CPP 10: Function should return a value in function main( )**

3) **return** statement was missing then the following warning message appeared but the program was compiled successfully.

> **Compiling XX.CPP:**
> **Warning XX.CPP 11: Function should return a value in function main( )**

In the previous program, which is shown in diagram 34, no **return** statement is necessary. **Why is it so?**

When **void type** value to be returned, there is no need to include **return** statement. **void** means empty, that is no value to be returned.

Practical Hints

- Each function's body is within its own braces { }.

- A function name must not begin with an underscore.

- A function name must be a unique name. It can be in theory upto 32 letters long.

- A function name cannot be split up with spaces, but you can use name like sumSquare.

- A function definition contains complete function, header, and code within its body.

- A prototype does not contain the actual code for particular function, except some essential information as explained above.

Diagram 37

The program is designed to illustrate that a function has its own variables. Besides the function **main**, we have another function called wages.

Local Variales

Within the function wages definition, we have declared variables namely **b**, **o** , and **wages** of **int** type. These variables are **local variables**, as they are available only to the function wages. **int** wages is computed by using the values of **b** and **o**. The flow of this program is simple to follow.

The program execution commences at function **main**. This function invokes the function wages. The statements within this function are executed sequentially. When the last statement within this function is executed, the program terminates, as there are no more functions to pass control. The output is shown at the bottom of this diagram.

```
#include <iostream.h>
// Using functions - a function has its own data
int main (void)
{
                            // prototype
void wages (void);
 wages ( );

}
                            // function wages
void wages (void)
{
 int b, o,  wages ;
 cout << " Enter a value for b which stands for basic wage: " ;
 cin  >> b;
 cout << " Enter a value for o which stands for overtime: ";
 cin  >> o;
 wages = ( b + o );
 cout << " ..................................." << endl;
 cout << " Total wages this week = £ " << wages << endl;
 cout << " ..................................";
}
```

// prototype or declaration.

// call to function wages.

Definition of function wages.

===================== Program Output =====================

　　Enter a value for b which stands for basic wage: 120
　　Enter a value for o which stands for overtime: 34

　.................. ....
　Total wages this week = £ 154
　..................

Diagram 37

Global Variables

Diagram 38

DON'T USE GLOBAL VARIABLES.
See Sam's P.68.

The program in this diagram illustrates the use of **Global** and **Local variables**. **Global** Variables are declared outside any particular function, and are available to other functions. Global variables may not be available to all parts of the program, but only to those parts of the program that come after their declaration.

Explanation

This program has four global **int** type variables namely a, b, c, and d. Their numeric values are already assigned. These variables are declared outside the function **main**, and thus they are external to all functions in this program. There are two functions **main** and **Av**.

The function **main** makes use of global variables in the statement:

$$\textbf{average } = (\textbf{ x} + \textbf{y} + \textbf{a} + \textbf{b} + \textbf{c} + \textbf{d })\textbf{/6;}$$

The execution of the program started at function **main**. It called the function **Av**, which is the first statement within it. Thus the control passed to this function, and the following statements in the function definition were executed sequentially.

```
cout << " Average of global variables = " << ( a + b+ c + d )/4 << endl;
 cout <<"\n";
```

When the execution of the function **Av** has ended, the control returned to the statement :

```
int  x = 10, y = 20, average ;
```

This is the statement that follows the function call. It is in the body of function **main**. Then, within this function execution continued sequentially. At the end of the execution, the program was terminated. Its desired output is shown in the diagram under program output.

Average of global variables = 200 is the first program output. **<u>Why is it so?</u>**

You can see in diagram 38 the prototype of function **Av** is the first item within the body of the function **main**. The program execution started at function **main**. The function **Av** was called immediately. It is for this reason that this average value was computed first, and displayed. If you declare function **Av** prototype at the end of the last statement in function **main**, "**Average of global variables = 200**", would be displayed underneath: Average using both global and local variables = 138, which is the output of function **main**. The program output is shown below.

```
==========================Program Ouput==========================
Average of global variables = 200

Average using both global and local variables = 138
-------------------------------------------------------
```

```
# include <iostream.h>
// Global variables/data
// Use local and global variables to calculate average
int a = 100, b = 150, c = 350, d = 200;                    // Global Data
void  main (void)
{
 void Av ( );
 Av ( );
 int  x  = 10, y  =  20,  average ;
 average  = ( x + y + a + b + c + d )/6;
 cout << " Average using both global and local variables" << " = " << average << endl;
 cout << " ------------------------------------------------------" << endl;
 cout << " " << endl;
}
void Av ( )
{
 cout << " Average of global variables = " << ( a + b+ c + d )/4 << endl;
 cout <<"\n";
}
```

Diagram 38

Function Scope

The scope of a **local variable** is limited to the extent of a function definition. It is accessible only within a particular function. Variables can also have a **file scope**. A variable that has a file scope is accessible throughout the file in which it is declared. It is then a global variable within that file. You can change the scope of a local variable by using the **scope resolution operator (::)** to file scope. The following example illustrates the application of resolution operator.

Diagram 39

The program calculates averages and sum, using both local and global variables. It displays the required averages and sum on the screen. It has **Add ( ), Av ( )** functions, and two variables. These are declared outside the function **main**, and thus their scope includes the entire file.

Explanation

There are two variables namely x and y in this program. These variables are declared three times in the program. Each set of x and y is assigned different numeric values. The first set of x and y values is global. Thus, their scope is file scope. The second set of x and y values is within the function **main**, therefore it has local scope. It is accessible only within function **main**. The third set of x and y values is within function **Add ( )**, so it has local scope.

It is desirable to use global variables together with local variables to calculate the average value in the function **main**. C++ allows you to do so by using the scope operator ::. For this purpose we must change the syntax of the relevant statement within the function **main**. We have done so, as shown below.

$$\textbf{average} = (\text{x} + \text{y} + \underset{\downarrow}{\underline{::}}\ \underset{\downarrow}{\underline{\text{x}}} + \underset{\downarrow}{\underline{::}\ \underline{\text{y}}})/4;$$

                                resolution   global   global variable
                                operator   variable

It is also required to add global variable **y** to the local variable **y** in the function **Add ( )**, instead of adding only local variables together. It has been achieved as shown below.

```
cout << " The sum of one local and one global variable = " << ( x+:: y ) << endl;
```

The rest of the program follows the pattern of the previous programs involving functions. The program execution started at function **main ( )**. Statements within this function are sequentially executed. This function worked out the average, using both local and global variables and displayed it.

When the execution reached **Add ( )** statement, then the control passed to the function **Add ( )**, and statements within this function sequentially executed. The function computed the sum of local variables, and then the sum of one local and one global variable, and displayed these as required.

When the function had finished execution, the control returned to the statement **Av ( )** following the function call. All statements within this function were sequentially executed. This function calculated the average of global variables, and displayed it. When function had finished execution, control returned to the statement following the function call. With the execution of the following statement, the program was terminated.

```
cout << "\t\t\t THE END OF THIS PROGRAM. BYE FOR NOW!" << endl;
```

```
#include <iostream.h>
// Global variables/data - Function Scope
void Add ( );                                              // global
void Av ( );                                               // global
int x = 350, y = 200;                         //   global
void  main (void)
{                                             // starts scope of main ( )
  int x = 10 , y =  20 , average ;
  average = ( x + y +:: x + :: y )/4;          // The scope resolution operator ::
  cout << "\t\t average" << " = " << average << endl;
  cout << "\t\t ............" << "......" << endl;
  cout << " This average value included two global data items." << endl;
Add ( );
  Av ( );
  cout << "\t\t\t THE END OF THIS PROGRAM. BYE FOR NOW!" << endl;
  cout << "\t\t\t _____ " << endl;
}                                             // ends scope of main ( )
 void Add ( )
{                                             // starts scope of Add ( )
        int x = 400, y = 250;
        cout << " The sum of local variables = " << ( x + y ) << endl;
        cout << " " << endl;
        cout << " The sum of one local and one global variable = " << ( x+:: y ) << endl;
}
                                                          // ends scope of Add ( )
void Av ( )
{                                             // begins scope of Av ( )
        cout << " The average  of global variables = "
                    << ( x+ y )/2 << endl;
}                                             // ends scope of Av ( )
```

--**Program Output**--

        average = 145
        ....

This average value included two global data items.
....

The sum of local variables = 650

The sum of one local and one global variable = 600
The average of global variables = 275

                    THE END OF THIS PROGRAM. BYE FOR NOW!

Diagram 39

Passing a parameter or parameters to a function

A variable's name within the brackets in the function name is called a parameter. The following examples illustrate the position of parameters in two function's headers:

Function 1   **Function 2**

void wages (<u>int x, int y</u>)   int add (<u>int x</u>)
                    ↓   ↓
              two parameters   one parameter x of **int** type
              x and y of **int** type

You have already met these parameters in function prototypes and in function headers. A parameter is also known as **argument.** When we say an argument, it has nothing to do with any argument between people. It is another jargon. Indeed, it is a bit confusing.

You have learnt that functions communicate with each other by **calling**. Often data has to be passed from one function to another function, so that a function can perform its task. The passing of data may be:

- **passing by value method or call by value method**
- **passing by reference method or call by reference method**

What happens when data (variables) are passed call by value method?

The actual contents of the variable are **not** passed, but a copy is passed. It does not in any way change the contents of variables in the calling function. Passing by value is only a duplicate of the actual parameter (argument).

Are there any disadvantages of passing by value method?

The function returns only one value. When data is passed by this method, it is only a duplicate. Because this approach creates duplication, more program memory is required.

What happens when data (variables) are passed call by reference method?

By this method, it is the address of the parameter is passed. It can alter the actual parameters in the calling function. It requires less program memory than the call by reference approach.

In what circumstances is the passing by reference method more useful than passing by value?

When a function has to return more than one value than passing by reference is the best approach to use. In C++ passing by value method is the default method. It is a popular method.

```cpp
# include <iostream.h>
// Passing by value method the computed average  value to another function for printing

int main ( void )
{
 int average;
int a = 280, b = 400, c = 580, d = 350, e = 350, f = 600, g = 300, h = 425,
               i = 400, j = 385;
 average = ( a + b + c + d + e + f + g + h + i + j )/10 ;
 void dispAver( int sal );
 dispAver ( average );
 return ( 0 );
}
 void dispAver (int sal )
{
cout << " Average weekly salary of 10 employees = " << "£" << sal << endl;
cout << " _____ " << endl;
}
```

—————————————————————— Program Output ——————————————————————

Average weekly salary of 10 employees = £407

_____

Diagram 40

Diagram 40

This program is designed to demonstrate how data is **passed by value method** to a function. It will work-out the average weekly salary and print it.

Explanation

There are two functions in this program. The execution of the program started at function **main**, It read 10 numeric values, and computed their average value. When the execution reached statement:

void dispAver(int sal);

it called upon the function **dispAver**, and passed to it the computed average value, as a parameter.The task of function **disAver** was to use the value passed to it, and print it. It did so in accordance with the statements within this function. When the function had printed the following desired output:

Average weekly salary of 10 employees = £407

Control returned to the statement: return (0); terminating the execution of the program.

Diagram 41

The program illustrates how more than one data item can be passed to a function by passing value method. It asks the user to input data, and then passes this data to the other function so that it can perform its task. It prints the desired result. The program is interactive.

Explanation

Besides the function **main**, there is another function called **wages**. The execution of the program started at function **main**, and statements within this function executed sequentially as follows:

The user was asked to input basic wage and the user was allowed to enter **150**. After this the user was asked to enter a numeric vale for the overtime this week. In response to this, the user entered **35**. At this stage, the control passed to function wages: **void wages (int x, int y);**

This function needed data to calculate the gross wages this week. These two data items were then passed to this statement: **wages (w, o);**

The execution of statements within this function's definition began sequentially. The user was asked to input surname, first and second initials. At this stage, the execution reached the following statement:

wages = (x + y);

The parameters which were passed to this function were substituted in this statement to compute wages. After this, the following statements were executed sequentially in order to print the required output

```
cout << " Gross wages this week for " <<" " << f <<" "<< sec <<" " << s;
cout << " = £" << wages << endl;
cout << " ................................................ ";
```

When the execution reached the last statement in the above segment of the function wages, the control returned to the statement following the function call: **return (0);** and the program was terminated.

```
# include <iostream.h>
// Passing more than one parameter ( data items ) to a function. passing by value method
int main ( void )
{
 int w, o;
 cout << " Please enter basic wage: " ;
 cin  >> w;
 cout << " Please enter overtime this week: ";
 cin  >> o;
void wages ( int x, int y );
 wages ( w, o );
 return ( 0 );
}
void wages ( int x, int y )              // wages function
{ int wages;
 char s [40], f, sec ;                   // [ ] More about it when we discuss arrays
 cout << " Please enter surname: ";
 cin  >> s;
 cout << " Please enter first initial: ";
 cin  >> f;
 cout << " Please enter second initial, if none enter - : ";
 cin  >> sec ;
 cout << " ................................................." << endl;
 wages = ( x + y );
 cout << " Gross wages this week for " <<" " << f <<" "<< sec <<" " << s;
 cout << " = £" << wages << endl;
 cout << " ................................................." ;
}
```

Program Output

```
Please enter basic wage: 150
Please enter overtime this week: 35
Please enter surname: Smith
Please enter first initial: V
Please enter second initial, if none enter - : D
.................................................
Gross wages this week for  V D Smith = £185
.................................................
```

Diagram 41

Practical Hints

- The order of parameters in both calling and called functions must be the same order.
- Parameters must match both in calling and called functions, e.g. don't use float for **int**.
- When a value is to be passed to a function and it must not be changed, then apply passing by value method. By this method, the function is self-contained and protected.
- When a function should return a single value, use passing by value method.
- In passing by value method, the variable is a read-only parameter.
- In passing by reference method, the variable is read-write parameter.
- Use passing by reference method when the function has to return more than one value. When a value is to be passed to a function and it is to be changed then apply passing by reference method. Run yourself solved examples to analyse results by both methods.

Diagrams 42 & 42A

The program is designed to demonstrate the application of **passing data by reference method** to a function. This program asks the user to input any three items of data. It calculates their average and prints it.

Explanation

This program has two functions. The function **Av** performs calcluations by using three variables that are accepted by function **main**. The function **Av's** declaration (prototype) is analysed below.

float Av (<u>float x, float y, float z,</u> <u>float &sum,</u> <u>float &av</u>);

three variables **x, y, z**   reference variable **sum**   reference variable **av**

The reference operator **&** (ampersand) makes **sum** and **av float tpe** synonyms for the actual parameters passed to the function.

What actually happened?

The user was allowed to input three values for three variables. They were accepted by the function **main**. Then these data items were <u>passed by value method</u> to the function **Av**. These values were not themselves changed; but they were used in the following segment of the code to calculate the required sum and average values:

```
sum = ( x + y + z );
av  = ( x + y + z )/3;
```

What had to be changed?

You can see in the above analysis of the function header two reference values namely **float &sum** and **float &av**. These reference variables held the calculated values of **sum** and **av**.

These values were then passed back to the calling function in order to change **sum** and **av** in **Av (x, y, z , sum, av)** statement in the function **main**. The function **main** used these reference values to print the required sum and average.

```
# include <iostream.h>
// Reference  parameters - Passing by reference method

int main (void)
{
float Av ( float x, float y, float z, float &sum, float &av );        // function Av header
float a, b, c, sum, av ;
cout <<" Please type any number" << endl;
cin >> a;
cout <<" Please type another number" << endl;
cin >> b;
cout <<" Please type last number" << endl;
cin >> c;
Av ( a, b, c, sum, av );
cout << " sum is " << sum <<endl;
cout << " " << endl;
cout << " average is " << av << endl;
return ( 0 );
}

                        // on receipt of values, it adds three numbers and finds average

float Av ( float x, float y, float z, float &sum, float &av )
{
        sum  =  ( x + y + z );
        av  =  ( x + y + z )/3;
                              // computed values are passed back to the calling function
}
```

Diagram 42

Output from the Program

Please type any number
45.90
Please type another number
60.00
Please type last number
100.10
sum is 206

average is 68.6667

Diagram 42A

Diagrams 43 & 43A

This program demonstrates the **swap ( )** function that uses passing by reference method for data communication between functions.

Explanation

Besides the function **main**, there is the following function:

$$\text{void swap (} \underline{\text{int\& x, int\& y}} \text{)}$$
$$\downarrow$$
reference parameters

In the function **main**, two **int** type variables are declared. These variables are assigned values:

> **int s = 250, w = 200.** We want the function to swap their values.

The function swap allows you to swap <u>s</u> for <u>w</u> , and <u>w</u> for <u>s</u>. This way <u>s</u> can can have <u>w</u>'s value, and w can have <u>s</u>'s value. It certainly interchanges the objects that are passed to it. What is an object?

C++ is an object-oriented programming language (OOP). We will discuss this in sufficient detail later on in this book; suffice to say that variables are often termed as objects. So **s** and **w** here are two objects that are passed to function **swap** for interchange.

In function **swap (int& x, int& y)** int& x and int& y are aliases for actual parameters that were passed to the function. When the execution reached **swap (s, w)**, then the function created two local reference values namely **x** and **y**. This way x became s, and y became w. Then the local variable **hold** initialised with the value of s, and s assigned the w, and w is assigned the value of **hold**. These swaps are depicted below.

Code Segment	Swapping	Assigned Values
int hold = x; →	local variable **hold** initialised	250
x = y; →	s assigned the value of **w**	200
y = hold; →	**w** assigned the value of hold	250

As a result of this swap, **salary** became **wages** = 200, and **wages** became **salary** = 250, as shown in the output from the program. You can appreciate the effects of passing by reference method. It changed the value of variables. When the function terminated, both parameters ended up with different values. Thus these parameters are **read-write**.

```
# include <iostream.h>
// Reference Parameters - Passing by reference
int main (void)
{
 void swap ( int&  x,  int&  y );
 cout << "\t The swap or exchange function" << endl;
  cout << "\t ............................................" << endl;
 int s = 250, w = 200;
 cout <<  "\t Salary = " << s << " wages = " << w << endl;
 cout << " " << endl;
 swap ( s, w );
 cout << " By exchanging or swapping salary became wages = " << s << endl;
 cout << " ..............................................................." << endl;
 cout << " At the same time wages became salary = " << w << endl;
 cout << " ............................................................" << endl;
}
                                // The swap Function to exchange value
void swap ( int&  x,  int&  y )
{
 int hold  = x;                 // local variable hold
  x = y;
 y = hold;
}
```

Diagram 43

============== Output from the Program ==================

The swap or exchange function
....
Salary = 250 wages = 200

By exchanging or swapping salary became wages = 200
....
At the same time wages became salary = 250
....

Diagram 43A

Diagram 44

The program illustrates the difference and effects of passing data by value method and by reference method to a function. Passing by reference method changes the value of a parameter, and passing by value method has no effect on the value of the parameter. It is demonstrated below.

Explanation

The program has four variables namely **Salary**, **grossSalary**, **Wages**, and **GrossWages**. These variables are assigned values **int** type in the function **main**. The function:

void pay (int& s, int g, int w, int& G) { s = 270; g = 320; w = 240; G = 280; }

↓

has assigned its own data shown above

The declaration is made outside the **main**. The function **main** has assigned four values:

int Salary = 300, grossSalary = 350, Wages = 200, GrossWages = 245;

The execution of the program started at function **main**. When the execution reached:
pay (Salary, grossSalary, Wages, GrossWages); then the call passed the following values:

a) **salary** was passed by reference to **s**. But **s** is an alias for the variable **Salary** whose value is 300. The function assigned 270 to **s**. In fact, 270 was assigned to salary, because **s** is an alias for Salary as shown above. The effect of passing by reference in this case was the changing of value, and thus **Salary became 270**, replacing **300**. The parameter **Salary is read-write**.

b) **grossSalary** was passed to **g** by **value method**. Then **g** became a local variable. It was assigned the value of **grossSalary = 350**. The function had assigned **g =320,** but it had **no effects** on grossSalary. The parameter **grossSalary** is **read-only**.

c) **Wages** was passed to **w** by **value method**. Then **w** became a local variable. It was assigned the value of **wages = 200**, whilst the function had assigned it **245**, but it had **no effects** on **Wages**. The parameter Wages is **read-only**.

d) **GrossWages** was passed to **G** by **reference value method**. But **G** is an alias for the variable **Gross-Wages** whose value is <u>245</u>. The function assigned <u>280</u> to **G**.

In doing so, <u>280</u> was assigned to **GrossWages** , because **G** is an alias as shown above. In this case, the effect of passing a parameter by reference method was the change in the value of **GrossWages**. Thus **GrossWages became 280**, replacing **245**. The parameter **GrossWages** is **read-write**.

When execution was terminated, **GrossSalary** and **GrossWages** had new values of 270 and 280 respectively, whilst Wages and **GrossSalary** still had there own original values.

================**Output from the Program in Diagram 44**===============

Table: Local Values assigned to four variables
•••

```
            Salary = 300
            Wages = 200
            Gross Salary = 350
            Gross Wages = 245
```
•••

Table: Effects of the call on Salary and Gross Wages
•••

```
            Salary = 270
            Wages = 200
            Gross Salary = 350
            Gross Wages = 280
```
•••

```
# include <iostream.h>
// Local values and Reference parameters
// The effect of passing data to a function by value and by reference methods
// ------------------------------------------------------------------------
void pay( int& s, int g, int w, int& G ){s = 270; g = 320; w = 245; G = 280;}
void main (void)
{
 cout << " Table: Local Values assigned to four variables" << endl;
 cout << " ...........................................................\n" << endl;
 int Salary = 300, grossSalary = 350, Wages = 200, GrossWages = 245;
 cout << "\t\t Salary = " << Salary << endl;
 cout << " \t\t Wages = " << Wages << endl;
 cout << "\t\t Gross Salary = " << grossSalary << endl;
 cout << "\t\t Gross Wages = " << GrossWages << endl;
 cout << " ...........................................................\n" << endl;
 cout << " Table: Effects of the call on Salary and Gross Wages" << endl;
 cout << " ...........................................................\n" << endl;
 pay ( Salary, grossSalary, Wages, GrossWages);
 cout << "\t\t Salary = " << Salary << endl;
 cout << " \t\t Wages = " << Wages << endl;
 cout << "\t\t Gross Salary = " << grossSalary << endl;
 cout << "\t\t Gross Wages = " << GrossWages << endl;
 cout << " ------------------------------------------------------------\n" << endl;
}
```

Diagram 44

Practical Hints

. A function must be declared first before any callsto it.

. A parameter that is passed by value method is duplicated by its corresponding actual parameter.

. A parameter that is passed by reference is re-named by its corresponding actual parameter.

Library functions

A software library is a collection of definitions, functions, classes and constants that come with a C++ compiler package. Borland compiler package comes with several libraries that include a collection of functions. These functions can be incorporated into your own program. These functions are written using a precise formal definitions. They have their identifiers (names). They are written because they are used often or the formula is too complex or too long to write. You have already met some of these functions through some of our programs. For example, we have already used **srand ( ), rand ( ), max ( ),** and some other functions. The use of library function requires the name of the header file in which the required function is stored. For instance, in order to use the **exit ( )** function, you must put the following pre-processor directive at the top of your program file: **# include <stdlib.h>**

It may be that on your college computing system libraries are not currently stored. Before you can use any of these functions, first make sure that the required file or files containing these functions are available for use.

The maths Library Functions

They include common mathematical functions such as square root, etc. These are defined in the **<math.h>** header file. This header file declares mathematical functions and should be put near the top of the program file as: **# include <math.h>**.

When for example, the program includes the **cube ( )** function, then the compiler is looking for the definition of the cube function. This pre-processor directive informs the compiler that the function **cube ( )** is declared in the **(math.h>** header file.

It should be noted that **<math.h>** is in fact Standard C Library header file, but it is also available with C++ compilers just like **<stdlib.h>** and some other C header files.

What is hidden?

The standard library functions do not show on the screen how these functions were developed. The processes involved in designing these functions are hidden. These functions are programs, and thus have all the input-process-output components of a program.

For instance, if you use function **cube ( )** to find the cube of 4, the answer will be given 64, which is correct. So we know that the output 64 is the result of input 4, as the cube of 4 is (4* 4* 4). But the process of giving this answer is hidden. We can be sure that all mathematical types and other types of library functions have the required properties. The following examples illustrate the use of some library functions.

Exit Function

It is a library function which can be used anywhere in a program to terminate it.

Diagram 45

It contains a simple program that demonstrates the application of the function **exit ( ).**

Explanation

The program allowed the user to enter any registration number. The user entered **2345**. It was passed to **int reg (int x)** function. In this function, it was tested against the condition **if (x == 0) exit (0)**. Since the number was not **0**, the next statement **return x** was executed. The value of x = 2345 returned to the **main**, where 2345 replaced **x** in **reg (x)** in the following code:

cout << "\t\t Your registration number = " << reg (x) << endl;

The execution of this statement generated the required output as shown in this **diagram 45A**. The user run the program again and entered **0**, which was tested against the test condition. Since it met the condition, the program was terminated from within the **reg ( )** function without any further attempt to return **x**. The following program output confirms this, as after **0** nothing happened. You can see this effect in the bottom part of **diagram 45A**.

```
# include <iostream.h>
# include <stdlib.h>
int reg ( int x )
{
if ( x == 0 )  exit ( 0 );
 return x;
}
main ( )
{
int x;
cout << "\t\t Please enter your registration number = ";
cin >> x ;
cout << " " << endl;
cout << "\t\t Your registration number = " << reg (x)<< endl;
cout << "\t\t ----------------------------";
return (0);
}
```

Diagram 45

```
================= Program output when 2345 was entered ==========================

      Please enter your registration number = 2345

      Your registration number = 2345
      -----------------------------------

---------------------------Program  was terminated when 0 was entered -----------------------------
      Please enter your registration number = 0
```

Diagram 45A

Diagram 46

The program in this diagram illustrates the application of the standard mathematical library function **sqrt**. It prints square roots of **10** numbers between **1-10**.

Explanation

In addition to <iostream.h> header file, We needed <math.h> header file for sqrt ( ) function. In order to generate 4 square roots, we declared variable **number** of int type in **main**, and gave it an initial value of 1. The **for loop** was used to evaluate the **sqrt (number)**. When the **counter** in the following code was

> **for (number = 1 ; number <= 4 ; number ++)**

equal to 1, 2, 3 and 4 the square root function was evaluated. Thus, the function sqrt was called 4 times, and each time its **argument** had a different square root value in the following code. Thus the actual parameter or the argument was passed by value to the sqrt function.

> **cout << "\t"<< number << "\t" << sqrt (number)<< endl;**

When number = 1, the value 1 was passed to the sqrt function by the call sqrt (number), which then returned the value **1** to the function **main**. **Why 1?** Because the square root of 1 is 1.

When the number = 2 in the **for loop**, the value 2 was passed to the sqrt function by the call sqrt (number), which then returned the value **1.41421** to the function **main**.

When the number = 3 in the **for loop** statement, then the value of 3 was passed to the sqrt function by the call sqrt (number), which then returned the value **1.73205** to the function **main**.

This process continued until the counter reached **4**. Then the final call was executed and the value **2** was returned to the **main ( )**. At each call its value was substituted in the above **cout** code, and printed. At the end of 10 calls the function was terminated. The output is shown in this diagram..

```
# include <iostream.h>
# include <math.h>
// Maths - square root function - sqrt ( )
int main (void)
{
cout << "\tNumber" <<"\tSquare Root" << endl;
cout << "\t------" <<"\t--------------" << endl;
int number;
for ( number = 1 ; number <= 4 ; number ++ )
cout << "\t"<< number << "\t" << sqrt (number)<< endl;
 }
```

========================= **Program Output** =========================

```
    Number  Square Root
    --------  ---------------
    1       1
    2       1.41421
    3       1.73205
    4       2
```

Diagram 46

Inline Functions: The general format is as follows:

inline type Name of Function (argument)
{

}
Example: inline int SalaryMin (int x).

It should be remembered that a function header is preceded by the keyword **inline**. **What is the difference between the normal function and the inline function?**

In C++ inline functions are special functions. They are useful when little functions are called upon a number of times within a program. When normal functions are called the compiler has to create extra code, allocate extra storage for the local variables, copy actual arguments, pass actual arguments, etc. When an inline function is invoked, all the normal function's such overheads as mentioned here are avoided.

Diagram 46

The program in this diagram illustrates the use of an inline function. The inline function defines the function **salaryMin ( )**, and prints the value of the smallest salary. To the human's eye, an inline function and a normal function differ only in their headers, but to the compiler an inline function makes a big different. In this case, the compiler was directed to substitute the code shown in the body of the function **salaryMin** into the **main** function.

if (s1 , s2) return (s1); else return (s2) ;

This resulted in printing the smallest salary, as shown in the program output.

```
# include <iostream.h>
// how to use inline function
inline int salaryMin ( int s1,int s2 )
{
 if (s1 , s2 ) return (s1);
  else return ( s2 );
}
void main ( void )
{
int s1 = 20000, s2 = 24000;
cout << " The smallest of these two salaries = " <<"£ " << salaryMin ( s1, s2 ) << endl;
cout << " ................................................." << endl;
}
======================= Program Output =======================
 The smallest of these two salaries = £ 20000
..............................................
```

Diagram 46

Overloading

This is another important feature of C++. It allows you to give the same name to more than one function.

How does C++ compiler distinguish between different functions within the same program?

It is essential that each function must have a unique argument list. This can be achieved if each argument list has at least one parameter of a different type or the number of parameters vary or both the number of parameters and the types of arguments are different in each list. Let us analyse this rule by examining the following examples.

Example 1.
```
int wagesMin ( int , int );
int wagesMin ( int, int, int );
```

In this example, each prototype differs from the other. Because first prototype **wagesMin** has only two parameters, whilst the second prototype **wagesMin** has three parameters. Both prototypes are of the **int** type, and return **int** type value. Thus the compiler will accept these prototypes having the same name **wagesMin** for two different functions.

Example 2.
```
float salaryMax ( int x, int y );
int salaryMax  ( int x, int y ) ;
```

In this example both prototypes have equal numbers of parameters and both are of the same **int** type. These are not acceptable to the compiler as two different prototypes for two different functions. They do not differ from each other. It is true to say that they have different return types, one returns **float** type, and the other **int** type. A function is overloaded when its argument list differs from the argument of the other function.

Example 3:
```
int averageSales ( int x,  inty );
float averageSales ( float x,  float y,  float z  ) ;
```

In this example, both **averageSales** prototypes are different.

Diagram 47

The program in this diagram is designed to illustrate the operation of overload functions. Besides the function **main**, it has two more functions whose prototypes are given just above the function **main**. Both functions are called averageLength. The program calculates the average length of three variables. One function prints the average length in whole meters, whilst the other function does so to the nearest centimeters (meters.centimeters).

Explanation

Both functions are overloaded. The compiler selects the correct function on the basis of the parameters in the arguments listed in these functions. The execution started at function **main.** When the following segment of the code was executed:

cout <<" Average length whole meters =" << " "
<< averageLength(23, 25 , 30) << endl;

the function call passed three integer values to check the lists to match which one had three integers in it. The list (int x, int y, int z) was matched and called the following function to return the average value to the **main**, which was inserted in the above code.

int averageLength (int x, int y, int z)

The **cout** output stream printed the required output. On the second call, the process was repeated. The output of this program is shown in diagram 48 below.

```
# include <iostream.h>
// Demonstration of overloading function
int averageLength ( int , int , int );
double averageLength ( double, double, double );
void main ( void )
{
cout <<" Average length whole meters = " << " "
        << averageLength( 23, 25 , 30) << endl;
cout <<" Average length to the nearest centimeters = " << " "
        << averageLength ( 23.90, 24.00 , 24.20 ) << endl;
}
int averageLength ( int x, int y, int z)
{
 return ( x+ y + z)/3;
 }
  double averageLength ( double x, double y, double z )
  {
        return (x + y + z)/3;
}
===================== Program Output =====================

Average length whole meters  =  26
Average length to the nearest centimeters  =  24.0333
```

<u>Diagram 48</u>

Diagrams 49 & 49A

The program in this diagram illustrates **single character function**. It displays two lines, which will be formed from '-' and '|' two different characters. Its output is in **diagram 49A**.

Explanation

The function **singleLine (char singleChar, int length)** generates two single lines formed from '-' and '|'. In the argument **singleChar** is a name for any character but we have used '-' and '|' characters. Their type is **char** type. The second parameter is for the **length** of the line to be formed. Its type is **int**. This function has two **for** loops, because it is required to print two vertical lines, separated from each other. In the following segment of code, 3 is the length of the line, which means each character is repeated 3 times in each line.

singleLine ('-', 3); singleLine ('|',3);

```
#include <iostream.h>
// Single character output
int main (void)
{
 cout << "\t\t Single Character Output" << endl;
 cout << "\t\t ...................…………..." << endl;
 cout << " " << endl;
                                    // prototype

singleLine ( char singleChar, int length);
 singleLine ( '-', 3);
 singleLine ( '|',3);
 return (0);
}
void singleLine ( char singleChar, int length)
{
  int count ;
   {
    for ( count = 1; count <= length; count ++ ) cout <<" " << singleChar << endl;
   }
   {
    for( count = 1; count <= length; count ++ ) cout <<"\t\t " << singleChar << endl;
   }
}
```

Diagram 49

============ **Output from Program Shown in Diagram 49** =============

Single Character Output

·······································.···

\-

\-

\-

        \-

        \-

        \-

|

|

|

        |

        |

        |

Diagram 49A

Programming Exercises

1 Write and test the function **void AddAv (void)** that has its own three data items. It
must calculate the sum and average of these variables; and
display on the screen sum and average values, each on a separate line.

2 Write and test a program that allows the user to input data, and then use the input data
in the following **void sumDiffAv ( )** function that returns the sum, difference, and mean
of any two numbers.

    void sumDiffAv (int x, int y, int z, int &sum, int &diff, int &av);

3 Write and test a Boolean function for the leap year. A user should be allowed to enter
any year such as 1990, and advise the user whether the input year is a leap year or not.

Chapter 6

Arrays

What is an array?

A computer's ability to store and manipulate data is an important aspect of learning programming. So far, in our programs we have presented single data value to the computer. This single value was stored in a variable in order to manipulate it. Often we have to store and manipulate a group of related data items. These related data items are presented to the computer as a single set. This grouping of related data items is known as **data structure**. Array is one method of data structure. It makes it easy for the programmer to process data in a particular way which is suited for the purpose of presenting data to the computer.

We can define an array as a set of the same type data items grouped together which has a specific name. This specific name is known as "**identifier**". Arrays are classified as one-dimensional array, two-dimensional array or multi-dimensional array. Let's examine the following example to understand the nature of one-dimensional array.

One-dimensional Array or a List

Example

Jan	Name [1]	**Identifier is Name**
		Subscript are **1, 2, 3, 4, 5** - these are in <u>square brackets</u>
James	Name [2]	An array subscript is also known as **index**
		Data items are **Jan, James, Bill, Robin** and **Chris**
Bill	Name [3]	Often data items are termed as **elements**.
		Thus we can say that our list **Name** has five elements.
Robin	Name [4]	Because it has only one column of **indexes** it is called
		one-dimensional array
Chris	Name [5]	We can **declare** this array as **char Name [5];**

char **Name [5];**
↓　　　↓　　　↓
data type　Identifier　size of array.

<u>**Size should be a constant expression**</u>. <u>**Data type can be int, float or char**</u>.

The name of this array is **Name** and it consists of **5** elements. These are called Name [0] through to Name [4]. The method of numbering elements is called **Zero-based indexing**. In this example, its initial element is Name [0]. **The general rule is that if the array has *n* elements, their names are *n-1*.** Thus in this example, these names are Name [0], name [1], name [2], name [3], and name [4].

. **What is the value of Name [3] ?** Its value is **Robin**. Its position is determined
by applying Zero-based indexing.

. **What is a subscripted variable?** It is an individual element of an array. In our above
example Name [2] is a subscripted variable.

Diagram 50

The program is designed to illustrate how to initialise one-dimensional array. It also demonstrates zero-based indexing. It prints 10 elements of array Account with their respective values.

Explanation

The variable **Account** was declared as **int** type. The following initialisation contains 10 values, as there are 10 elements in the array called **Account**. The list is within { } curly brackets. This list is the initialiser list for this array.

int <u>**Account**</u> [10] = { <u>10, 11, 12, 13, 56, 89, 20, 89, 67, 100</u> };
　　　↓　　　　　　　　　　　　↓
Array Account　　　　10 values to match the size of array Account

A **for** loop was initialised to zero. It was used to step through the array 10 times. Each time it substituted the element and its value in the following code.

cout << " Account [" << s << "] = " << Account [s] << endl;
　　　　　　　　↓　　　　　　　　　　　↓
　　　　position of an element　　Value of the variable Account corresponding to
　　　　in array **Account**　　the position of an element in this list

Output stream **cout** printed the results as shown in this diagram. **The major advantage** of using this list of accounts as an array is that instead of 10 different account names, we have used only one variable namely **account**, under which all accounts are grouped together. This makes the list more manageable and shortened the code.

```
# include <iostream.h>
// First step towards Arrays - elements of an array
void main (void)
{
cout <<"  A simple program to illustrate how to initialise an Array" <<endl;
cout <<" ...............................................................\n" << endl;
 int Account [10] = { 10, 11, 12, 13, 56, 89, 20, 89, 67, 100 };
int s ;
for
          ( s = 0;  s < 10;  s++ )
cout << "  Account [ " << s << " ] = " << Account [s] << endl;
}
============================== Program Output ==========================
A simple program to illustrate how to initialise an Array
..........................................................................

          Account [ 0 ] = 10
          Account [ 1 ] = 11
          Account [ 2 ] = 12
          Account [ 3 ] = 13
          Account [ 4 ] = 56
          Account [ 5 ] = 89
          Account [ 6 ] = 20
          Account [ 7 ] = 89
          Account [ 8 ] = 67
          Account [ 9 ] = 100
```

Diagram 50

Practical Hints

. **What happens when there are more elements than values in the list?** As many elements as corresponding missing values are initialised to zero. If your list contains **more** values than elements, you will get the following error message. Your program will not be compiled successfully.

```
Message                                                    _ □ ×
Compiling NONAME16.CPP:
Error NONAME16.CPP 9: Too many initializers in function main()
```

. If you do not include an initialiser list, you will get meaningless values as shown above. A simple program to illustrate how to initialise an Array

....

Account [0] = 9315
Account [1] = 13883
Account [2] = 25015
Account [3] = 25031
Account [4] = 14018
Account [5] = 25015
Account [6] = 9361
Account [7] = 18220
Account [8] = 24807
Account [9] = -1

These values were output by the above
program, without the initialiser list. Code
int Account [10];
was used - list was excluded.

Just garbage output by the computer.

Diagram 51

It contains a simple program that calculates and displays the sum of both real and whole numbers.

Explanation

This program followed the pattern of the previous program. However, there are some differences, which should be discussed. The array number is of **float** type. Data list contains both real and whole numbers. If you had declared as **int** type, the sum would have been **519** which is incorrect.

float number [ ] has no **size** specifier within [ ]. You can omit it when the initialiser list is provided. The code:

sum += number [n];

has += an addition assignment operator, instead of = sign. If you replace += with =, the compiler will not display an error message. It will compile and run the program. You will get **120** as an output, which is meaningless. The sum of these numbers = **522.17** not **120**.

```
# include <iostream.h>
// floating-point.
// IDE automatically links the floating-point math package with double
// _____

 void main (void)
{
float sum = 0.0 ;
float number [ ] = {10, 12.78,20,24,67.90,66.00,10.50, 100, 90.99, 120 };
for ( int n = 0 ; n < 10 ; n ++ )
sum += number [n];
cout << "\t The sum of these numbers = " << sum << endl;
cout << "\t ......................................................." << endl;
}
==================== Program Output ================================

            The sum of these numbers = 522.17
            ...................................................
```

Diagram 51

Passing Arrays & Elements to a Function

Just like simple variables, arrays can be passed from one function to another function. For instance in our diagram 53, **int s [ ]** is passed to **int salary (int s [ ], int x, int y)**. All arrays are passed by call- by- reference method. This is the default mode for all arrays.

.Why is this so ? When the compiler receives the initialiser list **int s [ ]**, it learns that the array is called **s** and the elements of **s** will be of **int** type. The array **s** will occupy a block of consecutive memory locations. It does not matter if the size of the array, that is the number of elements in the array **s,** is not given to the compiler. Since the array's name **s** is the address to the first element, **s** stores the array **s**'s **memory address**. It does not store the actual value of the element. When an array is passed to another function, it is only the address of the memory location, of the first element, which is actually passed. This is a reference. This is how it is called by the call-by reference method.

.How about elements of the array?
The elements have to be passed by using another integer variable.

When the function **int salary (int s [ ], int x, int y)** is called, it gains access to the actual elements in the array **s**'s list by directly accessing the memory locations where the array's elements are stored. The elements of an array are passed to a function by call-by-value method. This is the default mode for all arrays. Let's examine the program in diagram 52.

Diagrams 52 & 52 A

The program in this diagram reads a list of weekly salaries of 40 employees. It allows the user to input any figure for a weekly salary. In response to this input the computer prints out the frequency occurrence of this input figure. If this figure is not shown in this salary list, then a zero is output for non occurrence.

Explanation

The program has two functions. In function **main** array **s** is declared as **int** type. It is initialised with a list of 40 salary figures. Two integer variables **x** and **y** are also declared. The variable **x** is assigned **40.** The variable **x** is that variable which is used to pass the elements of this array to the called function. The other variable **y** represents the answer input by the user in response to "How many employees are paid weekly salary £ ? ".

The other function is prototype as <u>**int salary**</u> **(int s [ ], int x, int y);**

We can analyse its argument now: **(<u>int s [ ]</u> , <u>int x</u> , <u>int y</u>)**

                            ↓   ↓   ↓

                  name of the array **s**   integer   integer variable for input value

                  elements of **int** type   variable

                                       to access elements

In function **salary** a for loop: **(int i = 0; i < x; i++)** is set up to step through the array **s**.
Another variable **count** is inatialised to **0**. Its purpose is to keep a record of steps in the following conditional statement:

             if (s <u>[i]</u> == y) ++ <u>count</u> ;

                   ↓   ↓

      value of elements   increment the initial **count 0** which is matched with **y**

The value of variable **count** is a whole number, **int** type, which tells how many times **y** is matched. It is incremented each time **y** is matched. This is the value which is returned to the function **main** for inserting in the following code:

cout << "\t\t Salary per week £" << <u>y</u> << " is paid to " << salary(<u>s, x, y</u>) << " employee(s)" << endl;

                                ↓   ↓

           This value is the figure user input   x is here number of times y occurs in array S

Note that the order of **s, x, y** in **salary (s,x,y)** is very important. If you put **y in** the middle of **s** and **x**, you will not get the required result. It will print only the first matched value from the list. If you alter the position of **s**, you will get a long error message. **Be careful!**

```
# include <iostream.h>
//  Salary information
int  salary ( int s [ ], int x, int y  );              // Prototype
int main ( void )
{
  int s [ ] = { 140,200,200,210,150,150,175,190,210,205,300, 320, 275,200,
              164,150,150,200,210,175,190,200,150,210,250, 250, 310,
              150,180,175,200,175,200,150,177,200,150,200, 240, 275 };

int x = 40, y;
cout << " " << endl;
cout << "\t Weekly Salary Information" << endl;
cout << "\t .........................................\n" << endl;
cout << "\t Please answer the question below. Please  enter a figure.\n" << endl;
cout << "\t\t How many employees are paid weekly salary £ ? ";
cin  >> y;
cout << " " << endl;
cout << "\t\t Salary per week £"  << y << " is paid to "
     << salary( s, x, y) << " employee(s)" << endl;
}
int salary ( int s [ ], int x, int y )
{
  int count = 0;
  for ( int i = 0; i < x; i++ )
  if ( s  [ i ] = = y )++ count ;
  return count;
}
```

Diagram 52

Program Output

The program was compiled successfully. In response to the question displayed, the user input 300. The computer searched the list and found out that it was earned weekly by only one employee. The user ran the program again and input 379. This salary was not paid to any employees. The user ran the program once more and input 200. This salary is paid weekly to 9 employees, and once again it was the correct answer. It worked very well.

Output from the Program Shown in Diagram 52

Weekly Salary Information
....

Please answer the question below. Please enter a figure.

How many employees are paid weekly salary £ ? **300**

Salary per week £300 is paid to 1 employe(s)

===

Weekly Salary Information
....

Please answer the question below. Please enter a figure.

How many employees are paid weekly salary £ ? **379**

Salary per week £379 is paid to 0 employee(s)

===

Weekly Salary Information
....

Please answer the question below. Please enter a figure.

How many employees are paid weekly salary £ ? **200**

Salary per week £200 is paid to 9 employee(s)

Diagram 52A

Two-dimensional array

On a piece of paper a two-dimensional array is a table which consists of a number of **rows** and **columns**. The following table consists of 3 rows and 6 columns. The product figures of any of the three products could be stored in a one-dimensional array. Instead of storing three products' data in three different one-dimensional arrays, we can do so in the form of two-dimensional array.

In fact in C++ a two-dimensional array is an array of one-dimensional arrays. The following array is called **Table** which has **3** rows and **6** columns. The **Table [3] [6]** is thus a two-dimensional array.

In this table, if we want to know the location of a particular product, we have to know the intersection of a particular row and a column. For example, product 2 sales information for May is obtained by referring to **Table [2] [5];** which is where the value for product 2 for May is stored. It is the intersection of row 2 of the 5th column. C++ code for storing this information

Similarly, **Table [0] [0];** is where the value for product 1 for Jan is stored.

Table: Product sales Information for the last six months

	Jan	Feb	Mar	Apr	May	Jun
Product 1	20	30	12	34	50	45
Product 2	34	40	50	55	57	55
Product 3	30	45	55	60	67	59

Diagrams 53 & 53 A

The program in this diagram is designed to generate the above two-dimensional array. The output is shown in **diagram 53 A**.

Explanation

It has three rows of products and six columns of months. In arrays' terminology, each row (product) has 6 elements (columns). The figures (values of elements) are whole numbers.We already know these values. The array is called Table. It is declared as **int** type, and it is **initialised** with a single list. A nested **for** loop is used to access or read each element in the list, and print each element in its place in the correct row.

```
for ( int r = 0; r < 3; r++ ){ cout << "Product" << r+1;
    for ( int c = 0; c < 6; c++ ) cout << "\t  " << Table[ r ] [ c ]; }
```

The first **for** loop steps through for generating rows. Output stream **cout** prints the heading of each row. The second **for** loop steps through columns (or the elements of each row), and second **cout** prints the required array. The output from this program is shown in this diagram. It was compiled and tested successfully. You should test it on your system.

Output

Within this nested **for** loop, the last segment of code is **cout << " " << endl;** is an important statement in this code. Without this statement in this loop, your output format will not meet your requirements. This simple statement controls the layout of this array. The following output was obtained when the program was compiled and tested. It was compiled successfully but the result is unintelligible. The last statement in this program is outside the **for** loop because it is not a part of the array except to draw a line.

Table: Product sales Information for the last six months

	Jan	Feb	Mar	Apr	May	Jun
Product1	20	30	12	34	50	45
Product2	34	40	50	55	57	55
Product3	30	45	55	60	67	59

=========================== Program Output ===========================

Table: Product sales Information for the last six months

	Jan	Feb	Mar	Apr	May	Jun
Product1	**20**	**30**	**12**	**34**	**50**	**45**
Product2	**34**	**40**	**50**	**55**	**57**	**55**
Product3	**30**	**45**	**55**	**60**	**67**	**59**

Diagram 53 A

Practical Hints

- One-dimensional array has only set of brackets [ ].

- Two-dimensional array has two sets of brackets [ ] [ ].

- In Two-dimensional array the first set of brackets is unspecified. For example: [ ] [4]

- Arrays of more than one dimension are known as **multi-dimensional** arrays.

- You can have more than two dimensions of arrays but three dimensions are practical.
  A three-dimensional array is one-dimensional array of two-dimensional array. **Think!!!**

```cpp
# include <iostream.h>
// Two-dimensional arrays
void main (void)
{
 int Table [ ] [ 6 ] = {20,30,12,34,50,45,34,40,50,55,57,55,30,45,55,60,67,59};
cout << "Table: Product sales Information for the last six months" << endl;
cout << "..........................................................\n" << endl;
cout <<"\t\t Jan" <<"\t Feb" <<"\t Mar" <<"\t Apr" <<"\t May" <<"\t Jun" << endl;
cout <<"\t\t ..." <<"\t ..." <<"\t ..." <<"\t ..." <<"\t ..." <<"\t ...\n" << endl;
  for ( int r = 0; r < 3; r++ ){
        cout << "Product" << r+1;

                for ( int c = 0; c < 6; c++ )
                cout << "\t  " << Table[ r ] [ c ];

                cout << " " << endl;
}
 cout << ".........................................................." << endl;
}
```

Diagram 53

The next program illustrates how data is input in two-dimensional arrays.

Diagrams 54 & 55

This program is designed to demonstrate how the computer prompts the user to input data in two-dimensional array. The program has **input data function** which allows the user to input product information for the last six months in 1997. The **print function** of this program uses the input data to generate the required information in the form of a table.

Explanation

Programs in diagrams 54 and 55 have some C++ statements which are the same in both programs. Both programs handle arrays of the same size, but one has an initialiser list, because of this there was no need to have a segment of the code for data input, enabling the user to enter from the keyboard the value for each element of the array. The previous program has only function **main**, all the steps necessary to **generate** and **print** the required array are within the **main**.

Data Input Function: product

It has the capability of allowing the user to input data from the keyboard. Firstly, it displays the title of table to be generated, and then tells the user to enter **18 whole numbers**. After this, it prompts the user to enter the value for each element of the **array Table**. The statement:

cout << "product = " << r+1 <<" Enter monthly figures:" << endl; displays the message:
                              product = 1 Enter monthly figures:

Once the user has finished entering the sixth figue (value), the **product = 2 Enter monthly figures**: appears and the process is repeated, until all 18 figures have been entered. It should be noted that **cout** statement is within the nested **for** loop, which has two for statements to step through the array's rows and columns.

Data Output Function: Print

It makes use of nested **for** loop to generate and print the array. Within this function are **cout** statements that are executed first in order to print headings. When the execution reaches the **for** loop, the function **Product** passes the data as 18 consecutive elements of array **Table**. Within this nested loop are output statements which print headings of rows as product 1 to product 3, and print the values of each element in the same consecutive order as they are passed by function product.

Program Output: diagram 55

It was compiled and tested successfully. The user was prompted to enter 18 values. The values entered are shown in **diagram 55**. At the end of data input, the required table was printed as shown in the same diagram.

```
# include <iostream.h>
// Two-dimensional arrays
                                    // prototype
void product  (int Table [  ] [ 6 ] );
void print  (  int Table [  ] [ 6 ] );

void main (void)
{
 int Table [ 3 ] [ 6 ];
 product ( Table );
 print ( Table );
 }
 void product (  int Table [   ] [  6  ] )
 {
 cout <<"\t\t Data Input" << endl;
cout << "\t\t _____ \n" << endl;
cout <<" Table: Product Information July - December 1997" << endl;
cout <<" .............................................."<< endl;
 cout <<" Enter 18 whole numbers:" << endl;
 cout <<" -------------------------" << endl;
                   for (  int r = 0;  r < 3;  r ++  ) {
                           cout << "product = " << r+1 <<" Enter monthly figures:" << endl;
                                 for (  int c = 0;  c < 6;  c++  )
                                 cin >> Table[ r ] [ c ];
                   }
}
void print ( int Table [  ] [ 6 ] )
{
cout << "\t\t Information Output" << endl;
cout << "\t\t _____\n" << endl;
cout << "   Table: Product sales Information July - December 1997" << endl;
cout << " ...............................................\n" << endl;
cout <<"\t\t Jul" <<"\t Aug" <<"\t Sept" <<"\t Oct" <<"\t Nov" <<"\t Dec" << endl;
cout <<"\t\t ..." <<"\t ..." <<"\t ...." <<"\t ..." <<"\t ..." <<"\t ...\n" << endl;
            for (  int r = 0;  r < 3;  r++  ){
                  cout  << "Product"  << r+1;
                     for (  int c = 0;  c < 6;  c++  )
                       cout << "\t  " << Table [ r ] [ c ];
                       cout << " " << endl;
}
 cout << "..........................................." <<endl;
}
```

Diagram 54

program Output

Data Input

_____

Table: Product Information July - December 1997

....

Enter 18 whole numbers:

----

product = 1 Enter monthly figures:
60
67
57
50
44
50
product = 2 Enter monthly figures:
60
65
55
49
55
50
product = 3 Enter monthly figures:
44
50
50
56
65
59

Information Output

_____

Table: Product sales Information July - December 1997

....

	Jul	Aug	Sept	Oct	Nov	Dec
	.....	......	......	....	......	......
Product1	60	67	57	50	44	50
Product2	60	65	55	49	55	50
Product3	44	50	50	56	65	59

....

Diagram 55

Programming Exercises

1. Write a program that uses an array to store number of days in each month of the year. The number of days in each month should be included in your program in the form of an initialiser list. Under an appropriate heading, the program should display on the screen 12 months and their respective days. **(note: February = 29 for this exercise)**

2. Write and test a program that will include **void print (long sales [ ] , long x) function** to print 12 months sales data on the screen.

3. Write and run a program that will perform the following tasks:

a) **store** 50 random sales commission data paid to 50 sales staff in the form of a table that contains **5 rows and 10 columns**; and

b) **sort** out randomly stored commission figures in the ascending order of commission paid.

Use the insertion sort method

Hint

```
int temp;
     For ( int  i = 1; i < x; i ++ ) { // sort in ascending order { comm  [ 0 ]......... comm [ i ]};
  temp = comm [ i ];
   for ( int y = i; y > 0 &&  comm [ y-1 ] > temp; y -- )
   comm [ y ] = comm [ y-1 ];
   comm [ y ] = temp;
```

It contains two loops.

The main loop is **for (int i = 1; i < x; i++) {// sort in ascending order {comm [0],...,comm [i]}:**

It steps through the array comm [50]. This is from 1 to x-1. It inserts the **comm [i]** element in the correct position among comm [0] ...... comm [49]. But to insert it in the correct position, elements that are greater have to be shifted to the right.

To do so , first the **comm [i]** element is placed in a temporary place **temp = comm [i];** and then the inner loop **for (int y = i; y > 0 && comm [y-1] > temp; y --)**
is used to shift all the elements, that are greater than **comm [i]** one place to the right. The value placed in the **temp** is copied into the element **comm [y]**. At the end of the main loop 50 data items are sorted in the ascending order.

<u>Chapter 7</u>

Pointers

<u>What is a pointer?</u>

A simple variable holds information/data in a memory location. The content of any variable is its value. This value can be accessed by using variable's name. It can also be accessed with a reference operator **&**. We have seen this in chapter 4, when parameters that held information passed back information to the calling function by means of reference operator **&**. There is one more method of accessing information that is through a **pointer variable**. The application of pointer variables makes program more efficient.

A pointer holds the address of another variable and thus points to the location of the other variable in the computer memory. The pointer variable is declared as illustrated below.

<u>int</u> * <u>point</u> ;
↓   ↓   ↓
type pointer pointer name/identifier
to int

It does not mean to say that the pointer is **int** type. What it actually means is that a pointer variable called **point** holds the address of an **int** type variable. The value of a pointer is an address. The value of the actual address is given in hexadecimal notation, which does not directly concern the programmer. Nevertheless, you will see below in diagram 58 how to find its value.

<u>**.How about char* m; declaration ?**</u> It defines the pointer m that holds the address of a **char** type variable. Let's consider the following declarations.

char employee;	char * employee_name;
This statement defines a variable called employee of **char** type	This statement defines a pointer variable called employee_name that will hold the address of variable **employee**

<u>**Where do we place asterisk * ?**</u> There are different views on its position in variable declarations. You can place it either closer to the type of the variable or the variable itself. As far as the compiler is concerned, it makes no difference.

Diagram 56

The program is designed to illustrate that a variable has a memory address.

Explanation

In this program we have declared three variables namely **a**, **b**, and **c**. These variables are of integer, float, and long integer types respectively. We have also assigned values to them. The code includes output stream **cout** statements to display both the values stored in these variables and memory addresses for each variable. For the address of each variable, the **ampersand &** is used with **cout** . When an ampersand is used as a prefix to a variable name, it returns the address of the variable.

The program output illustrates each variable has a unique memory address. These memory addresses are in hexadecimal, as each number begins with **0x**. These addresses for the same variables on a different computer system will most likely differ but still each variable will have a unique address.

```
# include <iostream.h>
//  addresses of variables in the computer memory - hexadecimal notations
 void main (  )
{
 int a = 78;
 float b = 100.89;
 long int  c = 120450;
 cout << " a is integer type variable = " << a << endl;
 cout << " The address of variable a : " << &a << endl;
 cout << " b is float type or a real number = " << b<< endl;
 cout << " The address of variable b : " << &b << endl;
 cout << " c is long integer type variable = " << c << endl;
 cout << " The address of c variable :" << &c << endl;
 }
===================== program Output =============================
a is integer type variable = 78
The address of variable a : 0x6d0f26fc
b is float type or a real number = 100.89
The address of variable b : 0x6d0f26f8
c is long integer type variable = 120450
The address of c variable :0x6d0f26f4
```

Diagram 56

Diagram 57

This diagram contains another program that is designed to demonstrate that a pointer value is an address of a variable. It points to another variable.

Explanation

. The variable declarations include **int a,** which is already assigned the value of 78.

. **Point** is the name of the pointer variable.

. **&a** is the address of variable **a**.

. **int* point** is a pointer to integer variable.

. The statement **point = &a;** declares the pointer **point** pointing to the variable **a.**
  It tells us that the address of **a** is stored in the pointer variable **point.**

Output stream **cout** statements are used to display the required output on the screen. You can see from the output that the address of variable **a,** and the value stored in the pointer **point** is the same hexadecimal value = **0x1d172466**, because the pointer points to another variable. You can access a variable either by using its name or a pointer to its address.

```
# include <iostream.h>
// pointers-
 void main ( )
 {
  int a = 78;
  int * point;                        // declaration of pointer to integer
  point  = &a;                 // initialise- the  pointer points to a'address
  cout << " a is integer type variable = " << a << endl;
  cout << " The address of variable a : " << &a << endl;
  cout << "\nThe value stored in the pointer = " << point << endl;
  cout << "The content of the pointer: " << *point << endl ;
 }
==================== Program Output ====================
a is integer type variable = 78
 The address of variable a : 0x1d172466

 The value stored in the pointer = 0x1d172466
The content of the pointer: 78
```

Diagram 57

Address Operator & and Dereference Operator *

In the above program **a** is the variable whose address was obtained by using **&a.point** obtained the value that was stored in the pointer. That value was the address of the variable **a**. The value stored at the memory location, which was the content of the pointer, was **pointed to** by the pointer ***point**. It was the ***pointer** that located the value of the variable **a**. Thus it demonstrates that ***point** is an alias to **a**. They have the same value **78**. When the pointer locates the value to which it points, it is called **dereferencing**. The value **78** was obtained by dereferencing.

Referencing

Referencing is the opposite of dereferencing. The program in **diagram 58** illustrates both dereferencing and referencing.

Explanation

The variable **a** of **int** type is declared and initialised. It is important to initialise it first so that it contains an address. <u>A variable without its initial value does not contain an address.</u> The other essential declarations that are included in this program are as follows:

- **int * point;**   It defines pointer to **integer**.
- **point = &a;**   The pointer **point** points to the variable **a**.
- **int& ref = *point;**   **ref** is a reference for the variable **a**.
  Its initial value is the same to which **point** points to.

A **cout** statement displayed the content of the pointer: **78**. This is **dereferencing**. Another **cout** statement displayed reference value: **78**. This is the result of **referencing**. both values are the same, because both ***point** and **int& ref are aliases** for the variable **a**.

Pointers and Arrays

Pointers and arrays are related topics. Both are used to access memory. Their distinct features are listed below

Arrays

Array's name is a pointer to its first element.
Array's name is thus a locked address to the array's first element.
Array's name is constant.

Pointers

Pointer variable holds the address in the memory of another variable.
pointer can be incremented and deincremented like integers. Can be used to access elements of an array.

```
# include <iostream.h>
// pointers -  Referencing and dereferencing
 void main ( )
 {
 // dereferencing
 int a = 78;
 int *  point;       // pointer to integer
 point  = &a;            // pointer points to a
 int&  ref = *point;                          // ref is a reference for a

                                 // pointer points to a
 cout << "\t\t Dereferencing" << endl;
 cout << "\t\t --------------\n" << endl;
 cout << " a is integer type variable: " << a << endl;
 cout << " The content of the pointer: " << *point << endl ;
 cout << " --------------------------\n" << endl;
 // referencing
 cout << "\t\t Referencing" << endl;
 cout << " \t\t------------\n" << endl;
 cout << " Reference value is the same as variable a: " << ref << endl;
 cout << " ----------------------------------------------" << endl;
}
================== ========Program Output ==============================

                        Dereferencing
                        ---------------

a is integer type variable: 78
The content of the pointer: 78
-----------------------------------

                        Referencing
                        ------------

Reference value is the same as variable a: 78
-----------------------------------------------
```

Diagram 58

Incremental Operators & Pointers

The program shown in **diagram 59** illustrates that a pointer can be incremented just like any integer.

value. It further demonstrates that the increase in the pointer's value is equivalent to the size in **bytes** of the object to which the pointer points.

Explanation

The program reads an array **a** which has an initialiser list which consists of three elements. A **for** loop is used to step through the values of this list. The code includes statements for calculating the sum of three values and displaying it. Within the **for** loop are **cout** statements for displaying the size of each increment. **sum += *point;** statement is within the **for loop**, so that at each step the next value can be added to the current value stored in **sum**. This is how **sum+= *point;** accumulated the sum. The following code which displays sum and its address is outside this loop because it is printed only once.

cout << "\n Sum of these 4 number = " << sum << " " << " It is at address: " <<point;

The program output in **boldface** shows that on this computer **integer** occupies **2 bytes** in its memory location. Since **point** is a pointer to **int**, each time it is incremented, it increases the value of the address by 2. You can see this pattern of increment, if you closely read these memory locations: 0x115f245a, 0x115f245c, 0x115f245e, 0x115f2460, 0x115f2462. They are in hexadecimal notations. This program also illustrates how pointer can be used with arrays to access elements from it.

Diagram 60

This program computes the total weekly salary and average weekly salary for 40 employees. The calculated values are displayed as required. The program illustrates the application of assessing arrays by means of pointers.

Explanation

The array **salary** is initialized with a single list of 40 employees' weekly salaries. It is declared float type so that values up to the last Penny can be stored. The declaration includes **float *point** which is a pointer to float variable. This float variable is **salary**.

Point = salary; is declared. This initialised the pointer **point** to the **salary's** address. This is **salary [0]**, the first element in the array. **Point = salary;** This statement assigned the address of the array **salary** to the pointer **point**. **Why is it so ?** You know that the name of an array is constant, and that it is an address to the first element in the array. Because of this it cannot be changed. However, a pointer can be changed, as you have already seen this change in the previous programs. In the

                for loop <u>*</u> (<u>point++</u>)
                    ↓   ↓

              dereferencing   steps through the array **salary**.
              operator access   At each step of the loop it is increased, and point
              salary figures   to the next element **salary** list until loop is
                                 completed

```
# include <iostream.h>
// to illustrate that a pointer can be incremented
void main ( )
{
 int a [  ] = {6,7,8,9};
 int sum = 0;
 int *point = a;
 for (int count =0; count < 40; count ++ ){
        sum+=  *( point++ );
        cout << " The element in the array a list = " << *point
                <<" Its memory location: " << point << endl;
        }
 cout << "\n Sum of these 4 number = " << sum << " "
                        << "  It is at address: " <<point;
}
================= Program Output =================

The element in the array a list = 6  its memory location: 0x0e87245a
The element in the array a list = 7  its memory location: 0x0e87245c
The element in the array a list = 8  its memory location: 0x0e87245e
The element in the array a list = 9  its memory location: 0x0e872460

Sum of these 4 number = 30    It is at address: 0x0e872462
```

Diagram 59

Practical Hints

sum+= (*point++); if you miss the * in the brackets, your program will not be compiled successfully. You will get the following error message. Why is it so? Because without * no de-referencing. If you write *** (point++),** your program will compile and run successfully.

```
Compiling ME16.CPP:
Error ME16.CPP 17: Illegal use of floating point in function main( )
Warning ME16.CPP 21: 'point' is assigned a value that is never used in function main[ ]
```

```
# include <iostream.h>
//  Salary information
void  main ( void )
{
 float salary [  ] = { 140, 200, 200, 210,150,150,175,190,210,205,300, 320, 275,200,
                164,150, 150, 200,210,175,190,200,150,210,250, 250, 310,
                150,180, 175, 200,175,200,150,177,200,150,200, 240, 275 };

float * point;
point = salary;
float sum = ( 0.0 );
float average;
cout << " Summary Weekly Salary Period Ended on 7 January 1997" << endl;
cout << " _____ \n" << endl;
for ( int count =0; count < 40; count ++ )
sum+= ( *point++ );
average = sum /40;
cout << "\t Total Weekly Salary =" <<" £ " << sum << endl;
cout << "\t Average Weekly Salary =" <<" £ " << average << endl;
}
```

======================= **Program Output** ===================================

Summary Weekly Sally Period Ended on 7 January 1997

_____

   Total Weekly Salary = £ 8006
   Average Weekly Salary = £ 200.15

Diagram 60

Dynamic Arrays

Lets' consider an array called **int <u>salary</u>**   **[<u>30</u>];**   ←**<u>Static type array</u>**

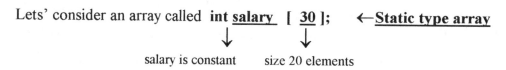

salary is constant   size 20 elements

The size has to be declared so that the compiler can allocate memory at compilation time. It is due to the fact that the pointer (array's name) in this example is constant. It may be that our array's size is unknown to us. In this the case, the compiler cannot allocate memory at compilation time.

How do we solve this problem?

In C++ this problem is overcome by making the **pointer non-constant**. This is achieved by including **new operator** in the code. This way the compiler allocates free memory at **run time** instead of at compilation time. Let's now consider the following example:

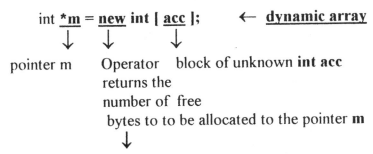

int **m** = **new** int [acc];   ← **dynamic array**

pointer m   Operator   block of unknown **int acc**
                 returns the
                 number of free
                 bytes to to be allocated to the pointer **m**

new operator allocates free memory of **n bytes** to the pointer.

This way **m** is initialised. **n bytes** is the size of an integer (2 bytes for an integer on this machine).

The **delete operator** is essential. If you do not free the allocated store, your program will work, but one day it may crash. Therefore, you must include **delete operator** in your program. This will free the memory used and then the memory will be returned to the **free store**. **delete (m);** will delete the memory allocated to **m** and then it will be returned to the free store.

Diagram 61

The program is designed to demonstrate the application of dynamic arrays. It prompts the user to enter the size of array and input data items. The program displays the output in the desired format. The program is interactive.

Explanation

The above explanation applies to this example. The value of **int acc** was input interactively so the array was created whilst the program was running. **new operator** allocated memory for **int acc**. **delete (m) ;** returned the freed memory to the store.

delete (m); Within the ( ) it must be non-constant **pointer;** otherwise the program will not be compiled successfully. If you place **int acc** or **int count** within ( ), the program will not be compiled successfully because none of them is a non-constant pointer.

```
# include <iostream.h>
# include <stdlib.h>                    //  needed for new and delete operators

//  An illustration of Dynamic Array
void main ( )
{
 int acc;
 cout << " Please type how many new accounts you wish to enter: " ;
 cin >> acc;
 int  * m = new int [acc ];
  for ( int count =0; count< acc; count ++ )
        {
                cout << " Element: " <<count+1 << endl;
                cin >> m [ count];
                cout << "\t you have entered: " << m [count] << endl;
                cout << "\t --------------------" << endl;
   delete ( m );                            // m is a non-constant pointer
            }
          }
```

========================== **Program Output** ==========================
```
 Please type how many new accounts you wish to enter: 4
 Element: 1
1234
         you have entered: 1234
         --------------------
 Element: 2
5678
         you have entered: 5678
         --------------------
 Element: 3
9876
         you have entered: 9876
         --------------------
 Element: 4
5567
         you have entered: 5567
         --------------------
```

Diagram 61

Programming Exercises

1. What is wrong with the following code?

```
int acc [ 50 ];
for ( int  i =  0; I <  50;  i++ );
*acc ++ = ( i+ 1 );
```

2. What is wrong with the following code?

```
int acc = 10;
float bal = 100;
int* p1  = & acc;
float  * p2 = & bal;
p1 = p2;
```

3. Write and test a program that makes use of pointers in order to pass arguments to two pointers **p1** and **p2.** You should include in your program **swap ( )** function in order to exchange the values of the current outstanding balance with the current balance. Display the amounts of outstanding balance and current balance, before and after the swapping of values.

Chapter 8

Character Strings

Strings & Initialisation

It is not only numbers that a computer system handles but it also manipulates sequences of characters such as employees' names, addresses, product textual details and the like. In C++, strings are considered as one-dimensional arrays, terminated by the **nul** character. The nul character is \0, and it is equivalent to zero. Consider the string:

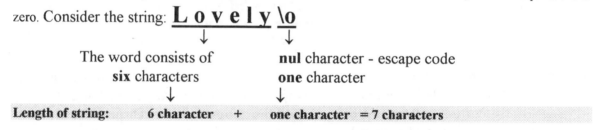

If you have to store the word 'lovely', you must include nul character in your string. Thus the length of this string is 7 characters long. The nul character terminates the string. It is stored internally at the end of the string.

We can initialise this string as **char word [ ] = { " lovely" };** We can also output it as an object. The following simple program illustrates how to declare, and output this string. The output stream **cout** has displayed the result, as shown in **diagram 62**.

```
 # include <iostream.h>
// how to initialise character strings
void main ( )
{
char  word [ ] = {" Lovely" };
cout << " The string is a word from English Language:" << word;
}
======================= Program Output =====================================
The string is a word from English Language: Lovely
```

Diagram 62

- **You can also declare string array as shown in diagram 63. Here no { } brackets are** used for the initialiser strings.

```
# include <iostream.h>
// how to initialise character strings
void main ( )
{
char  word [  ] = "Lovely " ;
cout << " The string is a word from English Language:" << word;
}
================================ Program Output ================================

The string is a word from English Language:Lovely
```

Diagram 63

- **The string array can be initialised as illustrated in <u>diagram 64</u>**. In this case, you must specify the size of the array that includes the **nul character**.

```
# include <iostream.h>
// how to initialise character strings
void main ( )
{
char word  [ 7 ];
                word [ 0 ] = 'L';
                word [ 1 ] = 'o';
                word [ 2 ] = 'v';
                word [ 3 ] = 'e';
                word [ 4 ] = 'l';
                word [ 5 ] = 'y' ;
                word [ 6 ] = '\0';
cout << " The string is a word from English Language:" << word;
}
================================ Program Output ================================
        The string is a word from English Language:Lovely
```

Diagram 64

Insertion Operator >> and Blank Space

The program in diagram 65 illustrates that for insertion operators any blank spaces between words are just terminating characters. It displays the output.

```
# include <iostream.h>
// how to initialise character strings
void main ( )
{
char str;
char word  [ 80 ];         // maximum characters in a string, including nul character
cout << " Please enter a string: ";
cin  >> str;
cout << " You have entered: " << str;
}
```
============================= Program Output =============================
```
Please enter a string: I am fine!
You have entered: I
```

Diagram 65

Explanation

The program is interactive which allows the user to enter a string of characters. The user typed: **I am fine!** The program output was: You have entered: I. **Why is it so?** In C++ the insertion operators consider a space as a terminator. Therefore, when the execution reached **cout << " You have entered: " << str;** the first character in the input string was **I**, which was displayed. All other characters were ignored because of a space between **I** and **am**. The execution did not pass the space. The program was terminated.

How do we overcome this problem ?

In C++, a more efficient facility exists. This is **cin . getline ( )**. This allows us to read the whole line together with spaces between words. It is one of the functions of the input stream object cin >>. The format is

$$\textbf{cin . getline (} \underline{\textbf{str}} \textbf{ , } \underline{\textbf{n}} \textbf{);}$$

              ↓   ↓

              name of string   number of characters in the string to be array

Diagram 66

This diagram contains the modified program shown in diagram 65.

Explanation

char str;

char word [80];

The above two statements in the previous program have been replaced by **char str [80];**

cin >> str; This statement in the previous program is now **cin.getline (str, 80);**

Now you can appreciate the efficiency of function **cin.getline ( )**, which is used for reading input character one by one.

```
# include <iostream.h>
// how to initialise character strings
void main ( )
{
char str [ 80 ];                    // maximum characters in a string. nul character included
cout << " Please enter a string: ";
cin.getline ( str, 80 );
cout << " You have entered: " << str;
}
```
======================== **Program Output** ========================
```
Please enter a string: I am fine!
You have entered: I am fine!
```

Diagram 66

Diagram 67

The program is designed to enter names and addresses in the address book. It illustrates the application of the input function cin. getline ( ). The program output is shown in **diagram 67 A**.

Explanation - see next page.

Here we have declared two one-dimensional arrays namely **name** and **add**. Their sizes have included an extra component for the **nul** character. A **while loop** is used in order to control the iteration process. The program design is interactive. It displays messages prior to the input process begins, so that the user can interact successfully.

Within the while loop, **cin. getline ( );** function reads **name**, the input from the keyboard. Each character is read individually. Similarly, **cin. getline ( );** function reads the input string **address**, character by character. The statement **while (*name);** controls the loop.

(***name**) is initially the same as **name [0]**. Therefore, it will be **non zero (true)** when it contains the **string**. When it contains only the **nul character** then it is an empty string. Under **DOS** on a PC, the loop is terminated, when **ctrl** and **z** keys are pressed simultaneously. This action loads the empty string into:

(*name)

which is a **nul character** and signals the end of file. From the program output you can see that the program is interactive. It showed the user how to input data and then allowed the user to enter sets of **names** and **addresses**. The user entered two such sets. The program was terminated when **ctrl** and **z** keys were pressed simultaneously. On my PC, the system does not print control +z that ended the loop. You should experiment with it on your machine.

```
#include <iostream.h>
// How to use cin.getnline ( ) function

void main ( void )
{
cout << "\t\tAddress Book" << endl;
cout << "\t\t_____ \n" <<endl;
cout << " Please enter initials and surname up to 24 characters" << endl;
cout << " Address up to 59 characters\n\n\n" << endl;
cout << " Press enter key at the end of each line" << endl;
cout << " To end input, press control and z keys simultaneously on a DOS PC\n" << endl;
char name [ 25 ];
char add  [60 ];
do
  {
        cin.getline( name, 25 );
        cin.getline ( add, 60 );
        }
         while ( *name );
}
```

Diagram 67

```
=========================== Program Output ===========================

        Address Book
        _____

    Please enter initials and surname up to 24 characters
    Address up to 59 characters




    Press enter key at the end of each line
    To end input, press control and z keys simultaneously on a DOS PC

    M K Smith .
    123 High Street Birmingham B1 6SS

    N V Major 1 Main Road London SW1 1AA
    1 Main Street London Sw1AA
```

Diagram 67A

Practical Hints

- ```
  while ( *name )
      {
      cin. getline ( name,25 );     ←  This code will generate the same output
      cin. getline ( add, 60 );        as was achieved by code do--- while
      cout << " " << endl;             loop in diagram 68.
      }
  ```

- The maximum length of a string should be declared.

- **cin.getlin ( )** does not read white space characters, such as blank spaces, new lines...

- In C++, it is not possible to assign the value of a string to another string. This can be achieved by copying strings.
  ```

```
# include <iostream.h>
# include <string.h>
// to illustrate how to copy strings
void main ( void )
 {
  cout << "\tAfter strings have been copied" << endl;
  cout << " \t-----------------------------\n" << endl;
  char London  [ 50 ] = " In winter London is far less colder than Moscow";
  char  Moscow  [ 50 ] ;
  strcpy ( Moscow," In winter Moscow is much Colder than London" );
  cout << Moscow << endl;
  strcpy ( Moscow, London );
  cout << Moscow << endl << endl;
  cout << "\tBefore strings are copied" << endl;
  cout << " \t-------------------------\n" << endl;
  .cout << " In winter London is far less colder than Moscow. " << endl;
  cout << " In winter Moscow is much Colder than London.\n" << endl;
}
```

=========================== Program Output ===========================

After strings have been copied

In winter Moscow is much Colder than London.
In winter London is far less colder than Moscow.

Before strings are copied

In winter London is far less colder than Moscow.
In winter Moscow is much Colder than London.

Diagram 68

Copying Strings

strcpy ( ) function

It is the string copy function, which is pre-defined in the **string.h** header file. Like **iostream.h** header file, it must be included, whenever you wish to use this function.

The program in **diagram 68** demonstrates how this function copies string **London's** contents into string Moscow's contents. We have declared London and Moscow as two character strings with an equal number of a maximum 50 characters in each string. The string London is initialised with, " **In winter London is far less colder than Moscow"**. See diagram on page 146 above.

Explanation

The directive # include has two header files. **iostream.h**, for input and output streams, and **string.h** for string handling function **strcpy ( ).**

The **strcpy( )** function is applied twice. The first **strcpy( ) function** call copies, **In winter Moscow is much Colder than London** into the string Moscow.

The second **strcpy ( )** function call copies the contents of string London into string Moscow.

The program output shows this copying output. Note that if you initialise string Moscow, the program will be compiled without any error messages displayed, but it will not copy strings correctly.

The strlen ( ) function

The strlen ( ) is known as string length function. It returns the number of characters in a string. It does not return **nul** character. It is one of the string library functions. You have to include in your # **include directive header** file <string.h> whenever you wish to use this or any other library functions.

Diagrams 69 & 70

Explanation

These diagrams contain two simple programs, designed to demonstrate **strlen ( )** function. In both programs, **string.h** file is included in the # include directive. In **diagram 69,** character string Moscow is ini-tialised with "Moscow". Note that there are no white spaces in this initialiser list,except the word Mos-cow. **strlen ( )** function is applied in output stream **cout**. It has actually output the length of this string as 6 characters long, as shown in **diagram 69**. This is correct.

Now examine the string Moscow in diagram 70. The output gives its length as 13 characters long. **Why is this so?** The declaration **char Moscow [ ] = " M o s c o w " ;** Here the initialiser list contains 6 charac-ters and 7 white space characters. Thus the string is 13 characters long.

```
# include <iostream.h>
# include <string.h>
// to illustrate how to copy strings
void main ( void )
 {
        char  Moscow [ ] = " M o s c o w " ;
        cout << " The string Moscow has: " << strlen (Moscow) <<" characters"  << endl;

}
```
===================== Program Output ===========================
```
The string Moscow has: 6 characters
```

Diagram 69

```
# include <iostream.h>
#include <string.h>
// to illustrate how to copy strings
void main ( void )
{
char Moscow [ ] = " M O S C O W ";
cout << " The string Moscow has: " << strlen (Moscow) << " characters" << endl;
}
```
========================= Program Output =========================

```
 The string Moscow has: 13 characters
```

Diagram 70

Appending Strings

stract ( ) function

This function is useful for appending or joining one string to another string. It is also known as the string **concatenation** function. The example in **diagram 71** illustrates the application of this function.

```
# include <iostream.h>
# include <string.h>
 // Illustration of strcat function
# define string_max 80

// stracat ( ) function illustration
void main ( void )
{
 char today [  ] = " Today is rather a dull day.",
                  umb [  ] = " Take your umbrella with you.",
         weather [string_max ];

 strcpy( weather, today );
 strcat ( weather, umb );
 strcat ( weather, " Don't get wet!");
 cout << weather << endl;
}
```

===================== **Program Output** =====================

Today is rather a dull day. Take your umbrella with you. Don't get .wet!

Diagram 71

Explanation

In this program the # include directive has two header files, one for input and output cin and cout routines. The **string.h** handles strings. **# define string_max 80** is declared and its size is initialised. It is equivalent to **const int string_max = 80;** You can declare a string in either way. string_max is just a name given to a string, and 80 is its maximum size. In the declaration **const int string_max = 80; const** is required. If you do not include it in this declaration, the compiler will issue an error message and your program will not be compiled successfully.

Three character arrays namely **today, umb** and **weather** are declared. Both **today** and **umb** are initialised but weather is not initialised. Two library functions **strcpy ( )**, and **strcat ( )** are used in this program. What do they do in this program ?

The function **strcpy ( )**, is used to copy the **today** string into **weather** string. Now **weather** stores, " **To-day is rather a dull day.**". This is followed by **strcat ( )** function call appends or concatenates, " **Take your umbrella with you.**" to the current contents of **weather** string. Now **weather** string contains, "Today is rather a dull day. Take your umbrella with you." The second function call appends, "Don't get wet!" to weather. **cout** has displayed the final contents of weather string. This is shown in the program output.

Arrays and Character Strings

Diagram 72

The program in this diagram demonstrates the application of two-dimensional arrays, and strings manipulation. It allows the user to enter 5 employees' names. Each name can have up-to 24 characters in it. These names are displayed as a list under a suitable heading.

Explanation

char employee [5] [25]; declares **char** type two-dimensional array called **employee. employee** can have 5 rows of names, each containing upto 25 characters, including the **nul** character.

Under arrays, it is said that a **two-dimensional** array is in fact a one-dimensional array. Therefore, each row of two-dimensional array is equivalent to one-dimensional array. In accordance with this rule, **employee** contains 5 one-dimensional arrays. Each of these arrays has a character string, whose length is 25 characters long. You can visualize it as a table of 5 rows and 25 columns. In this table you can store 100 bytes.

In order to read the whole string, **string cin.getline ( )** function is used. A **while loop** is set up so that values of each 5 rows can be read into **employee [ ]** . The following segment of the code controls the reading of 5 rows into the employee [count]

        while
          (cin.getline (employee [count ++], 25)) ;
                              ↓   ↓
                      up-date the loop   size of strings
                      reading of rows

for loop is used to print 5 rows of employees' names.

The program is interactive. It prompted the user how to input data. When the user entered **control - Z** , the cingetline ( ) returned 0, which terminated the while loop. Then the computer executed the next three **cout** statements. Next the **for loop** was executed. At each step of the loop, **employee [count]** was incremented and **cout** displayed each name (row) on a separate line as required.

```
# include <iostream.h>
// Two-dimensional arrays
void main (void)
{
        char employee [ 5 ] [ 25 ];    // maximum 24 characters ( 25 th is Nul Character )
        cout << "\t List of Employees" << endl;
        cout << "\t ----------------------\n" << endl;
        cout << " Please enter a name up to 24 characters long." << endl;
        cout << " Press enter at the end of each line." << endl;
        cout << " To end input routine, Press ctrl and z keys simultaneously." << end;
        cout << " ------------------------------------------------------------\n" << endl;
        cout << "\t Enter employee's full name" << endl;
        cout << "\t .........................\n" << endl;
        int count = 0;
         while
                ( cin.getline ( employee[count ++],25 )) ;
                cout << " " << endl;
                cout << "\t Staff List as at 24 March 1997" << endl;
                cout << "\t .............................\n" << endl;
                for
                        ( count  =0; count < 5 ; count++ )
                        cout <<"\t\t" << employee [count] << endl;
}
```

Diagram 72

Output from the Program is shown on next page

```
List of Employees
-----------------------

Please enter a name up to 24 characters long.
Press enter at the end of each line.
To end input routine, Press ctrl and z keys simultaneously.
------------------------------------------------------------------

        Enter employee's full name
        .................................

John N. Smith
Robert G, Johnson
Julia A. Roberts
Jane B. Blair
Terry C. Scott

        Staff List as at 24 March 1997
        ....................................................

            John N. Smith
            Robert G, Johnson
            Julia A. Roberts
            Jane B. Blair
            Terry C. Scott
```

Strings and Array of Pointers

Diagrams 73 & 73 A

The program in diagram 73 performs the same task as carried out by the previous program; even so there are some differences the way they allocate any storage for strings. The program in diagram 73 does not initially allocate any storage for strings. **It make use of a buffer area for storing all the input data.**

Explanation

Here all **5 string arrays which are names are stored as a single string in the buffer**. The size of each string is still 25 characters long, and the list of employees contains 5 names only. Since each character occupies **one byte** of memory, we need to declare the buffer size as 100 bytes.

This is done so by declaring :

```
char buffer [ 100 ];     // maximum 24 characters ( 25 th is Nul Character )
```

Char* employee [5]; employee is now a pointer to char. This way each **employee [s]** is the address of the first character of employee's name currently held in the buffer. Therefore. it is initialised as:

employee [0] = buffer;

The code **cin.getline (buffer, 100, 'z');** reads employee.

Each employee is read as a whole line. The letter **Z** signals the end of input. By applying this method all 5 elements of the array are stored in the buffer. The buffer has a maximum storage location for 100 bytes. These 5 strings are stored in the buffer in the same sequence as read into it. You may visualise it as one string in the buffer as:

James Baker\ Sarah Henderson\ David Johnson\ Robin Taylor\ John Major\

There are two for loops in this program. In the first **for** loop **pointer** is used to step through this single string stored in the buffer. Within this loop is **if** conditional statement. When the pointer meets '\n' character. the first name is then terminated in:

employee [++count] = pointer+1;

and '\0' is appended to the first string. that is **James Baker**. At the same time. **count** is incremented. Now count stores the address **pointer+1** of the first character of the next employee **Sarah Henderson** in employee [count]. This process is repeated for all strings.

The second **for** loop is used to output the data. **Diagram 73A** shows both input data and program output. You can see that the program prompted the user how to input data. The input was terminated when the user entered **z**. Note that z is not shown in the output list.

You have seen a number of string handling library functions in this chapter. There are a large number of similar functions which are used in similar ways. Some of these will be illustrated as we progress through this book.

```
# include <iostream.h>
// Pointers and character strings
void main (void)
{
        char buffer [ 100 ];     // maximum 24 characters ( 25 th is Nul Character )
        cout << "\t List of Employees" << endl;
        cout << "\t --------------------\n" << endl;
        cout << " Please enter a name up to 24 characters long." << endl;
        cout << " Press enter at the end of each line." << endl;
        cout << " To end input routine, Press z key ." << endl;
        cout << " ---------------------------------------\n" << endl;
        cout << "\t Enter employee's full name" << endl;
        cout << "\t .............................\n" << endl;
        cin.getline (buffer, 100,'z' );
        char*    employee [ 5 ];
        employee [ 0 ] = buffer;
        int count = 0;

            for ( char *pointer = buffer;  *pointer != '\0';  pointer++ )
              if ( *pointer == '\n' )
                {
                     ( *pointer )  = '\0';
                     employee [++count] = pointer+1;
                }
            cout << "\t Staff List as at 24 March 1997" << endl;
            cout << "\t .............................\n" << endl;
             for
                    ( int s = 0; s < count ; s++ )
                    cout <<"\t\t" << employee [ s ] << endl;
}
```

Diagram 73

```
================== Program Input Data ==========================
```

        List of Employees

Please enter a name up to 24 characters long.
Press enter at the end of each line.
To end input routine, Press z key.

        Enter employee's full name
        ....

James Baker
Sarah Henderson
David Johnson
Robin Taylor
John Major
z

```
================== Information Output ==========================
```

        Staff List as at 24 March 1997
        ....

                James Baker
                Sarah Henderson
                David Johnson
                Robin Taylor
                John Major

Diagram 73 A

Programming Exercises

1. Write a program that allows the course tutor to hold a computer file which will store information under three headings:

> student - all character;
> tel - all characters; and
> comments - all characters.

You should test the validity of this code for three students.

Hint

- Apply **for loop** technique for **x number** of data items to be input from the keyboard.

- Use cin.getline ( ) function for reading input character by character.

- Use **arrays of strings** of different sizes (number of characters in each string).

2. Write and test a program that counts the occurrences of a particular letter of the alphabet. You should use the string library function **cin.get ( )** in order to read character by character keyboard input. Your program should be user-friendly.

Hint

Include a **while loop**. This loop will allow you to enter as many characters from the keyboard as you wish. Press **control-z** at the end of your input.

Chapter 9

Mixed Data Structure

Introduction

You have learnt enough about arrays which allow elements of the same data type to be combined under its name, which can then be accessed. Data structure of arrays type is very practical in many circumstances but whenever you have to group related data of mixed types, arrays are not appropriate. In C++, you can handle mixed data structure.

Business data is often of mixed data types. How do we handle it ?

A file containing employees' personal information is a structure. Similarly, 2 years sales data kept by a company in a computer file is a structure. A sales invoice is a structure and so on. Let's examine the following illustration of a structure.

Structure

Staff Personal Information

Headings	C++ Declaration Types	
Surname	char name	[20];
Initials	char initials	[4]
Address	char address	[50];
National Insurance Number	char NI	[13];
Date of Birth	Int dob;	
Place of Birth	char pob;	[25];
Date Employment Commenced	int dec;	
Position	char	[20];
Current Salary	float salary;	
Qualification	char qual	[30];

The data items in the above example are related data because they are about an employee's personal record kept by the employers. They are of mixed data types, as shown under C++ declaration types. It is actually one unit of a record, that is a collection of data. This is what we call a **structure**. In this structure, we have grouped related data items, which are of different types. In C++, a structure is created by using the following syntax.

struct staff	←	**Struct** is a keyword. Type of structure is called **staff**.
{	←	It is required to begin structure staff's definition.
char name [20];	←	It is a member of the structure staff, its size is given.
char initials [4];	←	It is a member of the structure staff, with its size.
int dob;	←	It is another member . It is of **int** type.
};	←	The end of structure staff definition. A semicolon is needed, as this definition is a statement in C++.

This structure can be used to save staff information..

Diagram 74

The program uses a structure variable to store name, national insurance number, salary and place of birth of staff.

Explanation

As already explained **struct** is the keyword, which is followed by the structure name **staff**. **struct staff** specifies that the variable structure is called staff. Within the { } **braces** is a declaration of 4 elements of structure **staff**. Their types and sizes are also given. Note that **};** is required. As mentioned above, in C++ a structure definition is a statement. Therefore, a semicolon is essential. **};** this symbol marks the end of **structure staff definition.** You can think of this structure definition as the specification for user defined new data type called structure staff.

char cr; stands for character carriage return or a new line. This statement is the carriage return or new line declaration. It is used with **cin.get (cr);** in this program.

The statement **cin.get (cr)** receives the carriage return and saves it in **cr**. If you omit **char cr;** and **cin.get (cr);** statements, your program will compile without any error messages displayed on your screen. Your program will run, but it will not work successfully. You will not be able to input all data. Your screen will look like as shown below, after entering just one data item. From this computer output, you can see that the user was allowed to enter James Clark, and the computer did not allow the user to answer **Now enter NI Number:** instead it displayed the content of the next cout statement. This was not the requirement at all.

Please enter name: James Clark
Now enter NI Number: Next enter salary per annum £:

---

staff emp1; statements declares variable **emp1** (employee 1). Because of this statement storage is reserved for 4 members of the structure variable staff. These 4 members in fact can be visualised as 4 fields of a database, and that each field is a component of the record called **emp1**. Therefore, each field of this record can store a particular declared type variable.

<u>**Input data**</u> - Let's analyse the following segment of the code to understand how data is input:
cout << "Please enter name: ";   ← computer prompts the user to enter the data
cin.get (emp1.name, 25); ← **cin.get ( )** function puts the input data in the field **name** in
                                    record **emp1**
 cin.get (cr); ←   flushes carriage return - see above for its importance in this program
 The process is repeated for 3 **char** type data input. For the **int** type, the code:
cin >> emp1.salary; replaces cin.get (emp1.name, 25); In this case, **cin** puts the salary in the **emp1**
record.   ↓
                   The size of string name, included **nul character**

Output **Information** In order to output information about the employee, **cout** statements are used. In
cout << " Employee: " << <u>emp1.name</u> << endl;
                              ↓
                   compound name

all 4 members of the structure variable staff are displayed by referring to each member like this. This is how the compiler recognises these variables in this program.

From the program output shown below, you can see that the program is interactive. It prompts the user to enter the required data. The input data is the output in the desired format. Like other programs, you should compile and run this program.

Remember, practice makes perfect!

```
# include <iostream.h>
// Example of  structure
void main ( )
{
struct staff
{
 char name [ 25  ];
 char NI [ 15 ];
 int salary;
 char pob [ 25 ];
};
                         // data input
  char cr;                              // carriage return
  staff emp1;
  cout << "Please enter name: ";
  cin.get ( emp1.name, 25 );
  cin.get ( cr );
  cout << "Now enter NI Number: ";
  cin.get  (emp1.NI, 25 );
  cin.get ( cr );                       // flush carriage return
  cout << "Next enter salary per annum £: ";
  cin  >> emp1.salary;
  cin.get ( cr );
  cout << "Now enter Place of birth: ";
  cin.get (emp1.pob, 25 );
                               // Output information
cout <<"\n"<< "\t Staff Information" << endl;
cout << "\t ---------------------------\n" << endl;
cout << " Emplyee: " << emp1.name << endl;
cout << " National Insurance Number: " << emp1.NI << endl;
cout << " Salary per annum £: " << emp1.salary << endl;
cout << " Place of Birth: " << emp1.pob << endl;
 }
```

Diagram 74

=================== Output from program in diagram 74 ============

```
Please enter name: James Clark
Now enter NI Number: HY/76/02/80/D
Next enter salary per annum £: 21670
Now enter Place of birth: London


                    Staff Information
                    -------------------


Employee: James Clark
National Insurance Number: HY/76/02/80/D
Salary per annum £: 21670
Place of Birth: London
```

Diagram 74 A

Unions

A union is another data type. A union can hold only one data type at a time despite the fact that like the structure a union can declare a group several data types. The syntax of a union resembles a structure, as shown below.

```
union staff     ←  union called staff
{

 members;

} ;
```

It can be ended as: } **identifier;** An identifier is a label or a name.

The other method is to declare in function **main ( )**, just below { as **Exercise example;** where **Ex-ercise** is the name of union and **example** is an identifier. Note that there is no punctuation mark between the union name and the identifier label. In the following example, this method is applied.

You can see the definition of union **staff** looks very much like the definition of a structure. The difference is that the keyword **union** has replaced the keyword **structure**. This union has **n** numbers of members of character, integer, double and float types. However, **union staff** will hold only one active data type at a time but sufficient storage is allocated to hold the largest member.

Diagram 75

This program is designed to illustrate the use of a union. It demonstrates that a union can only hold one data item at a time, despite the fact that several data types can be declared within the union definition.

Explanation

Just below the comments line, union Exercise declaration begins. It has three members:

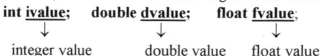

Like the structure declaration, **union Exercise** is terminated by a semicolon. Within the function **main ( )**, **Exercise example;** statement reserves memory space for **example** to hold the largest member of union **Exercise**.

example.ivalue = 1997; cout << example.ivalue << endl; statements enter 1997, and then unload 1997 from the union Exercise. The next four statements perform the same task of loading and unloading the data from the union. The following segment of program:

```
cout << example.ivalue << endl;
cout << example.fvalue << endl;
cout << example.dvalue << endl;
```

outputs each data value from the **union Exercise**. The statement

cout << " \t\tThe Size of the union is "<< sizeof(example) << " bytes" << endl;

displays the size of the union in bytes. It tells you memory size that holds the largest member in the union **Exercise**.

From the program output you can see that all three input data items are displayed correctly. Under data output heading, there is only one item that is displayed correctly. **1.23453e+16** is the only valid information. **Why is it so?** 1.23453e+16 was the last value loaded in the memory. A union only holds one value at a time and this was the only value held in the memory. Now you can appreciate that a union uses memory differently. The output shows that total memory located for union Exercise was 8 bytes. It is big enough to hold the largest member **double**.

```
# include <iostream.h>
// Example of  structure
union Exercise
{
 int  ivalue;
 double dvalue;
 float  fvalue;
} ;

void main ( void )
{
  Exercise  example;
  cout << "\t\t Data input" << endl;
  cout << "\t\t ------------" << endl;
  example.ivalue = 1997;
  cout << example.ivalue << endl;
  example.fvalue = 12.99;
  cout << example.fvalue << endl;
  example.dvalue = 12345.31E+12;
  cout << example.dvalue << endl;
  cout << "Data output invalid, except one valid item" << endl;
  cout << " _____\n" << endl;
  cout << example.ivalue << endl;
  cout << example.fvalue << endl;
  cout << example.dvalue << endl;
  cout << " \t\tThe Size of the union is "<< sizeof (example) << " bytes" << endl;
  cout << "\t\t --------------------------------" << endl;
  }
```

Diagram 75

Diagram 75A contains program input and output.

```
========================= Program Output =================================

                Data input
                ------------
1997
12.99
1.23453e+16
Data output invalid, except one valid item

_____

-27136
0.0186262
1.23453e+16
                The Size of the union is 8 bytes
                ---------------------------------------
```

Diagram 75A

Practical Hints

- Unions are set up like structures, but a union holds one data item at a time.

- Unions are not used widely.

- Structures enable you to group related data items of different data types.

- A structure is a collection or a group of related data.

- Structures are important in C++. The syntax of a structure is very much like the syntax of C++ classes.

- The understanding of structures and classes is essential for learning Object Oriented Programming (OOP). You will learn more about structures when we discuss classes.

Programming Exercises

1. Write and test a program that allows you to use a **structure variable customer** in order to store client's name, address, telephone number and contact's name in the customer's file. Use a **loop** so that the you can input data from the keyboard.

2. Write a program that uses **strcpy ( )** Library function with a structure variable. Assign strings to structure elements. **Data** items to be assigned are name, course and tutor. The following information to be output:

> student: his or her name
> course: its name
> tutor: his or her name

What is an object?

In Object Oriented Programming (OOP) a real world thing such as a book is considered as an object. This concept enables programmers to interpret real world objects such as printers, cars, monthly sales figures and the like as objects. Since a program in its essence is a simulation of the real world, where action takes place, objects interact under certain conditions at a given time. In OOP, a programmer can distinguish an object from another object by means of the task the object performs and the interaction it has with other objects under certain conditions. For instance, a sales file is an object because it can be displayed on the screen for your use. We can attach other attributes to it and represent these in a program. It can meet the required features of an object. It is discussed further under OOP.

Chapter 10

File Processing

A file is a collection of related records. It is usually stored on backing storage devices so that it can be used for a long time. Often there is insufficient available memory space in the main memory. Information has to be utilised. It must be available to both users and other programs. All of this can be achieved by holding information in files on backing stores (disks or tapes).

Input and output (I/O) Streams

The flow of data from one object to another object is known as a **stream**. For example:

- Data flow from keyboard (object) to display screen(object) is a stream; and

- Data flow from one file (object) to another file (object) is another stream.

If the file is **open for input**, then the flow of data is input stream. In this case, the file is input stream file. If the file is **open for output**, then the flow of data is output stream. The file is an output stream. In short, a **stream** is a flow of data. The understanding of streams is very important as it lays the foundation for comprehending object oriented programming.

C++ interprets a file as a sequence of bytes. The bits constituting a file are interpreted in accordance with some software system. When the file contains 8-bit groups as bytes, the **ASCII** code interprets it as a **text file**. A text file is processed by standard text editors. When a file has an executable program, its bits are interpreted by the compiler as instructions. Files can be accessed by using the **insertion** (<<) and extraction (>>) **operators**. The **cin** >> inputs data from the file on backing store into the random access memory (**RAM**) area. The **cout** << outputs data from **RAM** into the file which is on a backing store.

Library Classes for I/O

C++ does not itself include facilities for I/O, but the standard I/O library known as **iostream.h** provides this facility. **An input** stream manages the data flow into the program, whilst the **output** stream manages the flow of data out of the program. The **stream library** is a comprehensive collection of classes that are arranged in a complex hierarchy.

Summary Library Classes Support I/O

Input Operations	Output Operations	Linking File to an application
iostream class	**ostream class**	**fstream class**
↓	↓	↓
cin	**cout**	for linking a file for input-output
an object	an object	**ifstream class**
linked to a	linked to standard	↓
standard input	output	for linking a file for input only
	cerr	**ofstream class**
	↓	↓
	object linked to	for linking a file for ouput only
	standard error	
	unbuffered stream	
	clog	
	↓	
	object linked to standard error	
	buffered stream	

You have already met both input and output streams. **cin** and **cout** objects are always on the left hand side of operators >> and << respectively. **Files are declared as variables.**

Writing to an External File

When you have to create a file for reading and writing you must include:
 # include <fstream.h> header file. This header file includes **iostream.h** header. There is no need to include it in your directive.

Diagram 76 The program in diagram 76 illustrates how to create (open) a file in order to store (write) data in an external file.

Explanation

The purpose of this line is to create a file called **sales.data**. This file is to be stored on **drive c**. In this file monthly sales data to be held. This line is explained below:

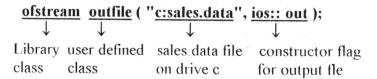

ofstream   outfile ("c:sales.data", ios:: out);

   Library user defined sales.data file constructor flag
   class   class   on drive c   for output fle

(a) As already discussed **ofstream** is a library class that is needed for file handling.

(b) **outfile** is defined by the user. You can give it any other suitable name. The **outfile** is now is a member of **ofstream** class. **outfile** is initialised to sales.data file.

(c) **sales.data** file is open for writing (output) on drive c. This is an **output file stream**.

(d) To read this file you need our program shown in Diagram 77.

(e) **ios::out** - it is known as file stream **constructor flag** for opening a file for writing. It specifies the output to the file.

The whole purpose of this statement is to define an **output file object** which is linked to the file name sales.data.

if (! outfile) statement is a check to make sure that the external file sales.data is opened on drive c correctly. If the file is not opened correctly, the message, **" Error: Unable to open 'sales.data' file "** is displayed on the screen and program execution is terminated. If the file is opened properly, the execution enters the **for** loop. The computer prompts the user to enter sales, and at the end of the last input from the keyboard, the statement **outfile << sales << endl;** is executed. It sends sales figures to sales.data file to be stored in it. Finally, **outfile.close ( );** statement is executed which terminates the program and at the same time closes the fiile.

Reading an External File

The program in diagram 76 has created a file. In this file 5 monthly sales figures are already stored. The external file is sales.data. This file can be read and information can also be displayed or printed. How do we achieve all this? The program shown in **diagram 77** is designed to perform this task.

```
# include <fstream.h>          // defines ofstream class - it includes output file streams
# include <stdlib.h>           // includes exit ( ) function
// Writing to an external file
void main ( void )
{
  ofstream outfile( "c:sales.data", ios::out );     // to create a file
  if (! outfile )
  {
  cerr << " Error: Unable to open 'sales.data' file \n";
  exit ( 1 );
}
 cout << " Monthly Sales Data" << endl;
  cout << " ----------------------\n" << endl;
  double sales;
 for ( int i = 0; i < 5; i++ )
 {
cin >> sales;
 outfile <<  sales << endl;
}
outfile.close ( );
}


==== Sales figures are stored  in file sales.data on drive c inthe following format =====
            Monthly Sales Information
            -------------------------------

                10345
                12346
                16000
                18000
                12546
```

Diagram 76

Diagram 77

This program demonstrates the technique of opening an existing disc file for reading from it. It also adds up sales data together and prints their sum in the desired format.

Explanation

This program makes use of **ifstream** library class. Here **infile** is defined as an object to be a member of **ifstream**.

ifstream infile("c:sales.data", ios::in); statement defines the input file object. **infile** is initialised to sales.data file. It opens sales.data file on drive c.

<u>**Here** the file sales.data is open for input data or reading data from it</u>

$$(\text{"c: sales.data " }, \underline{ios::in})$$
$$\downarrow$$
opens file for reading (input)

When a file is open for input, it is known as input file stream. **ios::in** input file stream constructor flag for opening a file for reading data from it.

Testing for errors

The following segment of the code tests to make sure that the file is opened properly. The file is set to zero by using the overloaded negation operator **!** with infile.

```
if (! infile ) {
 cerr << " Error: Unable to open ' sales.data' file \n";
 exit ( 1 );
}
```

If the file could not be opened, the error message is displayed and the program is terminated with a zero value. If there is no error in opening a file than the object returns a non-zero value. Like in the previous program, the error message is sent to **cerr**. This way the error message is separated from **cout** output.

```
while ( infile >> sales){
 sum += sales;
 i ++;                    // increment or counter
```

The above segment of the code is to read from the file sales data items and add them together. The **while** loop continues until the value of the file variable is non-zero and sales figures are added up together within the **while** loop. It will terminate if an error has occurred or the variable becomes zero at the end of sales.data file.

```
# include <fstream.h>            // defines ofstream class - it includes output file streams
# include <stdlib.h>             // includes exit ( ) function
// Reading from an external file
void main ( void )
{
 ifstream infile( "c:sales.data", ios::in );
 if (! infile )
 {
 cerr << " Error: Unable to open ' sales.data' file \n";
 exit ( 1 );
}
 cout << "\t Monthly Sales Information" << endl;
 cout << "\t -----------------------------\n" << endl;
 double  sales, sum;
 int I = 0;
 while ( infile >> sales){
 sum += sales;
 I ++;
 cout << "\tat" << sales << endl;
 }
 cout << "\t\t" << "------------" << endl;
 cout << " Total Sales £" << "\t" <<  sum << endl;
 cout << "\t\t" << "------------" << endl;

 infile.close (   );
 }
=========================== Program Output ================================
            Monthly Sales Information
            --------------------------------

                10345
                12346
                16000
                18000
                12546
                ------------
Total Sales £  69237
                ------------
```

Diagram 77

cout statements, with which you are familiar, are designed to direct the required output to the screen. You should compile and run this program to understand how it performs its task of reading from the existing file, adding data items together and finally, displaying information as required.

Diagram 78

Appending to a file

In order to add more information to an existing file sales.data, you need to run the program shown in **diagram 78**. The program in this diagram is designed to allow the user to append 5 data items to the existing file.

Explanation

The program is very similar to our program in diagram 76. It should be noted that the following statement which defines the outfile object uses a different constructor flag.

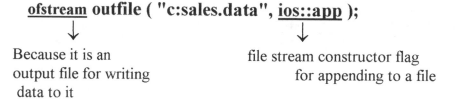

<u>ofstream</u> **outfile ("c:sales.data", <u>ios::app</u>);**

Because it is an
output file for writing
data to it

file stream constructor flag
for appending to a file

The variable **double sales** and **for** loop are the same as in the previous program.

Test Data in Diagram 78A

The program was run twice. Each time, 5 data items were entered, as the **for** loop is repeated only 5 times. These data items are shown in diagram 78 as two separate sets. In order to test that this program has in fact appended these two sets of figures to sales.data file, the program shown in diagram 77 was run again. Indeed, 10 data items were correctly appended to the existing file. This is shown in diagram 78A. It does prove that the program was compiled successfully and that both files were opened correctly and linked together.

```
#include <fstream.h>              // defines ofstream class - it includes output file streams
#include <stdlib.h>              // includes exit ( ) function
// Append or add to an existing file
void main ( void )
{
  ofstream outfile( "c:sales.data", ios::app );
  if (! outfile )
  {
  cerr << " Error: Unable to open 'sales.data' file \n";
  exit ( 1 );
}
  cout << " Monthly Sales Information" << endl;
  cout << " -------------------------------\n" << endl;
  double sales;
 for ( int i = 0; i < 5; i++ )
  {
 cin >> sales;
 outfile <<  sales << endl;
 }
outfile.close ( );
 }

======== The program in diagam 78 was run twice with the following sets of data =====
```

Monthly Sales Information	Monthly Sales Information
-------------------------------	-------------------------------
12500	12345
12495	34567
14000	43257
13750	45643
14800	34567

Diagram 78

```
        Monthly Sales Information
        ------------------------------

                10345
                12346
                16000
                18000
                12546
                12500
                12495
                14000
                13750
                14800
                12345
                34567
                43257
                45643
                34567
                ------------
Total Sales £307161
                ------------
```

Diagram 78A

Practical Hints

ios::out → this file stream constructor flag creates a file for writing.
ios::in → this file stream constructor flag opens file for reading from the existing file.
ios::app → this file stream constructor flag appends data to the end of an existing file.
ios:: binary → this file stream constructor opens binary file.
. When you append data items to a file, the new data items are added to the end of file.

Writing Strings to a File

The program in **diagram 79** is designed to demonstrate how the **get ( )** function can be used with a **for** loop to input character strings variables. This program allows the user to enter monthly sales information under agent, area and sales. The information is to be stored in a new file named **'agent.data'**.

Explanation

To the **insertion operator** >> a blank space is a terminating character. If it meets a string of words such as **'Chris Walker'** it will read 'Chris', the first word in the string, and because of the white space between 'Chris' and 'Walker' it will discard 'Walker'. To get round this problem, we must make use of the **get ( )** function.

The new file **agent.dat** has to be created to store agents' sales information. This requires **fstream.h** header file. We wish to include **if test** for checking that the file is properly opened. If it is not opened correctly then to terminate program execution and exit. The exit function is in the header file **stdlib.h**. Both header files are listed on the first two lines of this program.

Variable declarations include **char cr;** for carriage return. It is used in the following segment of the code.

```
cout << " Sales Value: " ;
 cin>> sales;0
 cin.get ( cr );                           // flush carriage return
```

What will happen if you do not include ci.get (cr); in this part of the code?

```
C:\TCWIN45\BIN\NONAME22.EXE                    _ □ ✕
Monthly Sales Information
--------------------------------
Agent: Chris Walker
Sales Value: 23457
Area:   Agent:                    ▉
```

As shown above without cin.get (cr) ; statement the program did not allow the user to input data for the variable area. Instead, it displayed the name of the next variable - agent.

The rest of the code is very similar to the code in previous programs in this chapter. The data items stored in this new file are listed in the diagram 79. It is suggested that first you compile and run this program with your own test data. You should also write, compile and run a program to read the stored data from this file.

This is the best way to gain both experience and confidence!

```
#include <fstream.h>              // defines ofstream class - it includes output file streams
#include <stdlib.h>              // includes exit ( ) function
void main ( void )
{
  ofstream outfile( "c:agent.data", ios::out );
  if (! outfile )
  {
  cerr << " Error: Unable to open 'agent.data' file \n";
  exit ( 1 );
}
  char cr;                                          // carriage
  cout << " Monthly Sales Information" << endl;
  cout << " --------------------------------" << endl;
  double sales; char agent [ 40 ],area [ 20 ];
  for ( int i = 0; i < 5; i++ )
  {
  cout << " Agent: ";
  cin.getline ( agent, 40 );
  cout << " Sales Value: " ;
  cin>> sales;
  cin.get( cr);                        // flush carriage return
  cout << " Area: ";
  cin.getline ( area, 20 );
}
outfile.close ( );
}
```

Diagram 79

See diagram 79A for program output

Binary Files

Binary files hold binary values in the same format as variables in **RAM**. Binary files do not hold **white space** characters (white spaces or tabs). The program in **diagram 80** is designed to demonstrate how a binary file is created. The program stores information on commission earned by sales agents. The user is prompted to enter from the keyboard commission figure, surname. first name and area for each sales agent.

```
============= The following information is stored in file 'agent.data' =========

Monthly Sales Information
-----------------------------
Agent: Martin Bell
Sales Value: 1234.00
Area: London
Agent: Alan Smith
Sales Value: 1000.89
Area: Birmingham
Agent: Robin Taylor
Sales Value: 1267.00
Area: Yorkshire
Agent: Alan Smith
Sales Value: 1000.00
Area: Birmingham
Agent: Roger Henderson
Sales Value: 1400.00
Area: Scotland
```

Diagram 79 A

Explanation

As in the previous programs in this chapter, two header files are listed in # include directive. This program has two functions **main ( )**, and **sales_data (rep&a)**, and uses a structure.

The **struct rep** is defined in order to group together 4 variables of different types. These are:

. Commission - **float** type (float comm) - float variable

. surname - **char** type (char sur) - a string

. first name - **char** type (char first) - a string

. area - **char** type (area) - a string

Here, **struct rep** is user defined type that is **rep**. It is the name the programmer has given.

```
void sales_data (rep&);
```

The above is the prototype, for function **sales_data**. Its task is to allow the user to enter data.

Function Main ( )

In function **main**, a variable **rep agent;** is declared. In this variable, data is stored.

ofstream <u>out_file</u> ("c:agent.data", <u>ios::binary</u>);
            ↓   ↓
    an object file   stream constructor opens binary file

The object out_file is linked to the file name agent.data, and the file is opened in the binary mode on drive c. This is followed by the fragment of the code which performs the task of checking that the file is opened properly. You have seen this test before. The statement :

   if (out_file) is meant to check the condition of the file. It checks for:
     (a) errors occurrence and   (b)   end-of-file marker.
If both (a) and (b) have not occurred then the following statements are executed:

```
{
        sales_data(agent);
        out_file.write  ( (char*) &agent,sizeof(agent) );
        cout << "Another agent? For yes enter y. For no enter n: ";
        cin >> c;
        cout <<"\n";
}
```

This loop is within **Do ---while**loop.

Thus the user within the **do---while** loop is prompted to answer by entering **y** or **n**, if there is another agent.

When the user enters, in either uppercase or lowercase, **y**, the loop is executed and the function **sales_data** **(rep&a)** is called. The user can now enter 4 data items for this agent. These data items are stored in this structure variable **agent**.

The process is repeated until the user enters **n**. The data that is stored in **agent** is written to the file **agent.data** on drive **c**.

```cpp
# include <fstream.h>
# include <stdlib.h>
 struct rep
 {
          float comm; char sur [ 20 ], first [ 15 ], area [ 20 ];
 };
 void sales_data ( rep& );                              // prototype
 void sales_data ( rep&a )
 {
 cout << " Commission Earned By Sales Agents " << endl;
 cout << " ------------------------------- \n"<< endl;
 cout << " Surname: ";
 cin >> a.sur;
 cout << " First Name: ";
 cin >> a.first;
 cout << " Area: ";
 cin >> a.area;
 cout << " Commission: ";
 cin >> a.comm;
 cout << " " << endl;
 }
 void main  ( void )
 {
 rep agent;                                 // structure variable
 ofstream out_file ( "c:agent.data", ios::binary );
 if ( !out_file )
 {
 cerr << " Error: Unable to open 'agent.data' file \n";
 exit ( 1 );
 }
 char c;       // Variable
 do {
                  if ( out_file )
                    {
                          sales_data( agent );
                          out_file.write  ( (char*) &agent,sizeof (agent) );
                          cout << "Another agent? For yes enter y. For no enter n: ";
                          cin >> c;
                          cout <<"\n";
                    }
 }while ( (c == 'y') || ( c == 'Y') ) ;
 out_file.close ( );
 }
```

Diagram 80

============ The following test data items for 2 agents were written ============

```
Commission Earned By Sales Agents
-------------------------------------------

Surname: Jameson
First Name: Susan
Area: London
Commission: 12000.00

Any more? For yes enter y. For no enter n: y

Commission Earned By Sales Agents
-------------------------------------------

Surname: Smith
First Name: Alan
Area: Manchester
Commission: 1145.89

Any more? For yes enter y. For no enter n: n
```

Diagram 80A

Copying File

It may be that you wish to check that there are no errors in **ofstream** or **ifstream** objects. It can be checked by making a copy file. We have an existing file called **staff.data** in which 5 data items are stored. The program that has created this external file to write in it is shown in diagram 81A.

Diagram 81

The program in diagram 81 is designed to copy data stored in file called **staff.data** into the file called **copy.data** which is also on **drive c**.

Explanation

The program in diagram 81 is similar to other programs you have met in this chapter; nevertheless it illustrates the method of copying existing data from an external file into another file.

The code begins with **fstream.h** file which is followed by a simple comment line. The function **main** is declared. You know that the execution of the program commences at main.

ifstream infile ("c:staff.data"); Like in the previous program the user defined object called infile is declared, initialised and linked to the external file **staff.data** that exists on drive **c**. This opens the file and also it allocates resources needed for this file.

ofstream copy_file ("c:copy.data"); This statement creates an **osftream** object called **copy_file**, initialises it and links it to the file **copy.data**, which is also on drive **c**.

if (! infile) and **if (!copy_file)** are declared. These invoke the overloaded operator !. Both statements ensure that files are opened correctly. If not opened properly, than an error message is displayed for each file and the program is terminated. Next 4 **cout** statements simply print headings so that the information is presented in the required format.

Within this **while (infile && copy_file)** loop, the following processes take place:

. a check is carried out to ensure that in **staff.data** file and in **copy_data** file, the **file-end** marker has not yet reached. If this is so (**logical true**), than the

. **getline ( )** function reads the string staff.data file until the **nul** character **\n** has reached.

.
$$\textbf{infile.\underline{getline} (\underline{staff} , \text{ sizeof (} \underline{staff} \text{));}}$$

getline function	sting is kept	size of the string is specified
Reads string from	in this argument	which is already declared.
the original file	of the function	This is the second argument of
	getline ( )	**getline( )** function

. **copy_file << staff << endl;** This statement writes the string to the copy_file.

. **cout << staff << endl;** this statement outputs the copied information in the required format for the user. It is because of this statement that you can see "Data copied from staff data file" which is shown in the lower part of diagram 81.

This program copies records of only 5 members of staff because the **for** loop was restricted to only 5 repetitions in the file created: ofstream outfile("c:staff.data", ios::out);

```
#include <fstream.h>      // defines ofstream class - it includes output file streams
#include <stdlib.h>              // includes exit ( ) function
// to create an external file to write in it
void main ( void )
{
  ofstream outfile( "c:staff.data", ios::out );
  if (! outfile )
  {
  cerr << " Error: Unable to open 'staff.data' file \n";
  exit ( 1 );
}

  cout << " Staff National Insurance Numbers" << endl;
  cout << " --------------------------------\n" << endl;
  char staff [ 40 ], NI [ 16];
  for ( int i = 0; i < 5; i++ )
  {
  cout << "staff";
  cin.getline ( staff, 40 ),
  cout << "\t\t NI Number";
  cin.getline ( NI,16 );
  outfile <<  staff <<"\t\t\t" << NI <<  endl;
  }
  outfile.close ( );
}
```

Diagram 81 A

Practical Hints

- Errors are possible when opening files. You should include a check when you open a file.

- A program must open a file before accessing it.

- A program can be written for both input and output. This can allow you to write to a file, and read from the same file.

```
# include <fstream.h>
// copying a file
void main ( void )
{
ifstream infile ( "c:staff.data" );     // open existing file

ofstream copy_file ( "c:copy.data"  );
 // Errors checking during opening file
if  ( ! infile )
 cout  << " Sorry could not open copy infile\n";
if  ( !copy_file )
cout << "Sorry could not open copy file\n";
{
cout << "\t Staff National Insurance Numbers" << endl;
cout << "\t -------------------------------\n" << endl;
cout << " Staff" << "\t\t\t NI Number" << endl;
cout << "------------" << "\t\t\t---------- " << endl;
}


                                 // copy file
while ( infile && copy_file )
{
char staff [ 40 ];
infile.getline ( staff, sizeof ( staff ) );
copy_file << staff << endl;
cout << staff << endl;
}
}
```

============== Data copied from staff.data file==================
            Staff National Insurance Numbers

Staff	NI Number
John Smith	NY/78/90/56/A
June Goldsmith	BN/89/67/45/N
Tony Blair	CV/67/55/45/V
Karen Wolf	DF/56/78/45/M
Jane Butler	MM/90/77/12/G

Diagram 81

Programming Exercises

1.

a) Write a program that will open a text file called **trade.data** on your hard disc **c** .
Write in this file the following table:

Monthly Purchases and Sales for the Period Jan - June 1996

Month	Supplies	Sales
-------	---------	------
January	25000	38000
February	24500	37000
March	20000	30708
April	24567	32759
May	25000	32450
June	20346	37543

b) Write a program that will open the above file **trade.data**.
It should allow you to append to this file the following trade figures:

Month	Purchases	Sales
-------	-----------	------
July	23348	34213
August	24976	31941
September	19432	29864
October	16854	21924
November	19865	22100
December	18800	29765

**These programs should include
an error message.**

c) Write another program that will open the **trade.data** file. This program should enable you to examine the whole year trade figures on your screen.

For b) and c) experiment. This is the only question in this book, which is partly answered. Follow other programs in this chapter.

<u>Chapter 11</u>

Object Oriented Programming (OOP)

<u>Introduction</u>

In OOP a program usually consists of related objects in a group. These related objects are organised under the **class data type**. These objects contain both **data** and **operations** that are performed on the data. This way the design combines both **data** and **functions**. OOP is not a C++ invention. The OOP methods have been applied in a number of other programming languages, such as FORTRAN. In simple terms, it is about grouping related data and functions together.

<u>Classes</u>

Let's consider the real world in which you have unlimited objects. For instance books, files, printers, computers, employees and buildings are all objects. Books can be classified in accordance with a particular classification used in a public library, under fiction and non-fiction. Each of these groups has its own sub-classification and these sub-classifications have their own sub- classifications, and so on.

For example, **C++ simplified** is one particular book that belongs to a broad category of books called computer literature. All computer literature books share some common properties. For instance, all computer books are sources of information on many aspects of computers. Whether a book from a computer literature library is on a particular programming language, or on types of computers, the fact is that both books are about the computer world. Thus, both books are members of the same group. <u>In OOP terminology this category is called a **class**</u>.

Why is it so desirable to identify real world objects in this way in OOP?

By referring to a class of objects, you are generalising the characteristics of the objects in that class. For instance, in a **class of employees**, every employee has a name, age, national insurance number, address and salary. If we have to store employees' personal records, we can create a class of employees. This concept helps us to <u>identify</u> all the relevant and common attributes of object (employees) in a **class employees**. Of course, employees' personal **data (called member data)** has to be maintained, stored, and retrieved. Thus, employees' data is subjected to some operations **(called member functions)**. By conceptualising real world objects in this way, objects hold both **member data** and **member functions** that operate on the member data.

In OOP a simple object such as **SalaryFile** can receive **messages**. The number of messages an object can receive is specified in the **class** to which it belongs.

What could be a message for the object **SalaryFile** ? Let's examine the following **class declaration** in order to understand the meaning of the message sent or received.

```
class staff {                        // class type
           char name [ 40 ];
           int wages, tax;
    public:
           void print (  );           // method
};
```

This definition looks like the definition of a structure. Here **staff** is user-defined type and can be used in a similar way to **Int** type, **char** type or **float** type. Within this class we can create an object by means of the statement: Staff SalaryFile;

This way we have also allocated sufficient memory space for our new object SalaryFile.

In the above **class staff** declaration the method **void print ( );** is a member function. **Why?** Because it is a member of the **class staff**. We can call this member function so that we can view the contents of this object. The call is   StaffSalary. print ( ); This way you send a message to an object. This allows you to print salary information. Thus you can manipulate this object **SalaryFile.** The possible message Which can be sent to an object is specified in the class declaration.

An **Object** as a member of a specified **class** can have its own **private** and **public** set of data. These are explained below. In OOP the program is divided into modules. A function is a module. This **modularity** is at the heart of OOP. This modulation means that not all data and functions are available to all modules within the program. Thus the data and functions that are for a particular module are inaccessible to other modules. This is called **information hiding**.

Furthermore, there may be a number of levels of **abstraction** in search of a modular solution. At the highest level of abstraction , the solution to a problem is outlined in broad terms ; but at the lowest level of abstraction it can be implemented.

A class definition **encapsulates** (it means here to collect) all of the related data items, initial values and member functions or methods.   Before we can put theory into practice we must analyse class syntax.

Class Syntax

class *customer*   ← **class definition**
                              begins with the keyword **class**.
                              It is followed by the class name (type) ***customer*. class**

{   ← **Body of the class begins here**

public: ← **Declaration of public members functions.**
                              can be used by other functions.
                              Functions can also be defined within the class

    function1; ←   note that the semicolon is needed here
        .
        .
        .
    function5 ←   semicolon is required here

private: ← **Declaration of private members (variables)**
                              by default members of a class are private. Accessible
                              by member functions and **friends** of the class.

    int acc;
    float bal;
        .
        .
        .

} *cust;*   ← **Body of class ends.** *cust* is a name associated with the class name

Diagram 82

Diagram 83

The program illustrates how a class could be implemented in a program. The program assigns two values of different types to two variables, and displays the result as required.

Explanation

It is important to note the following specific features as applied to class in a program.

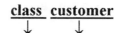

class customer

Keyword   name

Within { } are under **public:** are two **member functions namely:**

void assignData (int, float);

The purpose of this function is to assign one **int** type value to one variable and one **float** type value to another variable

void printData ( );

The purpose of this function is to print/display output stream values

Just below this segment of this code is **private: int accNum; float bal;**

These are two different variables. These are **members** of the **class customer**. In this program, there are only two variables. Private members (variables) can only be used by member functions. Private members can also be used by **friend of the class**. In this program, there are no friends of the class customer.

} cust ; It marks the end of the class declaration.

Will this program work successfully without cust ; which is associated with the customer?

It will compile and run without   **cust;** In fact, there is no need to include it here. It is shown here as in some cases your program will not be compiled successfully without such association with the class type.

The function prototype:

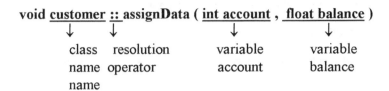

The class name customer is now linked with the function declaration made within the **class**. The scope resolution operator **::** is an essential component. Without both the **class** name **customer**, and **::** the compiler will not be able to link the function and the class together. As shown above, the compiler is able to verify that the function is used correctly.

This function's task is to assign values to variables **accNum = account; bal = balance;**

Similarly, **void customer::printData ( )** function is linked to **class customer**. This function makes use of **cout** output stream for displaying the output.

In the function **main ( ) customer　a ;**

an **instance** of the **customer** class. This way we
have created an **object** called a of the *customer* class. This object **a** has its own **internal** data members **acc** and **bal**. This object can call functions assignData ( ) and printData ( ).

How can an object call a member function?

Let's examine the following two member functions:

a . assignData (100, 178.90);	**a . printData ( );**
prefixing the function assignData ( ) with the name of the object **a**	prefixing the function printData ( ) with the name of the object **a**

Thus an object calls a member function by prefixing the name of the function with its own name. This prefixing requires you to place a '.' between the object name and the name of the function as shown above. This is the only way the object can call a member function. It is said that the object **a** owns the call.

You can say that an object is a variable whose type is a class. In C programming language, the word **object** refers to the storage location, where an item of data is to be stored.

How is the program executed?

The program execution starts at function **main ( )**. **customer a;** is executed first. This allocates storage area for the class object **a** in the memory. Then the control passes to the next statement:

a.assignData (100, 178.90);

This is a call by the **object a** to the member function. This call passes 100 and 178.90 as two parameters to function:

```
void customer::assignData ( int account, float balance )
{
 accNum = account;
 bal = balance;
}
```

The execution with { } begins, and values of **account** 100 and **balance** 178.90 are then assigned to **accNUm**, and **bal**. Next the control passes to **a.printData ( )**; This is a call to another member function by the object **a**.

Now the execution reaches function:

```
void customer::printData ( )
{
 cout << " Account Number: " << accNum << endl;
 cout << " Current Balance Outstanding: £" << bal << endl;

}
```

This function's task is to use **cout** output stream. This output stream (**cout**) displays the values of **accNum**, and **bal** that are passed to it by the function:

Void customer::assignData (int account, float balance)

Finally, the execution reaches } of the function **main ( )**, and the program is terminated.

Practical Hints

. Class definition resembles the **structure** definition.
. You don't have to finish the body of the class as } followed by the name assiciated with the class name.
   }; ends the body of class definition or declaration.
. You can declare private before public.
. Data is often private that is **information hiding**. This way it is protected and thus no access from outside.
. Functions are often public.
. Private and public sections divide the program into manageable sections, and make the program easier to follow, debug and maintain.
. An **object** is a variable whose **type** is a class. It is an **instance** of the class.
. A class combines both functions and data as members of the same class.

```
# include <iostream.h>
// Class Declaration
class customer
{
public:
                void assignData ( int, float );
                void printData (  );
private:
                int accNum;
                float bal;
}cust ;

void customer::assignData ( int account, float balance )
{
 accNum  =  account;
 bal  =  balance;
}

void customer::printData (  )
{
 cout << " Account Number: " << accNum << endl;
 cout << " Current Balance Outstanding: £" <<  bal << endl;

}
void main ( void )

{
        customer a;
        a.assignData ( 100, 178.90 );
        a.printData (  );
}
```

======================== Program Output ========================
Account Number: 100
Current Balance Outstanding: £178.9

Diagram 83

Diagrams 84 & 85

The program is designed to implement **customer class** for storing customer's name, contact's name, contact's status, telephone number, and credit limit agreed. The data is to be input by the user under the heading, ''Customer File'', and then to be displayed under ''Credit Control Information'' heading. In diagram 85 you can see both input data and output information.

Explanation

The code begins with two **# includes** files. You have met these library files before. As this program handles character strings, **char cr;** is declared. It is used with **cin.get (cr);**

The definition of **class customer** follows the pattern of the last program. There are 6 components of private section, of which 4 are character strings. These can be accessed by 2 member functions that are listed in the public section.

Function **input_data ( )** performs the task of allowing the user to enter data from the keyboard. This will create **Customer File**. The other function **data_output ( )** displays **Credit Control Information** as required. In function **main ( )**, an **object** called **sales_infor** is created by **class customer sales_infor;** The program output is shown in diagram 85.

The program operates in the same way as the previous program, except that it is interactive. It generates one customer credit control information; but by including in the **main ( )** a label and a goto statement you can use it for many records. However, a block of conditional statements in the **data_input** function can enable you to repeat data input for as many records as desired. **Try it yourself. Learn through practice!**
See diagrams on pages 193-194.

A comparison between structure and class specifiers (definitions/declarations)

Specifier for structure	Specifier for class
struct holiday	class holiday {
{	private:
int regular;	int regular, overtime, holidayMoney;
int overtime;	public:
int holidayMoney;	void print ( );
};	};

A class specifier is similar to structure specifier. Both are definitions.

```
#include <iostream.h>
#include <string.h>
// Strings & class
char  cr;
class customer{          // class name or tag is customer
private:
          char name     [ 40 ],
          contact       [ 40 ],
          status        [ 40 ],
          tel           [ 25 ];
          long limit;


public:
          void data_input ( void );          // Publicly available function
          void data_output ( void );         // Publicly available function
};

// Function to create information

void customer::data_input ( void )
{
 cout << "\t\t Customer File" << endl;
 cout << "\t\t ....................\n" << endl;
 cout  << " Enter customer's  full name: ";
 cin.get ( name, 39, ' \n' );
 cin.get ( cr );
 cout << " Enter contact's full name: ";
 cin.get ( contact, 39, ' \n' );
 cin.get ( cr );
 cout << " Enter contact's full status: ";
 cin.get ( status, 39, ' \n' );
 cin.get ( cr );
 cout << " Enter telephone number: ";
 cin.get ( tel, 24, ' \n' );
 cin.get ( cr );
 cout << " Enter agreed credit limit: ";
 cin >> limit;
 cin.get ( cr );
}
```

Diagram 84

```
// Function to output information created
 void customer::data_output ( void )
{
  cout << "\n" << endl;
  cout << "\t Credit Control Information" << endl;
  cout << "\t .........................\n" << endl;
  cout << "\t Customer's full name: " << name << endl;
  cout << "\t Contact's full name: " << contact << endl;
  cout << "\t Contact's full status: " << status << endl;
  cout << "\t Telephone number: " << tel << endl;
  cout << "\t limit agreed £: " << limit << endl;
  cout << "\n" << endl;
  }

void main ( void )
{
  class customer sales_infor;              // to create sales_infor object
  sales_infor.data_input ( );
  sales_infor.data_output( );
  }
```

================== **Input Data** ===============================
                      Customer File

                      ....

  Enter customer's full name: **CWS GMBH**
  Enter contact's full name: **Mr. Wolfgang Berg**
  Enter contact's full status: **Director**
  Enter telephone number: **0040 -7131 - 570016**
  Enter agreed credit limit: **15000**
====================== Output Information ========================
                Credit Control Information
                ....

Customer's full name: CWS GMBH
Contact's full name: Mr. Wolfgang Berg
Contact's full status: Director
Telephone number: 0040 -7131 - 570016
limit agreed £: 15000

Diagram 8 5

Combined Structure and Class

A structure can be nested within a class. The program in diagrams **86-89** illustrates the nesting of structures within a class.

Explanation

The program is designed to implement structures within a class. This program generates a weekly sales analysis under the following headings:

Desired Output

. Week ended on	. Product Code	. Product Name
. Unit price	. Number of items sold	. Total net value
. Salesperson's name	. Sales % commission rate	. Commission earned
. Total number new customers	. Enter any other related information	
. Sales territory	. Accumulated sales	

For generating the above information, the code includes a function called **sal_output ( )**.
In order to generate the above information, the program requires all relevant data be entered from the keyboard.

Input Data

Altogether there are 11 data items to be entered. These are the same items as listed above for the desired output except for two items, namely, **Total net value** and **Commission earned**. These data items are grouped together as shown below:

structures within the class sales

```
class sales{
        structure sal_ product {
                            prCode, pName, noSold, unitPrice, netValue* }
        struct sal_agent {
                        Person, misc, comRate, newCust, comEarned* }
          struct sal_order{
                    area, date, accSales }
.
.
.
}
```

Data items marked * are not input variables. Their values are calculated and then their respective values are printed as output. They are listed here because they are declared as members of structures. Function **sal_input ( )** allows the user to enter input data from the keyboard.

Diagrams 86 - 89

The code for generating the required output based on data input by the user is shown in diagrams 85 - 88.

Class Definition in Diagram 86

The **sales class** has three nested structures. These are outlined above, and named as product, agent and supplied. These names are associated with the **class sales**. Indeed, these structures are in **private** section of the **class sales** but in this program, the private section is not labelled as **private: You don't have to label this section as 'private:'.**

The **public** section has two functions. These are **sal_input ( )** and **sal_output ( )**.

Just below public section, the segment of the code for function **sal_input ( )** begins and continues in <u>diagram 87</u>. **cin. get ( )** function is used for reading input character by character into the **string** variables. For reading **int** and **float** type values input -output streams **cin** and **cout** are used.

<u>In diagram 88</u>, sal_output ( ) function makes use of output stream **cout** printing weekly sales analysis in the desired format.

The function **main ( )** contains only 4 statements. Here **sales_stats** object is created. This is associated with the sales class. To link it with the member functions, the **dot operator .** is used. The **sales_stats.sal_input ( );** is called to allow the user to input sales data and then **sales_stats.sal_output ( );** is called to calculate, 'Total net value, and 'Commission earned'. After that the function prints the entire output as weekly sales analysis.

<u>It is important to examine thoroughly **diagram 89**</u>. By including a block of conditional statements, or just amending the function **main ( )** as shown below, you can use this program for as many weeks as you wish. Try to debug and run this program with your own data.

```
void main ( void )
  {
again:
  class sales sales_stats;          // creates sales_stats object
  sales_stats.sal_input ( );
  sales_stats.sal_output ( );
goto again;
  }
```

```
# include <iostream.h>
# include <string.h>
// nested classes
char ( cr );
class sales{
        struct    sal_product  {
                char prCode  [ 10 ],
                            pName  [ 30 ];
            int noSold;
            float    unitPrice;
            long netValue;
}product;

        struct sal_agent {
                char  sPerson [ 30 ],
                 misc   [ 40 ];

                 float comEarned,
                comRate;
               int newCust;
}agent;

                struct sal_order{
                        char  area [ 20 ];
                        char date  [ 12 ];
                long int accSales;
}supplied ;
public:
                void  sal_input  ( void );
                void sal_output ( void );
};
                        // Function for collecting data items  through the keyboard
void sales::sal_input ( void  )
{
 cout << "\t Weekly Sales Analysis" << endl;
 cout << "\t ...................." << endl;
 cout << "\t Enter date week ended: \n";
```

Diagram 86

```
cin.get ( supplied.date, 11, '\n' );
cin.get ( cr );                         //  flash carriage return
cout << " Enter Product Code: ";
cin.get ( product.prCode, 9, '\n' );
cin.get ( cr );
cout << " Enter Product Name: ";
cin.get ( product.pName, 29, '\n' );
cin.get ( cr );
cout << " Enter number of items sold: ";
cin  >>  product.noSold;
cin.get ( cr );
cout << " Enter unit price: " ;
cin  >>  product.unitPrice;
cin.get ( cr );

cout << " Enter full name of salesperson: ";
cin.get ( agent.sPerson, 29 , '\n' );
cin.get ( cr );
cout << " Enter commission rate as percentage: ";
cin  >> agent.comRate;
cin.get ( cr );

cout << " Enter number of new customers: ";
cin  >> agent.newCust;
cin.get ( cr );
cout << " Enter any other related information: ";
cin.get ( agent.misc, 39, '\n' );
cin.get ( cr );
cout << " Enter sales territory: ";
cin.get ( supplied.area, 19, '\n' );
cin.get ( cr );
cout << " Accumulated sales: ";
cin  >> supplied.accSales ;
cin.get ( cr );
cout << "\t" << endl;
}
```

Diagram 87

```cpp
                        // Function for printing the program output
void sales::sal_output ( void )
{

cout << "\t" << endl;
cout << "\t Week ended on: " << supplied.date << endl;
cout << "   ..........................\n" << endl;
cout << " Product Code: "        <<  product.prCode << endl;
cout << " Product Name: "        << product.pName << endl;
cout << " Unit price: " << product.unitPrice << endl;
cout << " Number of items sold: "    << product.noSold << endl;

cout << " Total net value: "
                << ( product.unitPrice* product.noSold )<< endl;
cout << " Salesperson's name: " <<  agent.sPerson << endl;
cout << " sales %commission rate: " << agent.comRate << endl;
cout << " commission earned: "
        <<(product.unitPrice* product.noSold* agent.comRate/100)<< endl;
cout << " Total number new customers: " << agent.newCust << endl;
cout << " Enter any other related information: " << agent.misc << endl;
cout << " Sales territory: " << supplied.area << endl;
cout << " Accumulated sales: "
                << ((product.unitPrice* product.noSold )+ supplied.accSales) << endl;

cout << "\t" << endl;
}

void main ( void )
{
 class sales sales_stats;          // creates sales_stats object
sales_stats.sal_input ( );
sales_stats.sal_output ( );

}
```

Diagram 88

```
========================= Data Input =========================

    Weekly Sales Analysis
    ...................................

        Enter date week ended:
2.12.1996
Enter Product Code: A0123456
Enter Product Name: Computer Desk
Enter number of items ordered: 20
Enter unit price: 34.95
Enter full name of salesperson: John Bull
Enter commission rate as percentage: 1.4
Enter number of new customers: 1
Enter any other related information: It is a large company
Enter sales territory: London South
Accumulated sales: 129000


================= Weekly Sales Analysis Information ==================

        Week ended on: 2.12.1996
        .........................................

Product Code: A0123456
Product Name: Computer Desk
Unit price: 34.95
Number of items sold: 20
Total net value: 699
Salesperson's name: John Bull
sales %commission rate: 1.4
commission earned: 9.786
Total number new customers: 1
Enter any other related information: It is a large company
Sales territory: London South
Accumulated sales: 129699
```

Diagram 89

Diagrams 90-92

A program is designed **to collect/input** the following data about customers.

- Customer's full name
- Town/City
- Sales account number
- Customer's status new or regular or old
- Any condition/arrangements

- House number & street
- Post code
- Agreed credit limit
- Date account established
- %discount allowed. If none enter 0.00

and **output** the following information in the format shown below.

Credit Control Information

······································

Customer: **Peter Jones PLC**
House number & street: **200 Oxford Street**
Town/City: **London**
Post code: **W1A 2AB**
Sales account number: **1234**
Credit limit agreed: **30000**
Customer's status: Regular
Date account first established: **31.10.1988**
Any trade conditions/arrangements: **Trade discount on all orders**
%Discount rate, if applicable: **2.5**

Method

The code is designed to achieve the above requirements by implementing the **nesting structures** within the class **customer**. The 10 items of data are grouped together under two nested structures. These are **struct cust_name** and **struct cust_age**. In accordance with the nature of data items, **char**, **int** and **float** types are used in variables declaration.

Function **cust_input ( )** collects the data. It makes use of **cin.get ( )** function, and input and output streams to prompt the user to enter data items from the keyboard. The other function **cust_input ( )** prints the desired result by means of **cout** stream.

In the **main** function an object **sales_infor** is created. It is then linked to the other two functions. The execution of the program starts at **main** function. First **cust_input ( )** is called to allow the user to enter data, and then control is passed to **cust_output ( )** to print the information as per the segment of the code in the body of this function. It is strongly recommended that you run this program on your machine by using the data shown above in **boldface** or by using your own data.

```
#include <iostream.h>
#include <string.h>

char ( cr );            // to be used for carriage return

// Structures within a class and use of nesting
class customer{                         // class name or tag is customer
struct cust_name{                 // to group related data into a sigle record: cust_name
char name      [ 40 ],
     street    [ 40 ],
     town      [ 30 ],
     postCode  [ 10 ],
     status    [ 15 ];
int account;
long limit;
}sales;

struct cust_age{          // to group group related data into one record: cust_age
char newOld     [ 10 ],
        est     [ 12 ],
        cond    [ 40 ];
float discRate;

}age;

public:
        void cust_input ( void );       //  Publicly available function
        void cust_output( void );       //  Publicly available function
};

// Function to create information

void customer::cust_input ( void )
{
cout  << " Enter customer's full name: " ;
cin.get ( sales.name, 39, '\n' );
cin.get ( cr );
cout << " Enter house number & street: ";
cin.get ( sales.street, 39, '\n' );
cin.get ( cr );
cout << " Enter town/City: ";
```

Diagram 90

```
cin.get ( sales.town, 29,'\n' );
cin.get ( cr );
cout << " Enter Post code: ";
cin.get ( sales.postCode, 9,'\n' );
cin.get ( cr );
cout << " Enter sales account number: ";
cin  >>  sales.account ;
cin.get ( cr );
cout << " Enter agreed credit limit: ";
cin  >>  sales.limit ;
cin.get ( cr );
cout << " Enter customer's status new or regular/old: ";
cin.get ( age.newOld, 9, '\n' );
cin.get ( cr );
cout << " Enter date account established: ";
cin.get ( age.est, 13, '\n' );
cin.get ( cr );
cout << " Enter any condition/arrangements: ";
cin.get ( age.cond,39,'\n' );
cin.get ( cr );
cout << " Enter % discount allowed. If none enter 0.00: ";
cin  >> age.discRate ;
cin.get ( cr );
}

// Function to output information created

void customer::cust_output ( void )
{
 cout << "\n" << endl;
 cout << "\t Credit Control Information" << endl;
 cout << "\t ...................................\n" << endl;
 cout << "\t Customer: " << sales.name << endl;
 cout << "\t House number & street: " << sales.street << endl;
 cout << "\t Town/City: " << sales.town << endl;
 cout << "\t Post code: " << sales.postCode << endl;
```

Diagram 91

```
      cout << "\t Sales account number: " << sales.account << endl;
      cout << "\t Credit limit agreed: " << sales.limit << endl;
      cout << "\t Customer's status: " << age.newOld << endl;
      cout << "\t Date account first established: " << age.est << endl;
      cout << "\t Any trade conditions/arrangements: " << age.cond << endl;
      cout << "\t %Discount rate, if applicable: " << age.discRate << endl;
      cout << "\t" << endl;
      }
void main ( void )
{
 class customer  sales_infor;       // to create sales_infor object
 sales_infor.cust_input ( );
 sales_infor.cust_output( );
 }
```

============================ Input Data ============================
Enter customer's full name: **Peter Jones PLC**
Enter house number & street: **200 Oxford Street**
Enter town/City: **London**
Enter Post code: **W1A 2AB**
Enter sales account number: **1234**
Enter agreed credit limit: **30000**
Enter customer's status new or regular/old: **Regular**
Enter date account established: **31.10.1988**
Enter any condition/arrangements: **Trade discount on all orders**
Enter % discount allowed. If none enter 0.00: **2.5**

============================ Program output ============================

                   Credit Control Information

                   ....

                   Customer: Peter Jones PLC
                   House number & street: 200 Oxford Street
                   Town/City: London
                   Post code: W1A 2AB
                   Sales account number: 1234
                   Credit limit agreed: 30000
                   Customer's status: Regular
                   Date account first established: 31.10.1988
                   Any trade conditions/arrangements: Trade discount on all orders
                   %Discount rate, if applicable: 2.5

Diagram 92

Constructor & Destructor

A constructor is a class member function. A constructor is called automatically when an object is declared. It must have the same name as the class within which it is defined. It is declared without any return type. Constructors are useful for initialising class variables or allocating memory to objects when created as illustrated below. Constructors can accept an argument.

Diagram 93

The program in this diagram initialises the object by assigning the values to its member variables. The program has 2 variables namely **gross** and **deduct** which are **float** type. From the value of **gross** the value of **deduct** is subtracted. The program works out net salary and prints the required information.

Explanation

The following is a constructor salary function which uses the same name as the class salary within which it is declared. Notice that it does not return any value <u>not even void type</u>.

> **salary (float sal , float tax) { gross = sal; deduct = tax; }**

The constructor works the same way as assign ( ) function did in our program depicted in diagram 83. It initialises the **object a** and allocates storage for the values for its members.

The execution of the program begins at **main ( ).** When it executes **salary a (200, 35);**
the constructor is called automatically. The values 200 and 35 are passed to **sal** and **tax,** which are its parameters. The constructor salary assigns these values to **object a's** members (variables) **gross** and **deduct**.

When the call is made to function **a.printData ( )**, the statements within its body { } are executed. See the program output.

Class Destructor

Like the constructor, the destructor has the same name as the class within which it is defined; but its name is preceded by the character ~. A destructor is a logical complement of its constructor, therefore it destroys the object when it comes to an end. A destructor is automatically called when a program reaches the end of the scope of a class object. Destructors cannot accept an argument.

```
# include <iostream.h>
// Class constructor
class salary
{
public:
  salary ( float sal , float tax ){ gross = sal;  deduct = tax;}
                    void printData ( );
 private:
         float gross, deduct;
};
void salary::printData ( )
{
 cout << " Gross Salary: " << "£" << gross << endl;
 cout << " Deductions: " << "£" << deduct << endl;
 cout << " Net salary = " << "£" << ( gross - deduct ) << endl;
 }
void main ( void )

{
        salary a ( 200, 35 );              // object a is created and initialised
          a.printData ( );
}
======================= Program Output =========================================
Gross Salary: £200
Deductions: £35
Net salary = £165
```

Diagram 93

Diagram 94

Destructor It is the same program as shown above, except that it includes **destructor function:**
                     ~ **salary ( ) {cout << "\n\t*** Finished***"; }**.
This destructor contains a message that will be printed to the screen when it is called. When the **object a** is created and initialised, the costructor shown below is called automatically to manage this object.
                salary (float sal , float tax){ gross = sal; deduct = tax;}

When the **object a** reaches the end of its scope, then the destructor is automatically called. It prints the message on the screen, and destroys the object.

```
# include <iostream.h>
// Class constructor and destructor
class salary
{
public:
  salary ( float sal , float tax ){ gross = sal;  deduct = tax;}        // constructor
  ~ salary ( ) {cout << "\n\t*** Finished***"; }                        // destructor
                    void printData (  );
 private:
          float gross, deduct;
};
void salary::printData (   )
{
 cout << " Gross Salary: " << "£" << gross << endl;
 cout << " Deductions: " << "£" << deduct << endl;
 cout << " Net salary = " << "£" << ( gross - deduct ) << endl;
 }
void main ( void )

{
        salary a ( 200, 35 );            // object a is initialised
          a.printData (   ) ;
}
===================== Program output ========================================
 Gross Salary: £200
Deductions: £35
Net salary = £165

     *** Finished***
```

Diagram 94

A comparison between constructors and destructors

Constructor

A **class** can have several constructors.
A constructor is defined by **default** if
not defined by the programmer.
May be overloaded.
A constructor accepts an argument.
Creates object and allocates memory.

Destructor

A **class** can only have one destructor.
Defined by **default** if not defined by the
programmer.
May not be overloaded.
May not accept an argument.
Destroys object and free memory.

Constructor & destructor in one program

Diagrams 95 & 95 A

The program is designed to convert Deutsch Mark (DM) German currency into pounds sterling. It uses class constructor and a destructor to mark the beginning of the currency conversion, and the end of the conversion process.

Explanation

Both constructor and destructor are defined within the **class DM**. Besides the main ( ), there are two more functions. These are declared as member function within the class.
get_mark ( ) function. This function passes the number of DM to the variable **int number**. Function **pound_convert (double)** converts the DM into pounds sterling.

The constructor function contains only a message. Similarly, the destructor function also contains only a message in order to mark the end of the conversion process. When the message, "Start converting German DM into Sterling" appears on the screen , it is obvious that the constructor was automatically called which created the **object cash_in_mark.** Similarly, when the message, "**Finished Conversion!***" is displayed, it is clear that the object created has been destroyed. **You can see the program output in diagram 95 A.**

```
=================== Program Output ============================
    Enter German DM for conversion into pounds sterling: 1000

    ...............................................
    Start converting German DM into sterling
DM 1000
    converted to: £361.011
            ***Finished Conversion!***
```

Diagram 95 A

```
# include <iostream.h>
// Constructor and destructor
const double pound  = 2.77;    // current exchange tourist rate
class DM {
int number;
public:
    DM ( ) { cout << "\t Start converting German DM into sterling \n";}  // Constructor
   ~DM( ) { cout << "\n \t\t ***Finished Conversion!*** " ;}            // Destructor
        void get_mark ( double );
        double pound_convert ( double);
};
void DM::get_mark (double mark )
{
             number  =  mark;
         cout << " DM " ;
         cout << number << endl;
         cout << "\t converted to:" << " £";
}
double DM:: pound_convert ( double )
{
         cout <<   number / pound ;   return ( number / pound );
}
  void main ( void )
{
        int DM,  pounds;
        cout << "\t Enter German DM for conversion into pounds sterling: ";
        cin >> DM;
        cout << " \t................................................" << endl;
        class  DM cash_in_mark ; // associate the object with the class DM
        cash_in_mark.get_mark ( DM );
        pounds = cash_in_mark.pound_convert ( pounds );
}
```

Diagram 95

Inheritance & Derived Classes

A class can be derived from an existing class. The process of deriving classes from an **existing class** is known as **inheritance** and the class or classes derived are called **derived classes**.

The class from which other classes are derived is called the **base or parent class (or superclass)** , and the derived class is called the **child (or subclass) class**. The derived classes inherit all or some of the features of the parent class. The syntax for a derived class is as follows:

```
class derived_class_type : public parent_class_name
{
  .
  .
  .
};
```

Example of creating a derived class

```
_____class employees :  public people {
  .
  .
  .
};
```

In this example, **employees** is the derived class, and people is the base class. It is said that the **base** or **parent** class has **public visibility**. The class employees inherits the private and public members of the **base class people.**

Diagrams 96 - 100 A

The program is designed to illustrate the use of derived classes. The parent class is **staff**, and there are 2 child classes. These classes allow the user to input data from the keyboard. The input data is processed first, and then the information is printed on the screen.

Explanation

The following classes allow the user to enter data items that are listed below from the keyboard. The words which are typed in **boldface** are used in the code.

Parent class staff	Child class Salary	Child class work_schedule
----------------------	----------------------------	---
name - **name**	current salary - **cSal**	classroom teaching hours - **conHr**
department - **dept**	percentage salary increment	tutorial time/hours allocated
title - **title**	increment rate - **inRate**	per week - **tutHr**
qualification - **qual**	total increment - **inCr**	student's research project hours
commenced - **comm**	increased present salary - **inSal**	per week - **pSup**
		total allocated hours per week - **tot**

<u>**Within the class parent definition**</u>, the public section includes 2 functions. These are:

- . **data_input ( )** -   for allowing the user to enter staff basic data from the keyboard.
- . **data_output ( )** - for displaying staff basic information on the screen.

<u>**Within the child class:**</u>
class salary: public staff

in the public section, there are 2 functions. The function **salary_update ( )** allows the user to enter data items from the keyboard. The input values are used to calculate the amount of increment (**inCr**), and the increased present salary **(inSal)** of a named member of staff.

The other function **disp_salary record ( )** prints the salary information of the named member of staff on the screen.

<u>**Within the child class:**</u>
Class work_schedule: public staff

In the public section, there are 2 functions. The function **work_schedule_record ( )** is also interactive. It lets the user enter work schedule data. The second function **disp_weekly_hours ( )**. This function works out the total allocated hours per week (**tot**) for the named member of staff and then displays on the screen weekly work-schedule information (weekly Hours Record).

Data inheritance - Both child classes have inherited the basic data from the parent **class staff**.
The inherited data items are those which are collected by function **data_input ( )** within the parent class. In addition, both classes have also collected their own specific set of data.

The segment of the code in the **main ( )** function is designed to create a necessary link between objects, classes and functions in this program. Sufficient comments are added to assist you to follow it.

```
#include <iostream.h>
#include <string.h>
//  Illustration of Derived classes

char cr;
class staff {
        char name      [ 50 ],
              dept      [ 30 ],
              title     [ 40 ],
              qual      [ 70 ],
            comm        [ 12 ];

public:
                        void data_input   ( void );
                        void data_output ( void );
};

 void staff::data_input ( void )
{

cout   << "Enter employee's surname and initials: ";
cin.get    ( name, 49, '\n' );
cin.get  ( cr );
cout   << "Enter Department: " ;
cin.get  ( dept, 29, '\n' );
cin.get ( cr );
cout  << "Enter Qualifications: ";
cin.get ( qual, 69, '\n' );
cin.get ( cr );
cout  << "Enter Title: ";
cin.get ( title, 39, '\n' );
cin.get ( cr );
cout  << "Enter date employment commenced: ";
cin.get ( comm, 11, '\n' );
cin.get ( cr );
cout   << " " << endl;

}
```

Diagram 96

```
 void staff::data_output ( void )          // parent class - data output
{
cout << "Employee's name: " << title << name << endl;
cout << "Department: " << dept << endl;
cout << "Qualifications: " << qual << endl;
cout << "Date employment commenced: " << comm << endl;


}

class salary:public staff {                                    // child class

                          double cSal,  inRate,  inCr,  inSal;
public:
              void salary_update ( );
              void disp_salary_record ( );
};

void salary::salary_update ( )       child class - salary data input
{

        data_input ( );

cout  << "Enter Current salary per annum: ";
cin   >> cSal;
cout << "Enter Percentage salary increment: ";
cin   >> inRate;
inCr = ( cSal * inRate) ;
inSal = ( cSal+ inCr ) ;

cout  << " " << endl;
}
```

Diagram 97

```
void salary::disp_salary_record ( )              // child class - salary data output
{
        data_output ( );

cout  <<  "Current salary per annum:£ "  << cSal << endl;
cout  <<  "Percentage salary increment: " << inRate << endl;
cout  <<  "Increased salary per annum:£ " << inSal << endl;
cout << " " << endl;
}

class work_schedule:public staff {

                int  conHr, tutHr,  pSup,  tot;

public:

                void work_schedule_record ( );
                void disp_weekly_hours (
};

void work_schedule::work_schedule_record ( )      // child class work_schedule data input
{
                data_input ( );

cout << "Enter Classroom teaching hours per week: ";
cin  >> conHr;
cin.get ( cr );
cout << "Enter Tutorial time/ hours allocated per week: ";
cin  >> tutHr;
cin.get ( cr );
cout << "Enter Student's research project hours per week: ";
cin  >> pSup;
cin.get ( cr );
cout << " " << endl;
}
```

Diagram 98

```
void work_schedule::disp_weekly_hours ( )                    // child class weekly hours output

{

        data_output ( );

        cout << "Classroom teaching hours per week: " << conHr  << endl;
        cout << "Tutorial hours per week: " << tutHr << endl;
        cout << "Student's research project supervision per week :"<< pSup << endl;
        tot = ( conHr + tutHr + pSup );
        cout << "Allocated hours per week: " << tot << endl;
        cout << " " << endl;
}

void main ( void )
{
                                                         // linking variables with classes
 salary increment;
 work_schedule information;

                                                         //  Salary increment record
cout << "\t\t Salary Award " << endl;
cout << "\t\t ...................…..\n";
increment.salary_update ( );

                                                         // Work_schedule information
cout << "\t\t Weekly Hours Record " << endl;
cout << "\t\t ...............................…\n";
cin.get ( );
information.work_schedule_record ( );

                                                         // display  up-to-date staff Record
cout << "\t\t Salary Award" << endl;
cout << "\t\t ..........…………. \n";
increment.disp_salary_record ( );

                                                         // display  weekly hours records
cout << "\t\t weekly Hours Record" << endl;
cout << "\t\t ...............................\n";
information.disp_weekly_hours ( );
}
```

Diagram 99

```
========================= Data Input ==========================
        Salary Award

        ....................
Enter Employee's surname and initials: James Walker
Enter Department: Computing
Enter Qualifications: PhD
Enter Title: Dr.
Enter Date employment commenced: 12.12.1990
Enter Current salary per annum: 28500
Enter Percentage salary increment: .35


        Weekly Hours Record

        ...............................
Enter employee's surname and initials: Julie Johnson
Enter Department: Information systems
Enter Qualifications: MSc
Enter Title: Miss
Enter Date employment commenced: 01.01.1997
Enter Classroom teaching hours per week: 12
Enter Tutorial time/ hours allocated per week: 6
Enter Student's research project hours per week: 6

====================== Information Output ======================
        Salary Award

        ...................
Employee's name: Dr.James Walker
Department: Computing
Qualifications: PhD
Date employment commenced: 12.12.1990
Current salary per annum:£ 28500
Percentage salary increment: 0.35
Increased salary per annum:£ 38475
```

Diagram 100

```
============================ Information Output ============================

                    Weekly Hours Record
                    ..........................

Employee's name: Miss Julie Johnson
Department: Information systems
Qualifications: MSc
Date Employment Commenced: 01.01.1997
Classroom teaching hours per week: 12
Tutorial hours per week: 6
Student's research project supervision per week :6
Allocated hours per week: 24
```

Diagram 100A

Program Output

The information in **diagrams 100** and **100A** above should be studied carefully. This will help you to ana-lyse the whole code depicted in **diagrams 96 – 99**.

Miscellaneous Items

Inheritance allows a class to inherit properties from a class of objects. When a child or derived class in-herits its attributes from its single parent, it is called **single inheritance**. When an object inherits its prop-erties from several base (parent) classes or multiple parents, it is called **multiple inheritance**. This tech-nique allows re-use of a class. This hierarchy of classes leads to **polymorphism**. This means that there can be many types of related sub-classes. These sub-classes use the same functions but generate different re-sults. If you just imagine:

Base class	derived class	function
OfficeWork	sales, purchase and finance	office_work ( )

By applying the technique of polymorphism with one function **office_work ( )** you can do the office work for all the above derived classes. These are some powerful features of C++ software re-use programming techniques. **There is no more space in this chapter for further discussion. Programming exercises are listed on page 36 due to lack of space.**

Chapter 12

Suggested Programs & Outputs

Chapter 2

1.

```
# include <iostream.h>
// assignment statements
void main ( void )
{
int a, b, c, d,e, f;
a = 78;
b = 98;
c = 25;
d = ( a + b + c );
cout << " Simple Calculation" << endl;
cout << " -----------------------" << endl;
cout << " " << endl;
cout << " The sum of all given variables: " << d << endl;
e = ( a + b ) / c;
cout << " The sum of two variables divided by 3rd variable: " << e << endl;
f = ( a + b + c ) /3;
cout << " average value: " << f;
}
=========================== Program Output =====================================
 Simple Calculation
 -----------------------

 The sum of all given variables: 201
 The sum of two variables divided by 3rd variable: 7
 average value: 67
```

Programming Exercise. A suggested program for the required output

2.

The correct format for each statement:

cout >> " Why" ,　wrong　>> operators. Also **;** is required not **,** to end the statement.

　　　　　　　　　　Correct → cout << " Why";

cout << I am fine ;　"quotation marks are required "I am fine ";

　　　　　　　　　　Correct → cout << " I am fine" ;

cin << " Well done" ;　wrong operators, and remarks within quotation marks not allowed.

　　　　　　　　　　Correct → cin >> a;

cin >> n << endl;　　<< endl not allowed. **Correct** → cin >> n;

3.

The required assignment statements:

a) Balance = (OldBalance + CurrentBalance);

b) Discount = (sales + 0.05);

c) Y = L * (1 + X);

Chapters 3-4

1.

Gentlemen! This program can tell your retirement year.

....

Please type your age: 67
Sir you are a senior citizen. Keep enjoying yourself !

Gentlemen! This program can tell your retirement year.

....

Please type your age: 21
You will be happily retired in 44 years time. Be happy !

Program Output

The suggested program is shown on page 220

1.   **Suggested Program**

```cpp
# include <iostream.h>
// how to use if-else statement
// to work out  the year when a male will reach his statutory retirement age
int main(  )
{
 int age, retirement;
 char ans;
 cout <<" Gentlemen! This program can tell your retirement year." << endl;
 cout <<" ..................................................." << endl;
 cout <<" Please type your age: ";
 cin  >> age;

 if ( age >=65 ) {
                cout <<"Sir you are a senior citizen. Keep enjoying yourself !" << endl;
                return (0);
          }
                else
                        retirement = ( 65 - age);
                        cout <<" You will be happily retired in ";
                        cout << retirement << " years time. Be happy !" << endl;
                        return (0);
}
```

2.   **Suggested Program**

```cpp
#include <iostream.h>
// To demonstrate the use of if-else statement
// Pension date forecast for females
void main (void)
{
 int age, retirement, pension, currentYear, birth, retire ;
 char name [40];
 again:
 cout << " Ladies this program forecasts how many years are still" <<endl;
 cout << " left before you  will start your golden retirement age." << endl;
 cout << " Please type your age years: ";
 cin >> age;
 cout << " Please type now current year( 1997 or whatever):" ;
```

Program Output. Also see next page

```
#include <iostream.h>
// To demonstrate the use of if-else statement
// Pension date forecast for females
void main (void)
{
  int age, retirement, pension, currentYear, birth, retire ;
  char name [40];
  again:
  cout << " Ladies this program forecasts how many years are still" << endl;
  cout << " left before your will start your golden retirement age." << endl;
  cout << " Please type your age years: ";
  cin >> age;
  cout << " Please type now current Year( 1998 or whatever):" ;
  cin >> currentYear;
  if ( age >= 60){
  cout << " You are already a senior citizen." << endl;
  cout << " Enjoy madam your bus ride in the country!" << endl;
  pension = ( currentYear - age +60 );
  cout << " You reached your pension-able age in " << pension << endl;
  birth = ( pension - 60);
  cout << " I think you were born in " << birth << endl;
  cout << " ....................................." << endl;
  cout << " " << endl;
  goto again;
  }
  else
  cout << " Please now type your name: ";
  cin >> name;
  retirement = ( 60 - age );
  retire = ( currentYear + retirement);
  cout <<" " << endl;
  cout << " You will be retired in "<< retirement;
  cout << " years time." << endl;
  cout << " " << endl;
  cout << name << " Your pension-able age will begin in ";
  cout << retire <<"." << endl;
  cout << "         Be happy my friend!" << endl;
  birth  = ( currentYear - age);
  cout << "         you were born in " << birth << endl;
}
```

============== **The program output is shown below and continued on the next page** ==============

Ladies this program forecasts how many years are still
left before your will start your golden retirement age.
Please type your age years: **66**
Please type now current Year(1998 or whatever):**1996**
You are already a senior citizen.
Enjoy madam your bus ride in the country!
You reached your pension-able age in 1990
I think you were born in 1930
....

Ladies this program forecasts how many years are still
left before you will start your golden retirement age.
Please type your age years: 21
Please type now current year(1997 or whatever):1997
Please now type your name: Susan

You will be retired in 39 years time.

Susan Your pensionable age will begin in 2036.
　　　Be happy my friend!
　　　you were born in 1976

Program Output (completed)

3.

A suggested Program

```cpp
#include<iostream.h>
// single-character variable manipulation
// To test if b holds a digit

void  main(void )
{

char b;
int s;
s:
cout << " Enter a number: ";
cin >> b;
if ( ( b >= '0' ) && ( b <= '9') ) {
cout << " The number you have just entered is " << b << endl;

goto s;
}
else
cout << " Please enter a number not a letter " << endl;
goto s;
}
```

Suggested Program Output

Enter a number: **M**
Please enter a number not a letter

Enter a number: **8**
The number you have just entered is 8
Enter a number:

4   **Suggested program and Output**

```
# include <iostream.h>
// illustration while loop
void main ( void )
{
int b, c;
int n = 0;
cout << "Number" << "\t\tb values" << "\tc values" << endl;
cout << ".........." << "\t\t............." << "\t............" << endl;
                        while ( n < 6 ) {
                            n = n+1;
                            b = ( n +2 );
                            c = ( b * b);
                            cout << n << "\t\t" << b << "\t\t" << c << endl;
                }
                        cout << "........................................." << endl;

}
```

Output

Number	b values	c values
1	3	9
2	4	16
3	5	25
4	6	36
5	7	49
6	8	64

5.   **A Suggested Program & Output**

```
# include <iostream.h>
# include <stdlib.h>
// To generate random numbers by applying rand ( ) function.
void main ( void )
{
 cout << "\t\t The Random Number Program" << endl;
  cout << "\t\t -------------------------\n" << endl;
  cout << " The following random numbers are generated" << endl;
  cout << " ......................................\n" << endl;
  for (int s = 2 ; s < 10 ; s++ )
  cout << "\t" << rand ( )<< endl;
  cout << " ......................................\n" << endl;
}
```

The Random Number Program

The following random numbers are generated
....

        346
        130
        10982
        1090
        11656
        7117
        17595
        6415
....

6.

A Suggested Program & Output

```
# include <iostream.h>
# include <stdlib.h>
// To generate maximum random// number on my computer
void main ( void )
{
  cout << "\t\t Maximum Random Number on My PC:  " << RAND_MAX <<
}
```

```
        Maximum Random Number on My PC:   32767
        --------------------------------
```

7.   <u>**A suggested Program & Output**</u>

```
#include <iostream.h>
// If-else statment with goto statement
int main (void)
{
int y;
again :
 cout << " ...................................\n";
 cout << " This program can generate Leap Years\n";
 cout << " ...................................\n" << endl;
 cout << " Please enter any year of your choice: ";
 cin >> y;
 if (  y % 4 == 0 && y % 100 != 0 || y % 400 == 0)   // Leap Year condition
    {
          cout <<" " << y << "  is a Leap Year\n"; goto again;

    }
        else
        cout <<" " << y << "  is not a Leap Year \n";
goto again;

}
```

<u>**Program Output**</u>

....
This program can generate Leap Years
....

Please enter any year of your choice: **2000**
2000 is a Leap Year
....
This program can generate Leap Years
....

Please enter any year of your choice: **1998**
1998 is not a Leap Year
....
This program can generate Leap Years
....

Please enter any year of your choice:

8   <u>**Program Output**</u>

```
Please enter surname: Robinson
Please enter first initial: M
Please enter second initial: B
Please enter subject code: 101
Please enter final grade, using uppercase letter: P
M B Robinson your pass grade is P. Successful!
```

```
Please enter surname: Smith
Please enter first initial: J
Please enter second initial: S
Please enter subject code: 1204
Please enter final grade, using uppercase letter: F
J S Smith you are unsuccessful.
Please make an appointment to see your course tutor.
```

```
Please enter surname: Taylor
Please enter first initial: R
Please enter second initial: S
Please enter subject code: 103
Please enter final grade, using uppercase letter: R
R S Taylor your grade is referral.
You will receive a letter soon.
```

```
Please enter surname: Hobson
Please enter first initial: M
Please enter second initial: V
Please enter subject code: 103
Please enter final grade, using uppercase letter: M
M V Hobson your pass grade is merit. Good!
```

```
Please enter surname: Cooper
Please enter first initial: A
Please enter second initial: D
Please enter subject code: 123
Please enter final grade, using uppercase letter: D
A D Cooper Your grade is the highest pass grade. Well done!
```

```
Please enter surname: Clinton
Please enter first initial: T
Please enter second initial: P
Please enter subject code: 001
Please enter final grade, using uppercase letter: f
Error : grade is out of range
```

8. ## A Suggested Program

```cpp
# include <iostream.h>
// To illustrate how  switch , break and default statements work together
void main (void)
{
 char surname [40], firstInitial, secondInitial;
 int subcode;
 char grade;
 cout << " Please enter surname: " ;
 cin  >> surname;
 cout << " Please enter first initial: ";
 cin  >> firstInitial;
 cout << " Please enter second initial: ";  // enter - for no initial
 cin  >> secondInitial;
 cout << " Please enter subject code: " ;
 cin  >> subcode;
 cout << " " << endl;
 cout << " Please enter final grade, using uppercase letter: ";
 cin  >> grade;

 switch (grade){
 case 'P':  cout << " " << firstInitial<< " " <<  secondInitial << " ";
            cout << surname << " Your pass grade is p. Successful!" << endl; break;

 case 'F':  cout << " " << firstInitial << " " << secondInitial << " ";
            cout << surname << " you are unsuccessful." << endl;
            cout << " Please make an appointment to see your course tutor."; break;

 case 'R':  cout << " " << firstInitial <<" " << secondInitial << " ";
                                cout << surname << " your grade is referral." << endl;
            cout << " You will receive a letter soon." << endl; break;
 case 'M':  cout <<" " << firstInitial << " " << secondInitial << " ";
                                cout << surname;
                                cout << " Your pass grade is merit. Good!" << endl;  break;
 case 'D':  cout <<" " << firstInitial <<" " << secondInitial << " ";
                                cout <<  surname;
                                cout << " Your grade is the highest pass grade.";
                                cout << " Well done!" << endl; break;
 default:  cout << "Error : grade is out of range\n";
 }                         // end of switch statement
}
```

Chapter 5

1   **A suggested Program & Output**

```
# include <iostream.h>
// To compute sum and average of variables
// To display sum and average values, each on a separate line

int main ( void )
{
                                    // Function prototype
void AddAv ( void );
        AddAv ( );
        return ( 0 );          // Without this statement the compiler will list an error but it works
}
void AddAv (void)
{
        int sum,  Av,  a,  b,  c;

 a = 10,  b = 35,  c = 70 ;           // Function has its own data
sum = ( a + b + c ) ;
Av =   ( a + b + c ) /3 ;
cout << "\t The Result of Our Computation" << endl;
cout << "\t ................................" << endl;
cout <<  " " << endl;
cout << "\t The sum of given numbers = " << sum << endl;
cout << "\t The average of given numbers = " << Av << endl;
}
```

-------------------------------- **Program Output**---

        The Result of Our Computation
        ....

        The sum of given numbers = 115
        The average of given numbers = 38

2.   A suggested Program & Output

```
# include <iostream.h>
// Reference  parameters - Passing by reference
int main (void)
{
            void sumDiffAv ( int x,  int y, int  &sum, int  &diff,  int  &av );
            int a, b, sum, diff, av ;
            cout <<"Please type a whole number" << endl;
            cin >> a;
            cout <<"Please type another whole number" << endl;
            cin >> b;
            sumDiffAv ( a, b, sum, diff, av );
            cout <<"\t\t\t  sum is "<< sum <<endl;
            cout <<"\t\t\t  difference is " << diff << endl;
            cout << "\t\t\t average is " << av << endl;
 return(0);
}

// on receipt of values, it adds two numbers, subtracts one from the other and finds average value

void sumDiffAv ( int x, int y, int  &sum, int  &diff, int  &av )
{
            sum  =  ( x + y );
            diff  =  ( x - y);
            av  =  ( x + y )/2;
}
```

Program Output

```
Please type a whole number
33
Please type another whole number
67
                sum is 100
                difference is -34
                average is 50
```

3.   A Suggested Program & Output

```
#include <iostream.h>
// Boolean function - Evaluate a condition
int main (void)
{
int leap (int);
int y;
leap  ( y % 4 == 0 && y % 100 != 0 || y % 400 == 0 ); // Compound Condition
return (0);
}
int leap (int y)
{
start:
cout <<"\t\t Leap Year Function\n";
cout <<"\t\t ..............................." << endl;
cout <<" " << endl;
cout << " Please enter any year of your choice: ";
cin  >> y;
if ( y = = 0 ) exit ( y );              // exit (  ) function to terminate the program when y = 0
 if
            ( y % 4 == 0 && y % 100 != 0 || y % 400 == 0 )
            {
                    cout << " " << y << " is a leap year.\n" << endl; goto start;
            }
                else
                    cout << " " << y << " is not a Leap Year.\n" << endl; goto start;
}
===================================== Program Output =====================================
                        Leap Year Function
                        ...............................

Please enter any year of your choice: 2000
2000 is a leap year.


                        Leap Year Function
                        ...............................

Please enter any year of your choice: 1997
1997 is not a Leap Year.


                        Leap Year Function
                        ...............................

Please enter any year of your choice:
```

Chapter 6

1.   <u>**A Suggested Program & Output**</u>

```
#include <iostream.h>
#include <classlib/arrays.h>
// days in months of the year
void main (void)
{
  cout << " Number of Days in Months" << endl;
  cout << " ........................\n" << endl;
  int month [12 ]= {31,29, 31,30,31,30,31,31,30,31,30,31};
  int m;
  for
  (m = 0 ; m < 12;  m++)

        cout << " Month  [ " << m << "] =   " << month [ m ]<< endl;
}
```
================================ **Program Output** ==========================

Number of Days in Months
....

```
Month  [ 0] =   31
Month  [ 1] =   29
Month  [ 2] =   31
Month  [ 3] =   30
Month  [ 4] =   31
Month  [ 5] =   30
Month  [ 6] =   31
Month  [ 7] =   31
Month  [ 8] =   30
Month  [ 9] =   31
Month  [ 10] =   30
Month  [ 11] =   31
```

2.   <u>**A suggested Program & Output**</u>

```cpp
# include <iostream.h>
// Output function.  It shows on screen array as a table.
void main ( void )
{
            cout << "\t Random Monthly Sales Figures for the Year 1997-98 " << endl;
            cout << "\t ...........................................................\n" << endl;
            long sales [12 ] = {190000, 180500, 210215, 180568, 190885, 175678,

            155868, 151018, 152000,  177900,178900, 187890 };

                              // prototype
void print ( long sales [ ],  long x );
print ( sales, 12 );
}
                              // Print Function
void print ( long sales [ ], long x )
{
            cout << "\t\t Monthly Sales Figures" << endl;
            cout << "\t\t ..............................\n" << endl;
            for ( long s = 0; s < x   ; s++ ){
            cout << "\t\t\t" << sales [s ]<< endl;
}
            cout << "\t\t ...............………." << endl;

}
```

Output

```
Random Monthly Sales Figures for the Year 1997-98
...................................................................

       Monthly Sales Figures
       ...............................

              190000
              180500
              210215
              180568
              190885
              175678
              155868
              151018
              152000
              177900
              178900
              187890

       ..................................
```

3.   ## A Suggested Program

```cpp
# include <iostream.h>
// sorting out data items
void main ( void )
{
        cout << "\t Random Sales Commission Paid to 50 Sales Staff " << endl;
        cout << "\t ..................................................\n" << endl;
int comm [50 ]= { 140,200,280,210,160,150,175,145,210,185, 210,150,124,200,210,
                175,190,185,200,175, 150,180,200,180,200,180,198,177,200,275,
                190,125,250,200,175,159,210,200,195,175, 200,165,200,135,225,
                160,190,166,175,200};   // Commission Figures
void print ( int comm [ ],  int x );
void sort ( int comm [ ], int x );
print ( comm, 50 );
sort ( comm, 50 );
print ( comm, 50 );
}
        // To re-produce randomly entered Sales Commission
void print ( int comm [ ], int x )
{

    for ( int i = 0; i < x -1; i++ ){
        cout << comm [i]<< ", " ;
                        if (( i+1)%10  == 0 ) cout << endl;
  }
        cout << comm [x-1] <<  endl;
        cout << " \n" << endl;

}
    // To sort out randomly stored commission figures  in ascending order by insertion method
void sort ( int comm [ ], int x )
{
  cout << "\t Weekly Sales Commission Sorted Out in Ascending Order" << endl;
  cout << "\t ..................................................\n" << endl;
  int temp;
  for ( int i = 1; i < x; i++ ) {// sort in ascending order {comm [0],...,comm [s]} :
  temp = comm [ I ];
    for ( int y = i; y > 0 &&  comm [ y-1 ] > temp; y -- )
      comm [ y ] = comm [ y-1 ];
      comm [ y ] = temp;
    }
}
```

3.　　**Program Output (Program on page 233)**

```
        Random Sales Commission Paid to 50 Sales Staff
        ..............................................................

140, 200, 280, 210, 160, 150, 175, 145, 210, 185,
210, 150, 124, 200, 210, 175, 190, 185, 200, 175,
150, 180, 200, 180, 200, 180, 198, 177, 200, 275,
190, 125, 250, 200, 175, 159, 210, 200, 195, 175,
200, 165, 200, 135, 225, 160, 190, 166, 175, 200



        Weekly Sales Commission Sorted Out in Ascending Order
        ...................................................................

124, 125, 135, 140, 145, 150, 150, 150, 159, 160,
160, 165, 166, 175, 175, 175, 175, 175, 175, 177,
180, 180, 180, 185, 185, 190, 190, 190, 195, 198,
200, 200, 200, 200, 200, 200, 200, 200, 200, 200,
200, 210, 210, 210, 210, 210, 225, 250, 275, 280
```

Chapter 7

1.　The given piece of code needs to be modified as the array name is a constant pointer. A constant pointer cannot be incremented. Thus **acc** cannot be incremented. We re-write the given segment of the code as follows:

> **int acc [50];**
> **int* pointer = acc;**
> **for (int i = 0; i < 50; i++);**
> ***pointer++ = (i + 1);**

2.　The pointer **p1** is of **int** type but the pointer **p2** is of **float** type. When two pointers are of two different Types, it is illegal to assign the address in one pointer to another pointer. Your program will not be compiled successfully if you make this error.

3.　　**Program Output**

```
Before the swapping the outstanding balance = £2000
Before the swapping the current month balance = £15000

After swapping the outstanding balance = £15000
After swapping the current month balance = £2000
```

3.   **Suggested Program**

```
#include <iostream.h>
// swapping - passing arguments by pointers
void main ( void )
{
void swap ( long* bal, long* curr );
long balance = 20000;
long current = 15000;
cout << "Before the swapping the outstanding balance = £" << balance << endl;
cout << "Before the swaping the current month balance = £" << current << endl;
swap ( &balance, &current );

}
void swap ( long* bal, long* curr )
{
long temp;
temp = *bal;
*bal = *curr;
*curr = temp;
cout << " " << endl;
cout << "After swapping the outstanding balance = £" << *bal << endl;
cout << "After swapping the current balance = £" << *curr << endl;
}
```

Chapter 8

1.   **Program Output**

```
Enter some words containing letter m:
---------------------------------------

Manchester, London, Birmingham and Brighton are English cities.

The letter m was repeated 2 times.
---------------------------------------
```

1   A Suggested Program

```
#include <iostream.h>
// strings
void main ( )
{
char letter;
int appeared = 0;
cout << " Enter some words containing letter m: " << endl;
cout << " -------------------------------\n" << endl;
while ( cin.get (letter))
                          if ( letter  == 'm') ++ appeared ;
cout << " " << endl;
cout << " The letter m was repeated " << appeared << " times." << endl;
cout << " -------------------------------";
}
```

2.   A Suggested Program

```
#include <iostream.h>
// strings
void main ( )
{
void reverse ( char* any );
char anyString [ 80 ];
cout << " Please enter a string: ";
cin.getline ( anyString, 80 );
cout << " " << endl;
cout << " \t\tYou entered:  " << anyString << endl;
reverse (anyString) ;
cout << " " << endl;
cout << " You can have it in the reverse order: " << anyString << endl;
}
void reverse ( char* anyString )
{
for ( char* last = anyString; *last; last++ );
char temp;
while ( anyString < last -1  )
{
temp = *--last;
* last = *anyString;
*anyString++ = temp;
}
}
```

2. **Program Output**

Please enter a string: London is a large city.

You entered: London is a large city.
You can have it in the reverse order: .ytic egral a si nodnoL

Chapter 9

1. **Suggested Program**

```cpp
#include <iostream.h>
// How to create and use structure
void main ( void )
{
struct customer{       // struct is to group related data into a single record
char name [ 20 ];
char add [ 50 ];
 char tel [15 ];
char cont [ 20 ];
}customer;
  for ( int i =0; i < 2; i++ ){
cout << "\t\t Input Data \n" << endl;
cout  << " Enter clients: ";
cin.getline ( customer.name, 19,'\n');
cout << " Enter full address: ";
cin.getline ( customer.add ,49,'\n');
cout << " Enter contact name: ";
cin.getline (customer.cont, 19,'\n' );
cout << " Enter telephone number: ";
cin.getline ( customer.tel, 14,'\n');
cout << " " << endl;
cout << "\t\t\t  Customer file \n" << endl;
cout << "\t\t\t Clients: " << customer.name << endl;
cout << "\t\t\t Address: " << customer.add << endl;
cout << "\t\t\t Contact: " << customer.cont << endl;
 cout << "\t\t\t Telephone Number: " << customer.tel << endl;
}
}
```

1.

===========================Program Output =======================

```
Input Data

 Enter clients: Norwich Supplies
Enter full address: 12 Lower Street Norwich NR1 3VB
Enter contact name: Mr K smith
Enter telephone number: 0789 700 600


                        Customer file

                        Clients: Norwich Supplies
                         Address: 12 Lower Street Norwich NR1 3VB
                         Contact: Mr K smith
                         Telephone Number: 0789 700 600
Input Data

Enter clients : ABC PLC
Enter full address: ABC House John Mews Leeds LA2 7NN
Enter contact : Miss C Brown
Enter telephone number: 0123 700 5678


                        Customer file

                        Clients: ABC PLC
                         Address: ABC House John Mews Leeds LA2 7NN
                         Contact: Miss C Brown
                         Telephone Number: 0123 700 5678
```

2.   <u>**A suggested Program & Output**</u>

```
#include <iostream.h>
#include <string.h>
                                        // assigning strings to structure

void main ( void )
{
const int max = 80;

struct student
{
char name      [ max ];
char course    [ max ];
char tutor     [ max ];
};

student record;
strcpy ( record.name, " David Smith" );
strcpy (record.course," BSc(Computing)" );
strcpy (record.tutor,"   Julie Roberts" );
cout << " Student:" << record.name << endl;
cout << " Course:" << record.course << endl;
cout << " Tutor:"  << record.tutor << endl;
}
```

============================ Program Output ====================

```
Student: David Smith
Course: BSc (Computing)
Tutor:  Julie Roberts
```

Chapter 10

1.   **A Suggested Program**

```
# include <fstream.h>          // defines ofstream class - it includes output file streams
# include <stdlib.h>           // includes exit ( ) function
// Writing to an external file
void main ( void )
{

char month [ 15 ];
long supplies, sales;
ofstream outfile( "c:trade.data", ios::out );   // to read from the file
  if (! outfile )
  {
  cerr << " Error: Unable to open 'trade.data' file \n";
  exit ( 1 );
}

  cout << " Monthly Purchases and Sales for the Period Jan - June 1996"  << endl;
  cout << " --------------------------------------------------------------------------\n" << endl;
  cout << "Month" <<"\t\t Supplies" << "\t Sales" << endl;
  cout << "-----" <<"\t\t --------" << "\t -----" << endl;
  while (cin >> month >> supplies >> sales )
  {
  outfile << "\t" << month <<  supplies  << sales << endl;
  }
  outfile.close ( );
  }
```

Chapter 11

1.   **A suggested Program Part 1**

```
#include <iostream.h>

                                // How to create and use structure and class object

class customer{                 // class name or tag is customer

struct cust_name{               // struct is to group related data into a single record
char firstName [ 20 ];
char middleName [ 20 ];
char lastName [ 20 ];
char status [  10 ];
int account;
long limit;
}sales;

public:
        void cust_input ( void );           //  Publicly available function
        void cust_output ( void );          //  Publicly available function
};

                                // Function to create information

void customer::cust_input ( void )
{
 cout  << " Enter first Name: ";
 cin  >> sales.firstName;
 cout << " Enter middle Name: ";
 cin  >> sales.middleName;
 cout << " Enter last Name: ";
 cin  >> sales.lastName;
 cout << " Enter status such as Mr,  Mrs or any other abbreviation: ";
 cin  >> sales.status;
 cout << " Enter Account Number: ";
 cin  >> sales.account;
 cout << " Enter Credit Limit: ";
 cin  >> sales.limit;
}
```

1.   **A Suggested Program   Part 2**

```
// Function to output information created

 void customer::cust_output ( void )
{
 cout << "\n" << endl;
 cout << "\t Personal Finance Credit Control Information" << endl;
 cout << "\t ...........................................\n" << endl;
 cout << "\t First Name: ";
 cout << sales.firstName  << " " << endl;
 cout << "\t Middle Name: ";
 cout << sales.middleName << " " << endl;
 cout << "\t Last Name: ";
 cout << sales.lastName << " " << endl;
 cout << "\t status: ";
 cout << sales.status  << " " <<endl;
 cout << "\t Sales Account Number: ";
 cout << sales.account    << " " << endl;
 cout << "\t Credit Limit Allowed: ";
 cout << sales.limit  << " \n" << endl;
 }

void main ( void )
{

 class customer  sales_infor;     // to create sales_infor object
 sales_infor.cust_input ( );
 sales_infor.cust_output( );
}
```

1.   **Program Output**

```
======================= Data Input ==========================
Enter first Name: John
 Enter middle Name: David
 Enter last Name: Major
 Enter status such as Mr, Mrs or any other abbreviation: Mr
 Enter Account Number: 1000
 Enter Credit Limit: 1200
====================== Information Generated =================

                Personal Finance Credit Control Information
                ...............................................................

                First Name: John
                Middle Name: David
                Last Name: Major
                status: Mr
                 Sales Account Number: 1000
                 Credit Limit Allowed: 1200
```

2.   **A Suggested Program**   **Part 1**

```cpp
#include <iostream.h>
// nested classes.The Program creates a staff File for the personnel dept.
char ( cr );
class personnel{
                struct per_name{
                 char employee [ 40 ],
                 natInsNum    [ 20 ],
                       sex     [ 3 ],
                    MarStatus [ 10 ],
                        born   [12 ];
            int year;

}name;
```

2. <u>**A Suggested Program   Part 2**</u>

```
        struct per_qualif{
                char school        [ 70 ],
                        FurTech [ 70 ],
                        Univ       [ 70 ];
}qualif;

        struct per_experience {

                char  present [ 70 ],
                        Recent   [ 70 ],
                        past     [ 70 ];

}experience;

        struct per_post {

                char title [ 40 ],
                appointed [ 12 ],
                otherInfor [ 60 ];
                        int salary;
}post;

public:
        void per_input ( void  );
                void per_output ( void );
};
 void personnel::per_input ( void )
{
                        // Input personal data

cout << " " << endl;
cout << "\t\t  Staff File: Input Data" << endl;
cout << "\t\t  ................................\n" << endl;
cout << " Enter name: \n";
cin.get (name.employee ,39 ,'\n' );
cin.get ( cr );
cout << " Enter national insurance number: \n"  ;
cin.get ( name.natInsNum,19, '\n' );
```

2.   **A Suggested Program   Part 3**

```
cin.get ( cr );
 cout << " Enter date of birth: \n" ;
 cin.get ( name.born ,11 , '\n' );
 cin.get ( cr );
 cout << " Enter single/married/divorcee, widow or widower): \n";
 cin.get ( name.MarStatus , 9, '\n' );
 cin.get ( cr );
 cout << " Enter m for male, f for female: \n";
 cin.get ( name.sex ,2 , '\n' );
 cin.get ( cr );
 cout << " Enter the year employee was born: \n";
 cin >> name.year;
 cin.get ( cr );
```

// input qualifications data

```
cout << " Enter school qualifications: \n";
 cin.get ( qualif. school, 59, '\n' );
 cin.get ( cr );
 cout << " Enter further or technical qualifications gained: \n";
 cin.get ( qualif.FurTech, 59, '\n' );
 cin.get ( cr );
 cout << " Enter any higher/professional qualifications gained: \n";
 cin. get ( qualif.Univ , 59, '\n' );
 cin. get ( cr );
```

// input work experience data

```
cout << " Enter pesent  pst if any: \n" ;
 cin.get ( experience.present , 69, '\n' );
 cin.get ( cr );
 cout << " Enter  relevant recent experience: \n";
 cin.get ( experience.Recent , 69, '\n' );
 cin.get ( cr );
 cout << " Enter relevant past experience: \n ";
 cin.get ( experience.past, 69, '\n' );
 cin.get ( cr );
```

2.   <u>**A Suggested Program   Part 4**</u>

```
                      // input current post data
cout << " Enter post title: \n";
cin. get ( post.title, 39, '\n');
cin.get ( cr );
cout << " Enter date employment commenced: \n";
cin.get ( post.appointed, 14, '\n' );
cin.get ( cr );
cout << " Enter current salary: \n";
cin  >> post.salary;
cin.get ( cr );
cout << " Enter any other relevant information: \n";
cin.get ( post.otherInfor, 49, '\n' );
cin.get ( cr );
cout << " " << endl;
}
void personnel::per_output (void )          // Output section
{
        cout << "\t\t _____ " << endl;
        cout << "\t\t  Staff File: Information Held" << endl;
        cout << "\t\t _____\n" << endl;
        cout << " Name: " <<name.employee << endl;
        cout << " National Insurance Number: " << name.natInsNum << endl;
        cout << " Date of Birth: " << name.born << endl;
        cout << " Age at Next Birthday: " << (1997 - name.year)<< " years" << endl;
        cout << " Marital Status: " << name.MarStatus << endl;
        cout << " Sex: " << name.sex << endl;
        cout << " " << endl;
        cout << " School Qualifications: " << qualif.school << endl;
        cout << " Technical/FE Qualifications: " << qualif.FurTech << endl;
```

2.   <u>**A Suggested Program Part 5**</u>

```
cout << " University/Professional Qualifications: " << qualif.Univ << endl;
cout << " " << endl;
cout << " Present Post, if in employment: " << experience.present << endl;
cout << " Relevant Recent Experience: " << experience.Recent << endl;
cout << " Relevant Past Experience: " << experience.past << endl;
cout << " " << endl;
cout << " Post Title: " << post.title << endl;
cout << " Date Employment Commenced: " << post.appointed << endl;
cout << " Current Salary: " << " £ " << post.salary << endl;
cout << " Any Other Relevant Information: " << post.otherInfor << endl;
cout << " " << endl;
}
void main ( void )
{
int again;
again:
personnel staff_file;            // to create staff_file object
staff_file.per_input ( );
staff_file.per_output ( );
goto again;
}
```

2.   <u>**Program Output**</u>

<u>**See pages 248-249**</u>

2.

Staff File: Input Data

....

 Enter name:
Mr. V. M. Smith
 Enter national insurance number:
HY/53/63/02/72/D
 Enter date of birth:
12.06.1940
 Enter single/married/divorcee, widow or widower):
Married
 Enter m for male, f for female:
M
 Enter the year employee was born:
1940
 Enter school qualifications:
Matriculation Cert. London University 1955
 Enter further or technical qualifications gained:
Member AAT since 1989. All Examinations passed
 Enter any higher/professional qualifications gained:
None
 Enter Present post if any:
Area Accounts Manager
 Enter relevant recent experience:
 4 years computerised accounting experience
 Enter relevant past experience:
 20 years accounting experience
 Enter post title:
Accounts Manager (North)
 Enter date employment commenced:
02.01.1996
 Enter current salary:
28000
 Enter any other relevant information:
Able to audit clients' accounts and direct staff

---

2.   **Program Output   Part 2**

Staff File: Information Held

Name: **Mr.V. M. Smith**
National Insurance Number: **HY/53/63/02/72/D**
Date of Birth: **12.06.1940**
Age at Next Birthday: **57 years**
Marital Status: **Married**
Sex: **M**

School Qualifications: **Matriculation Cert. London University 1955**
Technical/FE Qualifications: **Member AAT since 1989. All Examinations passed**
University/Professional Qualifications: **None**

Present Post, if in employment: **Area Accounts Manager**
Relevant Recent Experience: **4 years computerised accounting experience**
Relevant Past Experience: **20 years accounting experience**

Post Title: **Accounts Manager (North)**
Date Employment Commenced: **02.01.1996**
Current Salary: **£ 28000**
Any Other Relevant Information: **Able to audit clients' accounts and direct staff**

Staff File: Input Data
...............................…....

Enter name:

Chapter 13

Glossary of Terms

abstraction - in programming abstraction means to concentrate on those elements that are relevant to a particular module instead of all elements concerning the whole program. This principle is applied in search of a modular solution. There may be several levels of abstraction. At the highest level of abstraction, the solution is outlined in general terms; but at the lowest of abstraction the solution is stated as such that it can be implemented.

address - it refers to a location (cell) in the computer memory. Memory locations are identified by variable names for the purpose of storing and retrieving data. See address operator variables.

address operator – it is the ampersand ' **&** ' that is used with the variable name to access the address of the variable to which it is attached. For example in the following code:

         int a = 100;

         cout << " &a = " << &a ; ← cout will print the address of **a** because of **&**.
See pointers.

algorithm - it is a step-by-step way of doing something. For instance, well prescribed instructions for making and serving a cup of tea to a guest is an algorithm. In fact a computer program is an algorithm.

alias – a reference parameter is an alias for the original variable. For instance:

         int a = 100;
         int & p = a;

Here **&p** is a reference parameter for the original value of **a** and thus it is an alias. Note the use of **&** which is essential with the reference parameter (operator).

argument - in any function it is a name given to a variable. For instance: **int add (int x)**. Here **x** is one parameter of integer type. See parameter.

Arrays – an array is a set of the same type of data items grouped together under a name called identifier. Arrays can be one-dimensional, two-dimensional or multi-dimensional. They are useful when dealing with tables or blocks of data. In C++, arrays are passed as reference parameters. See also elements, one-dimensional and two-dimensional arrays.

ASCII (or Ascii) code - acronym for American Standard Code for Information Interchange. It has been widely used since it was introduced in 1963. It has 128 different character values in the range 0–127.

For example:

- the ACII code for the symbol / (slash) is 47 - integer value
  and it is stored in 8-bit binary notation as **0010 1111**.
- the ACII code for the letter/character ' B' is 66 - integer value and it is
  stored in 8-bit binary notation as **0100 0010**.

The 8-bit binary code system is an extension of the ACII system.

assignment statement – its purpose is to assign initial values to variables. In C++, the general format of the assignment statement is given below:

Variable = expression;

Example: a = 10; b = 56;
          c = (a + b) – 15

The right hand side of the = is evaluated first, giving a value which is then assigned to the variable c on the left hand side of =. In this example **c becomes** 51 (not equals but becomes).

attributes - in OOP attributes of an object are the individual things that make an object different from another object in the class of objects. Each attribute has its own value. For instance, in **Employee** class, every employee has a name, date of birth and national insurance number, each having its values as shown below:

Attribute	Value
name	Smith
date of Birth	31.12.1967
national insurance number	PA/23/45/09/D

base class - see inheritance.

binary files – in C++, binary files hold data as a sequence of bytes as opposed to a series of characters in the text file.

blank space - in C++, the insertion operators consider blank space (white space or just space) as a terminator. See cin.getline ( ).

Boolean algebra – it is important in computing. Examples of Boolean logical operations are   TRUE, FALSE,   AND , OR or NOT. It is used to evaluate a condition involving   **if** , or **while** statement. It is named after George Boole , the 19th –century British mathematician.

Borland C++ Integrated Development Environment (IDE) - Borland C++ IDE contains all the necessary tools and utilities one needs for programming in C++. For instance, IDE enables you to create, compile, debug and save your program with ease.

break statement – it is used in both loops and switch statements. It terminates the iteration process or the loop. Its use in switch statement is also very important, as without it all statements from all cases would be executed one after another, and the program would not output the desired result.

call by reference – it is passing of parameters to functions. By this method it is the address of the parameter which is passed to function. In the calling function, it can alter the actual parameter. Its main advantage is that it allows the function to **return** several values.

call by value - it is passing of parameters to functions. The actual content of the variable is not passed but a copy is passed. This way, the variable in the calling function itself is not subjected to change. In C++, it is the default method of passing parameters (arguments) to a function. The disadvantage is that the function **returns** only one value.

cerr - it is a pre-defined stream object from library classes for I/O. It is an unbuffered output stream of ostream class. It is used for displaying an error message when a file is not correctly opened during file processing. Its use is as follows:

   cerr << "Error : unable to open sales.data file\n";

In this example the message, **Error: unable to open sales,data file** will only be displayed on the screen, if the file is incorrectly opened; and in this case, the program will be terminated.

char - any symbol on the keyboard. It is a keyword. It means character. All PCs have 256 different characters, and use a numeric value system in order to represent each character in its binary format. See also ASCII code.

In C++, **char** stands for the type of variable called **character**. For instance:
                        char name;
It declares variable called name whose type is character. See also char type below.

char cr – it stands for character carriage return or a new line. The statement: **char cr;** is the carriage return or new line declaration.

char type - it is an integer type and thus it can be used as integer. For instance in statements:
                        char a = 25;
                        char b = 5*a +7;

In this example, both char variables **a** and **b** are subjected to arithmetic operators.

character strings - a string is a sequence of characters within the double quotes. For instance:
                        " It is a fine day!"
is a string of characters. In C++, strings are manipulated as variables of type **char**. See also strings.

child class - see inheritance.

cin >> - it is pronounced as 'cin-in'. This is an abbreviation for 'console-input ', In C++, **cin** is the input stream, which is used with symbol >>. cin >> enables the user to input (key in) the required data one after another. For instance: **cin >> a;**

Which allows the user to key in required value (data) for the variable **a**. Similarly, **cin >> a >> b ;** will enable the user to key in two items of data , for variables called **a** and **b** . Note that a semicolon is needed to end a stament in C++. cin is the opposite of cout. When **cin** is used, data flows in from the input stream. See also extraction operator.

cin.getline ( ) - it is one of the functions of the input stream object cin >>. It is used for reading the whole line of characters (input) including spaces between characters. Its general format is:

cin.getline (str, n)

where **str** stands for the name of the string, and **n** number characters in the string including the nul character which is string terminator.

class - it is the basis of the concept object that is the central feature in object oriented programming. It is a broad category of things or objects that have similar features. For instance a **Car** class describes the features of all cars (body, engine, speed ,colour). The **Car** class thus serves as an abstract for the concept of a car. Of course, each car that is a specific **instance** of the **car** class can vary in features (small body, more powerful engine, maximum speed , different colour) from other cars – instances of the **car** class.

compiler - it translates the high level language whole source code into a self-contained program called object program. For instance C++ compiler translates the program you write in C++ into the object program so that it can perform its tasks.

constructor - a constructor is a class member function. It has the same name as the class within which it is defined. It is called automatically when the object is declared. A class can have several constructors. It creates objects and allocates memory.

continue statement - it is opposite of the break statement. It causes iteration by going back to the start of the loop's block in order to begin the next iteration. This way it returns control to the start of a loop's block. In C++, it is a keyword.

cout << - it is pronounced as 'see-out'. This is an abbreviation for 'console-output', which is the screen. In C++, sending data items to the screen, one after another, is called **output stream** of data. In order to send an item to data to the output stream, the symbol << is used with cout. For instance: **cout << " Hello"';** will send one item of data that is **hello** to the screen. But **cout << " Hello" << "John" ;** will send two items of data , **hello** and **John** to the screen. Note that a semicolon is needed to end a statement in C++. **cout** is the opposite of **cin**. When **cout** is used, data flows out to the output stream. See also insertion operator.

debugging - finding and removing of errors or bugs in a program. The debugging of programs is usually supported by **debug tool**. Borland C++ Compiler supports debugging, by providing all necessary tool under its Debug Menu. See testing.

decrement operator - the symbol -- is known as decrement operator. The use of this operator results in subtracting I from the number. It has two general formats as shown below:

--a this format is called **pre-increment operator**. The other format is a-- is called **post-increment** operator. Both -- must be placed next to the variable name without any space.

Both formats have the same effect that is to subtract 1 from the number as illustrated below:
            sum = 10; sum --;
            Here the value of sum will be decreased from 10 to 9.
See also increment operator.

dereferencing – when the pointer locates the value to which it points, it is called de-referencing. For example consider: int a = 10;

            int * point = &a ← **point** points to **a** and locates its value which is **10**, and point = 10. ***point** is an alias for **a**.

Here: **a** is simple variable. **Point** is the name of the pointer. **int * point** is a pointer of integer type and **&a** is the address of the variable **a**. See also referencing.

derived class – a class that is derived from the existing class is called derived class. The derived class inherits all or some of the features of the parent class. See inheritance.

destructor - a destructor is a class member function. It has the same name as the class within which it is defined; but its name is preceded by the character ~. It is a logical complement of its constructor, therefore it destroys the object when it comes to an end. It is automatically called when the program reaches the end of the scope of a class object. For instance, if the constructor **currency** converts Sterling into US dollars, the destructor would be used to print a message, say FINISHED and destroys the object **currency** and de-allocates the memory. This is why it is the logical complement of the constructor which dynamically allocates memory. See also constructor.

do-while loop - it executes the statement first and then evaluates or tests the condition at the end of the first iteration. It does so because it iterates at least once. It is a very useful statement when one does not know how many repetitions are executed.

double - it is a keyword. **double** is float type number, and it uses twice as many bytes as float. On my computer float is 4 bytes long and double is 10 bytes long. Use program in diagram 8 to find out integer types and their sizes on your PC.

elements - in the array, **name [5]** ,the number 5 within the brackets [ ] means that the array called **name** has 5 items which are known as elements. The elements of the array are numbered consecutively 0,

1, 2, 3,..... In this example, these elements are name [0], name [1], name [2], name [3], and name [4]. If you have to refer to a particular element in the array, say the 3rd, you have to refer to it as **name [2]**. The number within the brackets **[ ]** is called **subscript** or **index value**. The data stored in an array is accessed by referring to each subscript. See subscripted variable.

encapsulation - in OOP each object is an instance that combines its data structure (member data) and functions (member methods) into a single structure. This way, an object's internal structure is protected from the direct contact with other objects outside the class. The internal structure of the object can only be changed by its own member methods. This technique is known as encapsulation, which is also known as information hiding. This way, the object is an interface to the object itself and thus isolates its internal structure from outside the class. See also information hiding.

enum – it is keyword. It is used to define enumerated type data. Its general format is explained below by means of an example:

$$\text{enum day \{ mon, tue, wed, thr, fri, sat, sun \};}$$

It defines the enumerated type data called **day**. In this context, **day** is not a variable, but type of data chosen by the programmer. There are seven days (variables) in a week. These are within **{ }** brackets. Variables within **{ }** are known as enumerators.

enumerators - See enum.

enumeration (enumerated) type - a data type. It is explicitly defined by the programmer. Enumeration type data are easy to read. For instance, it is easier to read JAN, FEB, MAR and APR, the months of the year.

executable File - an object file together with the required library functions is known as executable file or program. It has the **.exe** extension. When it is loaded into the memory it can be executed directly. See also object file.

execution errors - same as Run-time errors. See run-time errors.

exit function - more precisely exit ( ) it performs three distinct tasks:

    a) writes all output to the file   **b)** closes all open files   and   **c)** terminates the program.

See also **stdlib.h**.

extraction operator (>>) – it refers to the standard input stream which is the keyboard. See also **cin >>**.

false – it is logical false. In accordance with the Boolean algebra, it evaluates to value of **0**. See true.

file - it is a collection of related records. For instance, employees personal information related to employment is kept in staff file. Files are kept on backing store so that they can be used when required. C++ interprets a file as a sequence of bytes (bits). When the file contains 8-bit groups as bytes, the ASCII code interprets it as a **text file**. See also binary file.

file scope - a variable that has a file scope is accessible throughout the file in which it is declared. It is then a global variable within the file. See also scope resolution operator.

float (or floating-point) - it is a real number. For example 34.90 is a float. See also double and long double. **float** is a keyword. See also double.

for statement - it is a counting loop. Its basic principle is that a section of the program is executed continuously with a counter taking successive values until the counter reaches the required number of times the loop is to be executed. The for loop has three parts as shown in its following general structure.

```
for ( initialisation value; condition to be tested ; update)          // three parts of for loop

{
    statement;
    statement;
}
```

One can construct a **for loop** without any condition to test, but such a loop will run forever. The only way, it can be stopped, is to switch off the computer, or reset the program. One uses it when one knows how many times the section of the program is to be executed.

friend function - a keyword. When a function is declared as a friend, it has access to all private, public and protected members of the class within which it is declared.

fstream class - it is a library class. It includes both *ifstream* class for linking a file for input-output, and *ofstream* class for linking output only. Thus, an *fstream class object* can be used to open a file for both input and output.

fstream.h − it is a header file which is required for file handling various facilities, as it supports file streams. When the header file *# include <fstream.h>* is shown near the top of your program, there is no need to have #include <iostream.h> in your program. #include<fstream.h> supports I/O various facilities.

function - a function performs some specific tasks. C++ compiler has powerful libraries of many predefined functions that the user can incorporate in his/her programs. For instance, the square root function **sqrt ( )**. In C++, functions are specific parts or modules of a program that can be coded separately. One can say that in C++, the programming task is carried out in terms of coding functions. All C++ programs must have at least one function called **main ( )**. See function main.

function call - usually a program has a number of functions. The program executions starts at function main ( ). **The function main ( ) invokes or calls (communicates with) the next function. The computer**

executes the statement(s) within this called function. When the execution of this function is completed, the control is returned to the function that invoked it, in this case, main ( ), which then calls the next function in the program. This way, one function calls another function until the execution of the program is completed.

function declaration - it informs the compiler of the type of data to be returned, the type of data and number of arguments the function will use. It is usually placed at the beginning of a program. It is also called function prototype or just prototyping. Prototyping declares in advance what the function is going to use. This enables the compiler to check that the function is correctly used. Example:

float balance (int m1, int m2, int m3, int p);

Here: float is the type of data the function named **balance** will return or produce when it is called. **int m1, int m2, int m3** and **int p** are four integer types arguments or parameters (values) will be required when the function is called. Note that function declaration ends with a **semicolon**.

function header - it looks like function declaration, but it <u>does not</u> end with a semicolon.

function main - See main ( ).

global variables – these are declared outside any particular function. They are available to all parts of the program which come after their declarations. See also file scope.

goto statement - it is useful when a repetition is desirable. It causes a jump, and therefore, the normal flow of control is broken by sending the control to another statement. Now-a-days, its use is declining as it can make a program more difficult to follow. C++ has better facilities, even so, sometimes, its application is unavoidable. See also label.

header file - it is provided by the compiler as pre-defined code that can be used with your source code. All header files are declared at the start of your program., and that is why we call them header files. Header files have **.h** which stands for header. For instance: **<string.h>** is a header file. The angle brackets are not part of the file; but these are used in order to show that **string.h** is a standard C++ library file. See also pre-processor directive/statement.

high level languages - use English-like words. This makes programming comparatively easier.

include directive – it is in fact **#include directive**. It is stated at the beginning of a program. It is:

#include <iostream.h>

without this directive in your program, input and output streams will not work. See also cin and cout.

increment operator - the symbol **++** is known as increment operator. This operator adds I to the number. It has two general formats as shown below:

++a this format is called **pre-increment operator**. The other format is **a++** that is called **post-increment** operator. Both ++ must be placed next to the variable name without any space. Both formats have the same effect that is add 1 to the number as illustrated below:

int a = 10;   a++;   Here the value of **a** is **11**. It is increased by one. See also decrement operator.

identifiers - an identifier is a name given to a variable, a function, a data type or any other element defined within the program. For instance the identifier:

int n;

declares variable called **n** which is numeric whole whose type is **integer**. See also variables.

ifstream - it is a library class file object. It is used for defining an input file object that is linked to the file name. For instance in the following statement:

ifstream infile ("c:sales.data", ios::in);

infile is an object. The object *infile* has been defined to be a member of the **ifstream** class, and associated with the file name shown within ( ) –sales.data. In order to use ifstream file objects, you must include near the top of your program #include<fstream.h> header file. There is no need to put #include <iostream.h> header file, because *fstream.h* supports all the necessary I/O facilities required for file handling.

index value - See elements and Zero-based indexing.

information hiding - it is an important principle of program development. In accordance with this principle, each module of a program should hide (**encapsulate)** a single design decision. What it really means is that data and functions for a particular module are **hidden** into a single entity (module) from other modules. This way the internal working of the module is protected from other modules that do not require any access to the module. This technique makes program modification easy as it is easier to alter each single module. It is another name for encapsulation. See also encapsulation.

inheritance – the process of deriving classes from an existing class is known as inheritance. The inheritance process is an important technique in OOP that allows you to create an object which inherits the existing object's member data fields and member functions. The existing class is called the **parent class** or the **base class** and the derived class is known as **child class**.

initialisation - it is associated with the assignment statement. See assignment statement.

inline functions - these are short functions whose code is inserted by the compiler when they are called. This way, they save time when they are called more than once within a program. They avoid all the normal function's overhead (such as allocating extra storage for the local variable) as the compiler inserts the code at the point of call.

input stream - when the file is open for input, then the flow of data is input stream.

insertion operator (<<) - it refers to the standard output stream which is the screen. See also **cout <<**.

instance - In OOP an instance is a specific thing or object that belongs to a particular class . See class.

instance Variables - different values given to attributes of an instance or object are sometimes called instance variables. These values can change. For instance national insurance number can change for an object

instantiation - the process of creating new instances or objects of a particular class is called instantiation.

int - it is a keyword for integer. See integer.

integer – it is a whole number. 1,7,9,-6 are some examples of integers. See **int** above.

interpreter - it translates and carries out the instruction immediately line by line as it meets each line in a source code. It is contrasted with compiler. See compiler.

invokes a function – it has the same meaning as a function calls another function or a function is called by another function. See also function call.

ios::append - it is called constructor flag for appending data to the end of a file. Its use is shown in the following general statement:

ofstream outfile ("c:payroll.data", ios:: app);

Here outfile is user defined class/object to be associated with ofstream file object. **c** is the drive on which payroll.data file is stored.

ios::binary - it is called constructor flag for opening file in binary mode. Its use is shown in the following general statement:

ofstream outfile ("c:payroll.data", ios:: binary);

Here outfile is user defined class/object to be associated with ofstream file object. **c** is the drive on which payroll.data file will be opened in binary mode. The default is text mode in C++.

ios class – it is the base class for derived stream classes. The broad category of derived classes are input stream classes, output stream classes, input-output stream classes and stream buffer classes. See ios use below.

ios::in - it is called constructor flag for opening a file for reading from it (input data). Its use is shown in the following general statement:

                 ofstream outfile ("c:payroll.data", ios:: in);

Here outfile is user defined class/object to be associated with ofstream file object. **c** is the drive on which the file called payroll.data is stored.

ios::out - it is called constructor flag for output file. It is required when a file has to be created for reading and writing. Its use is shown in the following general statement:

                 ofstream outfile ("c:payroll.data", ios:: out);

Here outfile is user defined class/object to be associated with ofstream file object. **c** is the drive on which the file is to be stored as an external file and payroll.data is the file to be created.

iostream class – it is the general purpose input and output class that is usually included in the source program.

iostream.h – it is a standard C++ library file in which information about input and output streams are kept. In **iostream.h** , **.h** tells us that it is a header file. It instructs the compiler to include in the source program facilities for handing input and output as and when required. #include <iostream.h> is the include directive. When it is required in a program, it is shown near the top of a source program.

iteration - it is the process of repetition. C++ has three types of iteration statements which are also known as loops. See loops.

label – it identifies a destination for a **goto** statement. Its general format is:
Label: again: (terminated by **:**)

           .   .
           .   .
           .   .
         goto;   goto again;

See also goto statement.

limit.h - it is written as <limit.h> which is a header file. It contains resources for handling limitations, ranges of integers and compile time. Use #include<limit.h> pre-processor directive to find ranges of integer types on your PC. For instance the statement: **cout << CHAR_MAX << endl;**
will display the maximum char on your PC.

linking error - it occurs when a compiled program is linked to a library function. It may be due to incorrect parameters or unavailability of the required function or subroutine.

local variable – these are declared within a function, and thus available to the function itself. See global variables.

logical error – these errors are the result of poor program design. These are recognised when the program outputs the wrong result or it just does not generate the required output.

loops - C++ has the following three types of loops statements. These are also called iteration statements, because of their repetition or cyclic nature.

> *. while* loop　　　　*. do . . . while* loop　　　　*. for* statement.

See also break, continue , for loop and iteration.

low level languages - use binary codes that cannot be easily transferred from one computer to another.

main ( ) function - it is where the program execution begins and ends. All C++ programs must have this function.

main ( ) - - the following shortest program performs no task that is called function main. Within the braces { } it has an empty body and thus does nothing, even so it is a legal C++ program.

```
Main ( )
{

}
```

math.h or <math.h> - it is a header file that has many maths functions, including all those functions that are found on a pocket calculator, and many other mathematical operations that can be incorporated into your program. For instance, when **sqrt ( )** function is used in the program, say in order to find the square root of 2, it will be used as **sqrt (2)** and it will **return 1. 41421**. The mathematical functions always return a *double* type. See double.

max ( ) function - it is C and C++ function that is used for comparing two values. It returns the larger of two values compared. In order to apply this library function, **#include <stdlib.h >** should be listed near the top of the program.

member data - in OOP variables within a class definition are known as member data as shown below:

```
class employee {              // class name employee
public:
       void cal ( );           // member function
       void print ( );         // member function
private:
       int wage, gross, tax, net;     //  member data

};
```

member functions - in OOP functions within a class definition are known as member functions as shown in the example under member data. Member functions are also known as methods.

methods - see member functions above.

min ( ) function – it is C and C++ function that is used for comparing two values. It returns the smaller of two values compared. In order to apply this library function, **#include <stdlib.h >** should be listed near the top of the program.

module - it is a component of a long program. A module deals with a particular section of the problem being tackled by the program. It can be separately developed and compiled. Modules make program alterations easy, as modifications are made to the internal working of a particular module.

multiple inheritance – when a child class inherits its attributes from several bases or parent classes, it is called multiple inheritance. See inheritance.

nested loops (or nesting) - Loops can be embedded within loops. There is no limit to nesting, but nesting can be complicated. It is better not to have too many nested conditions.

nul (null) character – it is \0 . In C++, strings (character strings) are terminated by the nul character. As it is an additional character, the size of the string is the total number of characters in the string plus the nul character. It is required in order to detect the end of the character string (one-dimensional array). It is equivalent to zero, and stored at the end of the string. See also strings.

object - an object is a specific thing that belongs to a particular class. Objects and instances are the same thing in OOP. Often the distinction between class and object is not obvious, because from an object one can create another class. One can also visualise an object as a unique thing that has its own data and functions. See also member data and member functions.

object file - the compiler converts the **source code** into an intermediate file which is known as object file or program. It contains machine code. The object file has the **.obj** extension. See also executable file.

object oriented programming (OOP) - in simple terms, this programming technique is about grouping related data and functions together. In OOP, the central feature is the object, which is an instance of a class. See classes above.

ofstream - it is a library class . It is needed for file handling. It is used for defining an output file object that is linked to the file name. For instance in the following statement:

ofstream outfile ("c:sales.data", ios::out);

<u>outfie</u> **is an object**.

The object *outfile* has been defined to be a member of the **ofstream** class, and associated with the file name shown within ( ) – sales.data. In order to use ofstream file objects, you must include near the top of your program #include<fstream.h> header file. There is no need to put #include <iostream.h> header file, because *fstream.h* supports all the necessary I/O facilities required for file handling.

one–dimensional array - it is a list of data items of the same type. For instance:

reference	the declaration
1001	int reference [3] declares **reference** as one-dimensional array
1200	of three elements (data items) of type integer.
1205	

reference is one-dimensional array. 1001,1200 and 1205 are reference numbers, but here we refer to them as three elements of the array reference. See also two-dimensional array.

ostream class - it is an output stream class that is used for general purpose output. Some other output stream can be derived from it.

output operator (<<) - see insertion operator.

output stream - when the file is open for output, the flow of data is output stream.

overflow – it is a run-time error due to maximum and minimum bounds of integer values. When the output of a program exceeds these bounds, it is called overflow. On my PC integer range that is 32767 and - 32767.

overloading - in C++, when a number of functions in the same program have the same name, it is called overloading. The essential requirement for overloading is that each function must have a unique list of arguments, and that each list must differ from the other list of arguments in terms of the types of arguments or number of arguments or even both the types and number of arguments.

overloading functions - it allows the programmer to give the same name to several functions within the same program. See overloading.

parameter - it is a variable's name within the brackets in both function declaration and function header. For instance the function header : **void cal (int a, int b)** has two parameters namely **a** and **b**. The required parameters are included in the function declaration (prototype), function header and in the function call as well. Arguments are the same things as parameters.

parent class – See inheritance.

passing by reference – when passing values to a calling function by this method, the address of the parameter is passed. It can alter the actual parameters in the calling function. This method requires less memory than passing by value method as outlined below.

passing by value - when passing values to a calling function by this method, the actual content of the variable is not passed, but a copy is passed. This method prevents changing values of variables passed, but requires more memory for duplication.

pointer - it holds the address of another variable and thus points to the location of other variable in the computer memory. It is thus a variable and also known as **pointer variable**. Like arrays, pointers are used to access memory. See address and de-referencing.

polymorphism – in practical terms it simply means different objects or related sub-classes or derived classes can produce different results by using the same **virtual function**. The following skeleton of a program illustrates this important technique.

```
class work {                          parent/ base class

            // ...
      public:

            virtual  void office_work ( void )       virtual function
        }
            //...

        }
    };
  class sales: public work {          sales is a sub-class/ derived class of work

        // ...
public:
        void office_work ( )
    }
            // ...
        }
};
    class purchase : public work {    purchase is a sub-class/derived class of  work

        // ...
public:
        void office_work ( )
    }
        //
};
    void main ( )
{
    // ..
slaes.office_work ( );                performs sales function
purchase.office_work ( );             performs purchase function
}
```

There is no need to use the keyword virtual as long as the function office_work ( ) is in the base class, it will be inherited by sub-classes due to the keyword public.

pre-processor directive/statement - it instructs the compiler to retrieve the code stored in a library file into the source code. It consists of include directive plus header file.

Directive + header file = pre-processor directive/ statement.

Example: #include <iostream.h>　　　　(**.h** indicates header)

See also #include directive under include.

private – private members (variables or data) can only be used by member functions and friends of the class. By default all members of a class are private. It is a common practice to declare data as private members. See also public. See also friend function.

procedure - the term procedure is often used for a section of a program that is able to carry out some well defined task. It can be coded and tested separately, prior to linking it with other procedures in the main program. See also module.

procedural programming - in procedural programming, the problem is analysed in terms of input-output and then the code is written.

program - a program is a set of instructions arranged in sequence for a computer. It tells a computer what to do and how to carry out a task step-by-step.

program specification - a precise statement of what the program is required to do without describing how this to be achieved.

prototyping - see function declaration.

public - it is a common practice to declare functions as public. This way, functions can be accessed by other functions outside the class.

Put to operator (<<) - see insertion operator.

rand ( ) function - random generator function. In order to use this function, the program should include <stdlib.h> header file. It will generate whole numbers between the range 0 – 32,767. This is the range on my PC. It is highly likely that your PC has the same range. Experiment! See also seed.

reference operator –it is ampersand - **&** . See alias.

reference parameter - See alias.

relational operator – it is used for a comparison between two operands (values). The appropriate operator is placed between two values and then a comparison is made. It returns a truth value if the condition or the relationship between the values is true (or 1); otherwise, the comparison is evaluated as false (or 0).

         For instance: **if (a > b) cout << a << endl;**
                                  else cout << b << endl;

Here the condition is **a** (operand) is greater than **b** (operand). The values of **a** and **b** are compared in order to find out which of them has a bigger value. If **a** has a bigger value than the condition is evaluated as **true or 1**; otherwise, the condition is evaluated as **false or 0**.

run-time errors - these errors are due to a breach of logical or mathematical rules. These errors are detected during program execution. For example the division by zero will give run-time error. See also overflow.

scope resolution operator (::) - by using (::) one can change the scope of local variables to that of global variables.

seed - when <sdlib.h> header file is included in your program to generate a sequence of pseudo-random numbers, the first random number is initialised by the computer. It is called the seed. The problem with this first number (seed) is that every time the program runs, the seed is the same. To avoid this undesirable situation, **use srand ( ) function**, because it allows the programmer to use one's own seed.
See also **rand ( )** function.

signed integer – a whole number whose bit pattern is interpreted as an integer type. It may be positive, negative or zero. For instance – 8 is signed integer. **signed** is a keyword.

single inheritance - when a child class inherits its attributes from its single parent class, it is called single inheritance. See inheritance.

sizeof - it is a keyword. It is used to find the size of variable.

source code - it is the program you write using C++ language. It is translated by the C++ compiler for conversion into the intermediate file or program called object file or program that contains machine code. It has the extension **.cpp**.

srand ( ) - See seed.

standard C++ library - it is a collection of software components that can be used in any C++ program. These components are pre-defined and tested functions, classes, objects, constant, I/O, sound and graphics. These libraries are usually supplied with the C++ compiler. You can also buy them from C++ compilers manufacturers.

stdlib.h or <stdlib.h> - it is a header file for handling standard library routines. For instance, in order to use the library routine function exit ( ) in your program, you must include in your program the following pre-processor directive:

#include<stdlib.h>   near the top of your program.

stract ( ) function - pre-defined function which is in **string.h** header file. It is used for appending or joining one string to another string. It is also known as concatenation function.

strcpy ( ) function - it is one of the functions in string.h header file. It is used for copying strings. The application of this function requires the name of the string array which contains the string, and the name of the string array into which the string is to be copied. Before you can use it, you must include near the top of your program **#include<string.h>** directive.

stream of data - In C++, sending data items to the screen, one after another, is called output stream of data. On the other hand, sending data from the keyboard (key in), one after another, is called input stream of data. See cin >> and cout << for input and output streams. See also input stream and output stream.

stream library - it is a comprehensive collection of classes that are arranged in a complex Hierarchy. All I/O objects defined in the iostream classes are derived from the base class known as **ios**.

string.h – it is a header file. It is needed for character-string handling functions provided by C++ standard library. Its format is : **#include<string.h>** and it is listed near the top of a source program.

strings (character strings) - in C++, strings are considered as one-dimensional arrays, terminated by the **nul** character. See also arrays and nul (or null) character.

string concatenation function - See stract ( ) function.

strlen ( ) function – it is a pre-defined string function from C++ standard library. This function is used to find out the length of any string. Thus it will count the number of characters in a string. In order to apply this function, #include <string.h> file must be listed near the top of a source program.

struct – it is a keyword which is an abbreviation for the word structure. It is used to create a structure. The keyword **struct** is followed by the type for the structure to be created. Its general format is as follows:

struct type   **// or name or identifier**

For instance:

struct staff

Here **staff** is user's own chosen type or name or identifier for the structure.

structure - in C++, a structure is one unit of record, that is a collection of related data items of mixed data types. For instance, a payslip is a structure which contains data items of several different types of data, but conveniently grouped together.

structure chart – it is similar to an organisation chart or a family tree. It helps to visualise the structure of a complex program. The main program is at the top of the structure. It is thus the **parent**. The functions called by the main program are underneath. These functions are the **children** as shown in the simple illustration below.

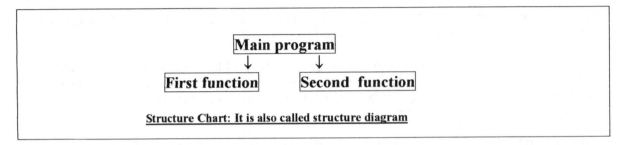

Structure Chart: It is also called structure diagram

structure definition – the general syntax for defining the structure is given below:

       struct **payslip**   payslip is type or name given by the programmer

     {
        data-type member1 ;
        data-type member2;
            :
            :
        data-type membern;

     };   // it can be ended as } **staff;**

The semicolon terminates the structure definition. Why ? It is necessary as in C++ structure definition is a statement. The definition of structure is very much like the definition of classes. See classes.

subscripts - in the array a number within **[ ]** is subscript. For instance , in the array clients [5] , number 5 within the brackets [ ] is subscript, in position 6 in the array called **clients**. It is due to the fact that in C++ first subscript start at **0** (zero). See also elements.

subscripted variable - in the array it consists of the name of the array followed by the element within the brackets [ ]. For instance, in the array name [5], name [2] is the scripted variable. The subscript 2 will give the value of name [2] stored in the memory. See also Zero-based indexing.

virtual function – see polymorphism.

swab function - it swaps bytes from s1 to s2. For this swap your program must include standard library file <sddlib.h>. It is not the same as swap ( ) below.

swap( ) function - it interchanges the two objects that are passed to it. It does so by reference method. The #include<iostream.h> header file handles this function

switch statement - it is used when the program offers multiple choices, or actions or cases to choose from. Of course, multiple **if - else** statements can also perform the task of multiple choices, but the switch statement can be neater. In multiple choices, **if -else** statement can be rather complicated. Its general format is shown below. As many cases as required can be included within { }.

```
switch (choice)        (choice is switching variable – a suitable name given by you)
{
    case 1:            (case is C++ reserved word)
            statement;
            break;
    case 2:
            statement;
            break;
    default :                              ( it is optional )
            statement;
}
```

syntax errors - these are due to violation of the rules of C++ languages for whatever reasons. These can be detected by the compiler.

testing - it searches for bug or errors in a program but it does not remove them. Before a program test begins by using the test data, the expected result is also worked out so that the actual output can be compared with the expected results. See debugging.

text files - these files are organised as a series of characters. They are simple to access by using the insertion and extraction operators (<< and >>).

The **cin >>** is used to input data from the file which is on backing store into the random access memory (RAM) area. The **cout <<** is used to output data from RAM into the file which is on backing store. See also file.

true - it is logical true. In accordance with the Boolean algebra, it evaluates to value of **1**. See false.

Two-dimensional array – a two-dimensional array is considered as one-dimensional array of one-dimensional array. For instance the following table is two-dimensional array.

Product	Jan	Feb	Mar	The declaration
	......	....	....	
Prod 1	56	70	75	int poduct [ ] [3] declares product as
Prod 2	77	74	69	two-dimensional array of two rows and
				three columns. Note that the first set of
				brackets is unspecified. In fact, it is
				int product [2] [3].

See also arrays.

union - it is a keyword. A union is a data type. Its following definition looks like the definition of the structure.   **union staff**   staff is the name or type of union.

```
{
   data-type member1;
   data-type member2;
   :
   :
};
```

It is not very often used. Unlike the structure, a union holds only one value at a time, and thus only one member data is active at a time, but sufficient storage is allocated to hold the largest member.

unsigned integer – it is a positive whole number whose bit pattern is interpreted as a natural type that is positive or zero. **unsigned** is a keyword.

variables - the computer memory consists of many thousands of locations (cells), where data can be stored. Each location is given an unique name or symbol that is called variable. We can place a value (data) in a variable and recall it by its unique name. In the following code:

```
int a;        // a is the name of variable
a = 10;       // 10 is stored in our variable called a
cout << a;    // cout will print 10 which is stored in variable a.
```

 See also address and identifiers.

variables declaration statement - it defines variables and their types to be used in the program. See also identifiers, local and global variables. Examples :

   . **int n;**   it declares single variable called n and it is integer type.
   . **char surname, first, last;**   it is a compound statement, declaring three variables of character type.

virtual function – it is a member function of a class. It is invoked through a pointer to a base class. See polymorphism.

while loop - it is executed continuously **while** some condition is true. It only ends when the condition becomes false. It is very useful where the number of repetitions required is uncertain.

Zero-based indexing – it is the method applied for numbering elements in the array. Its rule is that if the array has *n* elements, their names are *n-1*, because the first element starts at **0** position.

Chapter 14

Exploring Java

Introduction

The Java programming language was developed from 1990 at Sun Microsystems. It looks like C++ from which it has borrowed a lot. It has been growing in popularity since 1995. It has taken the Computer Industry by storm with the promise of "Write once. Run anywhere". Java is often linked to World Wide Web, Internet, applets, applications and beans programs that are written in this language.

Amongst other things, it has been described as object oriented, portable, multithreading and dynamically-linked programming language. C++ is also object oriented programming (OOP) language. The similarities between Java and C++ make it easy for anyone with C++ experience.

Aims

The aims of including this chapter in this C++ book are as follows:

. to introduce Java as another increasingly popular programming language;

. to enable a reader to discover for oneself some of its features;

. to furnish a reader with some practical information on Java development Kit (JDK), Java development environments such as Borland JBuilder 2 for developing Java programs, HTML, Browser, Web Server in relation to Java applets on the Internet;

. to let the reader find out the differences between the Java and traditional approaches to running a program;

. to introduce the reader to Java programming by means of a simple program so the reader can compare and contrast the structures of C++ and Java simple programs; and

. to provide an opportunity to the reader to discover the similarities and differences between C++ and Java programming languages.

The Java Development Kit

In order to develop Java programs, you would require Java development Kit **(JDK)**. One can download it from the JavaSoft Web site:

http://java.su.com/products/jdk/

The main Java Web site is at   **http: / /java.sun.com/**

There are some other sites concerning online information and help for Java users. The site at

http://www.gamelan.com/

is of particular interest for development resources. It contains many sample codes, applets, applications, and guidelines for Java language and development.

There have been many fast developments leading to a number of JDk's versions, and undoubtedly there will be some more soon. So far, JDK's versions are JDK 1.0.2, JDK 1.1.1, JDK 1.2. Each version has more features and is bigger in size than its predecessors. The JDK has numerous tools, documents and help pages. Some of its most important tools are as follows:

- **javac.exe** - the **compiler** for converting the source code into Java **bytecode** (described below).

- **java.exe** - the **interpreter** to execute the bytecode of a Java application (described below).

- **appletviewer.exe** – the **appletviewer** to view an HTML page which contains an applet. The HTML is briefly outlined in this chapter.

- **javap.exe** – the **decompiler** to convert the compiled program into a Java file. It is useful when you wish to find out how an applet was written.

Java program development tools

In order to develop Java programs, you can also use one of the commercially available Java development tools that are often called Integrated Development Environment **(IDE)**. **Microsoft Visual J++ 1.0**, and **Borland JBuilder 2** (for short JBuilder 2) are just two examples of such IDE's for developing Java programs. In fact, these IDE's are easier to use.

For example, I use JBuilder 2 which has graphical user-interface, integrated editor and debugger and other facilities that make my work easy. Your money will be well spent if you buy JBuilder 2 tools for learning Java. Indeed, it is a comprehensive set of visual development tools for creating pure Java business and database applications. It is available in three versions, which are standard, professional and professional upgrade. The tables 1-3 on pages 290-292 summarize the main features of each version. For the beginner, the standard version will be sufficient.

Types of Java programs

A Java program can be:

> . **applications**   . **applets**   **or**   . **beans**.

These are outlined below.

Applications

These are stand-alone programs. Any program that is designed for any business purpose or maintaining personal finance, can also be developed in Java. Like C++, Java is a programming language for all programming solutions. A program which is designed simply as an application <u>does not</u> need any Java-enabled **Web browser** (see below) to run it. It can be added at this stage, that a program can be both an applet and application. <u>The distinction between an applet and application can be made on the basis of their purposes, sizes, capabilities and program development methods.</u>

Applets

 These are small programs. In fact, often smaller than applications. They are designed specifically to run them by a Java-enabled **Web browser (or just browser)**, such as Netscape Navigator, on the **World Wide Web (WWW)**. You can also run applets by using Microsoft's Internet Explorer. Applets are embedded into the **HTML Web pages** (see below). They are, in fact, small networked applications that are designed to be dynamically downloaded across the Internet. It is fair enough to say that applets have made Java world wide famous in such a short space of time since 1995.

It is worth mentioning here that **WWW** is a distributed information service. It was developed, in the early 1990s, at CERN, the European Centre for Practical Physics. In short, the **Web** is the most exciting and popular part of the **Internet**, that is a computer communications network system. It was developed during the 1970s in the USA. It is now a huge collection of computer networks linked together world wide. Even you can link loosely your own PC system to the Internet.

Web Server

Nothing is possible on the internet without the Web server. For instance, your HTML document (see below) is accessed by other internet users on their computers through the Web server. A Web server is a computer system on a network that provides a service to other systems connected to the network. There are many commercial Web Server service providers to allow you to use the internet.

What is HTML?

HTML is an abbreviation for **Hypertext Mark-up Language**, which is used for presenting documents within the Web pages. You have to use it in order to create a Web page that contains your applet with the **<APPLET>tag** within the Web pages. Thus, it is essential to learn HTML, so that you can write HTML pages. It is not considered as a programming language, but **markup-language**. You can create and edit HTML documents by using any editing tools. You can use Microsoft Word for this purpose.

Whenever, you access a **Web** document, follow the hyperlinks by using your mouse pointer, see animated images on your screen, and so on, all these things are created by using the HTML language. The HTML enable you

- **to create pre-formated text**.

- **to format document** - you can choose numerous typeface styles.

- **to create hyperlinks** – the hyperlinks allow you to point to such things as multimedia files, other Web documents.

- **to create tables**.

- **to create graphical images and link these to other documents** – you can link these to other documents all over the internet.

- **interactive tasks** – a user can perform various tasks. For example, form completion.

- **other features** – such as downloading and running of Web pages on your system.

The HTML language has its own set of symbols and rules. The HTML language is a part of **http** which is also briefly outlined below for your benefit.

What is a Browser?

It is a piece of software that enables a user to explore the Internet. Two well-known WWW browsers are **Netscape Navigator** and **Microsoft Internet Explorer**. Web browsers communicate over the network with **Web Servers** by means of the:

> **Hyper Text Transfer Protocol** which is widely known as **http**. It is also

known as:

> . Transmission Control Protocol – **TCP** and
> . Internet Protocol – **IP**

The network protocol is a set of agreed symbols and rules that allows communication between computers in the network.

Are there other protocols used on the network?

Yes, there are many other protocols used on the network. These protocols have their own rules and symbols. One example of such a protocol is the **Electronic Mail**. It is also called file transfer. These protocols have a specific purpose.

It should be noted that the **http protocol** incorporates numerous network protocols, and thus it is the **multi-purpose** protocol. The Web browsers speak the **http** protocol. The **http protocol** enables the user by means of browser to access all kinds of services on the Internet.

What is Browsing?

In order to locate and retrieve information from a large information database set, you have to **dip** into that area of the **WWW** that interests you on the Internet. This **dip** which is in fact a searching method is called **browsing**. It is also known as **surfing**. A browser that supports Java applets is a **Java-enabled** browser. Netscape is a Java-enabled browser. Java applets are downloaded via a Java-enabled browser.

Web Server

Nothing is possible on the internet without the Web server. For instance, your HTML document is accessed by other internet users on their computers through the Web server. A Web server is a computer system on a network that provides a service to other systems connected to the network. There are many commercial Web Server service providers to allow you to use the internet.

The relationship between the Browser, HTML, http and Web Server is shown below in the same order as it happens. It is a simplification to illustrate their working tohether:

. **you** write a document in the **HTML** language;
. the **browser** reads and displays the document;
. **you** click the **hyperlink**;
. the **browser** by means of the **http protocol** sends a message for the data or document, specified by the HTML hyperlink, to a **Web Server**;
. the **Web Server** acts on the message by providing the required data or document though the **http protocol**;
. the **browser** reads and interprets the data or document which is in HTML language; and
. the **browser** presents the requested data or document to **you**.

The Relationship between Java, HTML, Browser, WWW & Local Computer

It can be depicted as follows:

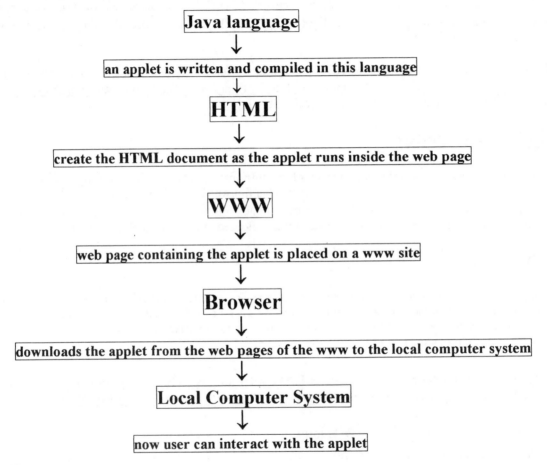

Beans

Java beans are re-useable software components. These beans can enable programmers to design applications, create beans and to write interfaces in order to manipulate beans. Java beans technology is rather new, but promises comprehensive software components that can be used across platforms world wide.

Running a Java program

A program written in Java language is machine independent at the source and binary levels. What does it mean? Let's examine how a Java program is executed and run by the Java development environment.

● **Java source program is first handled by the Java compiler**. The compiler is a part of Java development environment.

● **Compiler converts the source code into bytecode**, which is an intermediate code. This is **not** machine code, and thus compilation does not produce machine code in the same way as say, C++ compiler will do. The byte code resembles machine code, and is not specific to one particular processor. The source program at this stage is not an executable file yet. **Bytecode** instructions are not specific to any particular processor. They look like machine code instructions; but you can think of them as "half-way machine" code instructions.

●**The byte code has to be interpreted by the bytecode interpreter** (also called Java runtime interpreter). The Java interpreter is also known as **Java Virtual Machine (JVM)**. It is another part of the Java development environment, that translates the byte code into the **native machine code** and then runs it. Here by native, it means a particular system. For example, your own computer system is a native system. If a machine, say your PC has already installed the **JVM** which is a piece of software, such as Netscape 3.0 then this JVM will read the byte code and convert it into machine format and run it.

If you wish to run your Java program on a different platform that is equipped with the JVM, your Java program will be executed and run as required. It does not have to be the same JVM as it is on your own machine. To emphasise the fact that the JVM is an integral part of a web browser (for short browser). As long as the other platform has a Java-enabled browser, you can run your Java program on it.

Are there any likely disadvantages?

● Yes indeed, you may run into some difficulties if you use a browser that handles the old version of Java. There are several versions of Java, and probably there will be some more due to its continuing development. **Which version should one use?**

It is a sound investment to purchase JBuilder 2. **Why?** Because JBuilder 2 continues Borland's tradition of supporting the latest JDK. Amongst several new features, JBuilder 2 has a new feature that is **Swichable JDKs** for compiling against any JDK.

● There are built-in security checks in order to make sure that applets within the Java-enabled browser do not harm the local computer system. Applets cannot read/write to the disk on the local system, cannot execute any program on the reader's system, and only be downloaded from the server. The problem is that these security checks may not work on all Java-enabled browsers.

- Java program runs slower than C++ program, because JVM must first convert bytecode into the machine code.

Traditional approach Vs Java approach

The source program written say in C++ or any other high level language has to be translated into the machine code so that it can perform its task. Similarly, the source code written in Java has to be converted into the machine code for execution. The following diagrams illustrate the stages of running a program by both traditional and Java approaches.

Diagram 1   **Traditional approach**

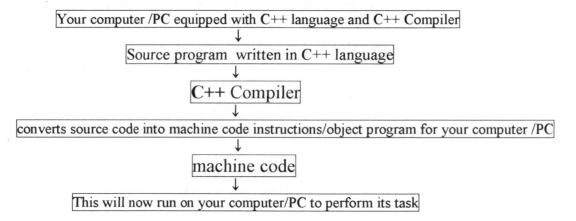

Diagram 2   **Java approach**

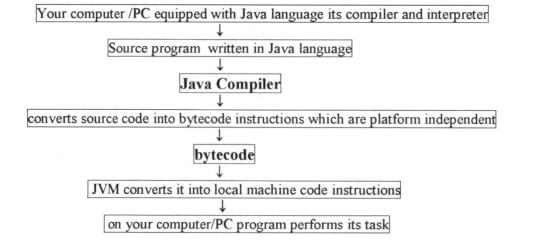

According to the Java approach, a program can run on any other system, providing it is equipped with the JVM. Thus, the Java program is **platform independent**.

Practical Hints

. Java applications do require the **Java interpreter** in order to run these applications. The interpreter comes with the Java language package.

. For running applets, your machine must have **bytecode interpreter – JVM**

. Java-enabled browsers have built-in bytecode interpreter.

. At present, a JVM does not come with the Java language package. But it is likely that soon it will be supplied the Java language package.

. Commercially available IDEs come with the JVM.

Let's now make a simple start towards Java programming by way of creating a Java application.

It can be seen from diagram 2 that the Java development environment has two components namely:

> . **Java compiler**   and   . **Java   interpreter**

The JBuilder 2 incorporates both aspects of Java environment.

Your first Java application

It is almost universal to introduce Java programming by using **class HelloWorld** example. This application is shortest, but it lays the foundation for much bigger applications.

================== **The Simplest Application Program** =========================

```
class HelloWorld
 {
         public static void main (String [  ] args)
         {

            system.out.println (" Hello  Java  Learners!" );

         }

 }
```

Purpose

The purpose of this simple Java application is to illustrate the structure of a Java program by printing the message "Hello Java Learners!".

Explanation

Like in C++, the class concept has the same meaning. You can think of Java program as a **class**.

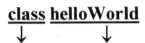

class helloWorld

class   class name always begins with a capital letter

• Within the outer **{ }** **pair of braces** is the entire program. The first line of code declares the **method** called **main ( )**. In all Java application, main ( ) is the point where Java interpreter starts **execution** of the program. The general format of the method main ( ) declaration is as follows:

public static void main (String [ ] args)

Let's examine each word in this statement:

• **Public** is a keyword in Java as in C++. In its simplest term, it means that the class to which it refers is accessible to other classes and objects outside of its package once it is loaded.

> **. Is the keyword public always applicable when creating the main ( ) ?**

> **.** The main ( ) is always declared as public.

• **static** is another keyword. It indicates that method is a class method.

• **void** is another keyword which you have met in C++. Here, it means that the method main ( ) does not return any value or whatsoever.

•

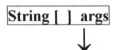

String [ ] args

        In Java it denotes **string object** of unspecified number of elements in the string called argument **(args)**. **Argument** is data that a method accepts in order to carry out its function. Strings in Java are objects. Unlike as in C++, in Java a string is not terminated by a **null** character. As you have already learnt in C++ that a string is an array. Like in C++, strings are also arrays in Java.

---

main (String [ ] args)

This statement sets up an array of string. It has unspecified number of elements/arguments **Why?** Because there is nothing enclosed within **[ ]**.

• The method main has a body (code) which is enclosed within the **inner** set of braces. In the above example, this body consists of only one line of the following code:

system.out.println("Hello Java learners!");

What does it do?

Here, the function of the method main ( ) is to print the message **Hello Java learners!** The **ln** will produce a line feed.

• At this stage, it is worth mentioning that the **system.out.print ( )** is a **method**. Inside ( ), it contains single string (data) that is called **argument**. Multiple values can also be represented by a single string within ( ).

In this simple example, the argument is just a message enclosed within the double quotes. **Why is it enclosed within " " ?** The argument (your text) should be placed within double quotes.

It prints the message or the output on the standard output of your computer system, which may be printer, screen or a special window whatsoever. It does not produce by itself line feed. This is why in this simple program, we have this code:

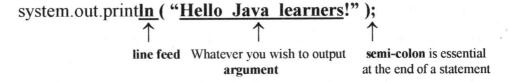

If you have used Borland Turbo C++ 4.5 or a similar product for your C++ programming exercises, you are well experienced in the use of integrated development environment (IDE) that has enabled you to create your source files, compiled your program and run it successfully. For Java programming, I use Borland JBuilder 2 which also has similar IDE for creating the source file. We do not have space in this book to discuss the comprehensive and powerful features of JBuilder 2 (see tables 1-3). Indeed, it has all the necessary capabilities that are required to create and compile your source file, and allow you to run your program.

The JBuilder 2's graphical IDE will enable you to create, save, compile and run this program as a stand-alone program. The J builder **AppBrowser** allows you to browse through the code and objects that are part of your application. AppBrowser makes easy program development tasks such as editing, debugging, and browsing for data/information. It facilitates edit, design, and debug all in one unified window.

Once the source file has been created, it has to be saved, under the same name as the class name, precisely written, using lower and upper case letters and punctuation as in the class name. The file name ends with the Java file extension. Thus the file will be saved as

HelloWorld. Java

What will happen if the file name does not fully match the name of the class it defines?

In such a case, your program will not be compiled at all. For instance, the file name **HeloWorld** is not acceptable as here one letter **l** is missing. **Helo** is not the same word as **Hello**. Thus, you will <u>not</u> be able to compile it. What a pity!

Is it similar to C++ program?

I am sure that you have already discovered that this simple application (stand-alone program) is similar to the programs you have met in this book. It is true to say that the format of the output statement differs to a certain extent, but the fact of the matter is that any one who is familiar with the C++ will find it easy to grasp Java and make good progress towards learning it.

Does it need an HTML browser?

No. A Java application does not run in an HTML browser. Furthermore, Java application is not subject to the security restrictions imposed on Java applets.

It has been said that any particular program can be both application and applet. If so, can I run my application as an applet?

Yes, an application can be run as an applet, but first it has to be embedded in an HTML page and then run in an HTML browser or applet viewer.

The major difference between an applet and an application is that an applet has to be incorporated into HTML document for it to be run and displayed inside a Web page. For this reason alone, applets development is more complex than the development of an application.

similarities and differences between JAVA and C++

Often one hears that JAVA looks like C++ and that if one knows C++ it helps to learn JAVA quickly. This section highlights some of the important similarities and differences between JAVA and C++ languages.

Java language

As you already know that before you can read or write a program in C++, you must learn first about C++ **syntax rules** and the **restrictions in** terms of what is legal and illegal. The syntax concerns the elements of the language, how these elements are put together in accordance with the established rules of the language to be meaningful to the computer system and the programmer. Like C++, Java also has its own language elements, syntax rules and restrictions to construct a meaningful program.

machine dependent

The source program written in C++ language has to be compiled into the object program by the C++ compiler. The compiler checks the source code for syntax errors and displays a list of errors and warnings.

Once the programmer has eliminated all errors, the compiler will convert the source code into the object code. The object code is the operation code or executable code. It is also known as machine code that is specific to a particular machine. **The object code can only run on the machine it was compiled on or a similar type of machine or platform.**

For instance, Apple Macintosh and Sun SPARC-station are two different platforms. Each different type of machine has its own unique way of converting source code into the object code. However, it is possible that by re-writing some components of the source code, you can re-compile the same source code on another type of machine.

machine independent

The source program written in Java language is also compiled by a Java compiler, but the code is not an executable code. It is an intermediate code called **bytecode**. The bytecode is not machine code, but generated in such a specific way that it can be executed on any **native machine** on which the **Java Virtual Machine (JVM)** is installed. Thus, Java allows cross-platform portability, and unlike the C++, **it is platform or machine independent.** It is because of this cross-platform portability that Java has been, in the late 1990's, revolutionising the computer industry.

pre-processor construct

In Java, there is no need for any kind of pre-processors. For instance in C++ program, you must have **#include** < >. A Java program does not require any such constructs or pre-processor directives.

primitive and non-primitive types

In Java, there are eight primitive data types. These are integers, characters, Boolean values and floating-point numbers. Primitive types are built into the system and are available to the user by the basic hardware.

On the other hand, **Objects** and **arrays** are of non-primitive types. This is not so in C++.

Primitive types are outlined below under integer, character, floating-point and Boolean types data. Unlike in C++, in Java, sizes, and signs of primitive types are pre-determined and thus platform independent. Furthermore, unlike in C++, in Java, all variables have defined default values.

integer types data

In C++, integer data types **int** may be signed or unsigned. Their sizes may vary from platform to platform. In Java, integer data types are machine-independent, their sizes are consistent and are all signed. Like in C++, **int** have different range of values . In Java, integer types are **byte**, **short**, **int** and **long** whose fixed sizes are 8,16,32 and 64 bits respectively. In Java , to write **long int** or **short int** is illegal. In Java, **unsigned** is not a reserved word, as it is in C++. These four types can hold either positive or negative numbers.

floating-point types data

In C++, you can declare real numbers as **float**, **double** and **long double**. Their sizes and precision are those used in a particular computer. In Java, the floating-point types are as shown below with their sizes and precision already determined.

type	size	Precision
float	32 bits	single
double	64 bits	double

character type data

In C++ as well as in Java character values represent characters, but Java uses **Unicode** character set. The Unicode is 16-bit code, defined by the Unicode Consortium. Java uses the data type **char** to store a single Unicode character. In C++, **char type** is 8-bit wide by default.

unicode

Unicode list consists of thousands of characters that are derived from the main written languages of Europe, America, Asia and Africa. Unicode character encoding is designed for world-wide interchange, processing and display of written text. You do not have to use it, if you don't need it. At present, across platforms, Unicode is not yet widely supported. However, Unicode makes Java acceptable at the international level, in particular in those countries where other languages are spoken and written. For instance, A Gujarati programmer in India can name classes in Gujarati alphabet. Unicode is a trade mark of the Unicode Consortium.

boolean type data

In C++, when the Boolean expression evaluates to **0,** it means **false.** When it evaluates to any **nonzero** value, it means **true**. In Java, the boolean expression cannot be evaluated to a number such as o or 1; but only to **false** or **true** value.

strings

" Java is the programming language for the year 2000 and beyond \n" is an example of string in programming. A series of characters that is enclosed within the double quotation marks. It will be obeyed by the computer without changing it. It is also called **string literal**. In C++, string literals are treated as arrays of characters.

In Java, string literals are instances of the **String class**. As string literals are widely used, Java allows the use of string literals, constructed within the double quotation marks. When a string is encountered in a program, Java creates an **instance** of String class. In Java, strings are not terminated by a null character as is the case in C++.

comments

Java supports C++ comment that begins with the symbol // for a single line comment . It also supports C language comment type, and a special **doc comment** that are used by the javadoc program in order to generate online documentation from the Java source code. doc comments begins with **/** and ends with */.

goto statement

goto statement is not included in Java. Of course, C++ supports it.

operators

Java borrows almost all operators from C/C++ languages. Almost all C/C++ operators can be used in Java. These standard C/C++ operators have the same level of precedence and association in Java. In addition, Java also has some new operators. These are outlined below.

. **+** it is used for string values.

. **instanceof** it is applied to **true** and **false** values. It has the same precedence as the <, >, <= and >= operators .

. **>>>** it is used with integral types of data in order to shift data.

. **&** and | these two operators are used with integral types of data to perform **bitwise AND** and **OR** operations.

In Java operators are **arithmetic**, **logical**, **comparison**, **assignment** and **bitwise**. Some operators are **unary** and others are **binary**.

operator Overloading

C++ allows operator overloading. Java does not support operator overloading.

if, else, do and while statements

These statements are syntactically exactly the same as they are in C++. The difference is that in Java, the conditional expression must evaluate to false or true only. Thus, it cannot return an integer value such as **0** or **1**. But in Java, there are two conditional statements namely **if** and **switch** statements.

for statement

Like C++, Java supports **for** statement, but you still have to learn the way Java compiler handles loop variables.

loop constructs

There are three loop constructs in Java. These are **while**, **do** and **for** loops.

switch statement

Like in C++, Java supports **switch** or **case** statement. As mentioned above switch is a conditional statement.

break and continue statements

break and **continue** statements are supported by Java. These statements act in the same way as they do in C++. In Java, there are additional facilities as options called **labelled break** and **labelled continue.** Labelled break allows to break any specified statement or loop outside nested loops. Labelled continue allows continue any specified statement or loop outside the current loop.

enumerated types

Unlike C++, Java does not support enumerated types.

functions

Java does not have functions that are defined outside classes in C++. On the other hand, Java has **methods** that are defined inside classes.

arguments

Methods, in Java, must have a specific number of arguments (data). Functions, in C++, can take a variable number of arguments.

unions

Unlike C++, Java does not support unions.

structures

Unlike C++, Java does not support **struct**.

local variable declarations

Java allows you to declare and initialize local variables anywhere. But usually they are grouped together at the beginning of a definition. It is the same feature in C++ that is borrowed by Java.

local variable declarations

Java allows you to declare and initialize local variables anywhere. But usually they are grouped together at the beginning of a definition. It is the same feature in C++ that is borrowed by Java.

global variables

Java does not have global variables, but C++ supports such variables.

null

In C++, null is equivalent to zero; and a string is terminated by the null character '\0'. On the other hand, in Java, null is a reserved keyword and a special value. It can be assigned to any variable of reference type. More when you learn Java.

pass by value

pass by value

The actual primitive types of data values are stored in variables. These are then passed to **methods**. As you already know that C++ does not have primitive types of data. Just to remind you that in C++ a copy of the contents of variables is passed to functions.

pass by reference

The non-primitive types data **(objects and arrays)** are also known as **reference types**. Their addresses are stored in variables, and when required are passed to methods.

& and * operators

In C++, the **&** (ampersand) operator is used with 'pass by reference' in order to obtain the address of the variable , and * (asterisk, star or times) is used for dereference or dereferencing (remember pointers) . These operators do not exist in Java.

pointers

Java does not have pointers. Pointers are used in C++. Java's **reference** technique is similar to pointers.

arrays

Like C++, Java supports arrays. The way arrays are handled in Java differs from that in C++. Java does not support multi dimensional arrays as in C++, but you can create arrays of arrays. In Java, arrays are class objects. The array's elements types are: primitive, composite and user-defined. The size of the array is not specified. In order to allocate memory for the array variables, Java requires the use of the ***new*** operator. It is similar to the new operator in C++.

keywords   Many of these keywords are borrowed from C++. We can categorise these in accordance with their functions as summarised below.

function category	Keyword
data declaration	float, int …
loops	for, continue…
conditional	if, else…
structure	class …
Modifier & access	private, public…
Exceptional	try, catch …
Miscellaneous	null, true

Diagram 3

Void

Void is support in Java like in C++. The difference is that in Java, it is not used with methods without arguments.

Java class libraries

C++ has no built-in libraries. On the other hand, **JDK 1.1** has an impressive library that has numerous support packages. Java class library has many packages. The most important package is called **java.lag** package. It is impossible to develop a Java program without using **java.lang**. The language package contains **classes** that are the main core of the Java language.

Object class

In this language package, the object class is the **parent class** of all Java classes. It implies that all other classes are derived from the object class. A **class** is a type definition. On the other hand, the **object** is a variable declaration. Classes and objects are at the heart of Java language.

Object-oriented programming(oop)

Java is pure object-oriented programming language as the core of data structure in Java is the **object**. On the other hand, C++ is also object-oriented language, but one can still write structured programs in it. This is not possible in Java, because it is purely object-oriented programming language.

JBuilder 2

The most comprehensive Java visual development tool

The following set of three tables summarizes the main features of three versions of Borland JBuilder 2.

. **Table 1** contains features common to all three versions. It is the **Standard version (STD)** .

. **Table 2** shows features, which are common to **Professional** and **Client Server** levels of this package. It is the **professional version (PRO)**.

.**Table 3** lists features that are available only for the **Client Server version** of this package. It is usually known as **Client Server Suit (C/S)**. Of course, one can purchase any of these versions. Academic organizations will find the full package worth buying for both academic and administrative purposes. The Standard and Professional Versions will indeed meet the need of most readers of this book.

Table 1

Borland JBuilder 2 Feature Matrix	STD	PRO	C/S
Pure Java applications, applets and Java Beans for cross platform development	√	√	√
Rapid Application Development for maximum productivity	√	√	√
NEW! Complete support for the latest Java standards including JDK 1.2, Java Beans, JFC/Swing, JDBC, RMI, Serialization, Customizers, JARs, JNI, and more	√	√	√
NEW! Switchable JDKs for compiling against any JDK	√	√	√
NEW! Integrated JFC/Swing components for drag-and-drop application development	√	√	√
100+ Robust Java Bean components including Layout, Button, Checkbox, Scrollbar List, Popupmenu, and many more	√	√	√
NEW! Beans Express with visual bean designers to reusable Java Beans	√	√	√
NEW! BeanInsight to diagnose and fix problem Java Beans	√	√	√
AppBrowser for integrated management of projects, classes, and source	√	√	√
Professional IDE with integrated AppBrowser, Editor, Debugger, Compiler	√	√	√
Pure Java Layout Managers for easy UI development	√	√	√
Pure Java Two-Way-Tools for complete control over your code	√	√	√
Java Explorer for easy access to your files	√	√	√
Comprehensive Graphical Debugger	√	√	√
Wizards for development and development of Application and Applets	√	√	√
NEW! CodeInsight to speed up coding and reduce syntax errors	√	√	√
New! Customizable code creation based on developer style preferences	√	√	√
Integrated HTML viewer	√	√	√

Table 1 continued

Fully Unicode enabled for international applications	√	√	√
Built-in Local Obfuscator to protect your Java sourcecode	√	√	√
NEW! Java Generic Library of optimized data structures	√	√	√
NEW! JBuilder Quick Start printed book with numerous examples and sample code	√	√	√

Table 2

Borland JBuilder 2 Feature Matrix	PRO	C/S
Fast Java compiler with SmartCecker for the fastest compiles	√	√
New! Servelt Wizard for easy development and deployment of Servlets	√	√
Complete JDBC database connectivity	√	√
NEW! Improved DataExpress components for drag-and-drop database applications. Includes QueryDataSet, QueryResolver, TableDataSet, TextDataFile, DataSetView, Navigator, and many more.	√	√
NEW! DbSwing data-aware JavaBeans with source code	√	√
NEW! Source code for 200+ JBCL and JFC/Swing beans	√	√
NEW! Improved programmable Grid Control with source code	√	√
Charting to visualize your data	√	√
Local InerBase Server for off-line-SQL database development	√	√
Full SQL92 query syntax support	√	√
Professional command line tools including Fast Compiler, Grep, Make, Touch JKD Tools, and more.	√	√
NEW! Project Folders and Resource Management for increased productivity	√	√
Multilingual On-Line Shopping sample application using JavaBeans with Source Code	√	√

Table 3

Borland JBuilder 2 Feature Matrix	C/S
NEW! Integrated VisiBroker for Java for CORBA/IIOP development	√
NEW! Integrated project management for CORBA development	√
NEW! Multi-tier CORBA sample application using VisiBroker with Source Code	√
RMI Wizards for building distributed Pure Java applications	√
NEW! Java Beans Express for Visually creating Enterprise Java Beans	√
NEW! Serializable Datasets for distributed computing solutuions	√
PrcodureDataSets to access and use data from Stored Procedure	√
NEW! DataStore for Pure Java, High-performance, data caching and persistent storage of data, objects, and files	√
NEW! Resourceable SQL to simplify management of SQL code	√
SQL Builder to visually create and edit SQL queries	√
SQL Monitor to test, debug , and tune SQL applications	√
SQL Explorer for visual database schema and content management	√
Integrated PVCS Version Management for team development	√
NEW! Express Development Server to seamlessly manage and deploy applications Across the network	√
DataGateway for Java (unlimited licence) high-performance native drivers for Oracle, DB2, Sybase, MS SQL Server, Infomix, InterBase, MS Access, FoxPro, Paradox, and DBASE	√

These tables contain the latest product information obtained from **INPRISE Corporation** at the time of preparing this chapter in July 1998. I thank the INPRISE Corporation for allowing me to include this information for the readers of this book.

Future Prospects

By now you will have learnt that Java is a modern programming language for the year 2000 and beyond. Its widely known capability of platform independence attracts young people to learn it. Java programmers can earn more money and improve their job prospects. From the programming perspective, Java is platform independent at source and binary levels. Thus it makes one believe, "Write once. Run Anywhere", and go for it.

Should you wish to learn more about Java, learn from:

Java Simplified

Adam Shaw

A new book in A.D.R. Student Simplified Text Series

ISBN 190 1197 88 3

Available in Spring 1999 from major bookstores and directly from A.D.R. England

---

A.D.R. Student Simplified Text Series
New Programming Books 1999

. **Windows Programming**
. **Visual Basic**
. **Internt**
. **Java**

INDEX

Symbols